TUNBRIDG

C000080762

IN THE SECOND
& THE YEARS OF AUSTERITY
1939-1953

*'Bredbury', Mount Ephraim,
the HQ of Civil Defence Region 12*

Ann Bates

Royal Tunbridge Wells Civic Society
Local History Monograph No.11
2009

The text is set in Bookman Old Style 8-10 pt.
and the cover in Bookman Old Style 12-30 pt

Front cover: Collage of period images.
Title page: Bredbury, Mount Ephraim.

Printed and bound by
The Inkpot Lithographic Printers
Southborough, Tunbridge Wells, Kent

CONTENTS

Page

FOREWORD   1

PART 1   INTRODUCTORY BACKGROUND

1. The World from 1914 to 1939   4

2. How the War affected the British   9

3. The Military Defence of South-East England   40

PART 2   TUNBRIDGE WELLS IN THE SECOND WORLD WAR

4. Preparing for War 1930–1938   54

5. Tunbridge Wells in 1939   64

6. The Darkest Years 1940 – 1942   87

7. Towards Victory 1943 – 1945   118

PART 3   TUNBRIDGE WELLS IN THE YEARS OF AUSTERITY

8. Post-War Austerity 1945 -1949   147

9. The Promise of a Better Future 1950–1953   178

POSTSCRIPT   190

APPENDICES

Appendix 1 – Properties Requisitioned in Tunbridge Wells
during World War II and the Post-War Years   191

Appendix 2 – Awards and Honours   194

Appendix 3 – Sources   196

Appendix 4 – Acronyms and Abbreviations   199

Appendix 5 – Conversion of Earlier £ Sterling Values
into 2009 Values   200

ACKNOWLEDGEMENTS   201

INDEX   202

LOCAL HISTORY GROUP PUBLICATIONS   209

KEEP CALM AND CARRY ON

A Ministry of Information poster of 1939 sets the mood for the Nation.

FOREWORD

I have lived in Tunbridge Wells all my life. I was seven years-old when the Second World War started and thirteen when it ended.

So I was particularly pleased to be asked by the Local History Group of the Royal Tunbridge Wells Civic Society to write, as part of their series of Local History Monographs, a history of Tunbridge Wells in World War II and the post-war period of austerity, for publication in 2009 - the 70th. Anniversary of the start of the Second World War. Obviously my perspective of these events has changed considerably over those seventy years, but it remains for me one of the most vivid and character-forming periods of my life.

In this book, I hope to give the reader some idea not only of what happened but also of what it felt like to live as a school girl in Tunbridge Wells during the years of War and the Post-War years. As a Coda to events, I have included extracts from the speeches of King George VI broadcast by the BBC, particularly on each Christmas Day, which became so much a part of the Christmases I remember; and the speeches of Churchill which were broadcast and were so inspiring (at least to adults!) during those dark days.

Although this history is mainly confined to the old Borough of Tunbridge Wells (the modern Borough and its boundaries were not created until 1974), events in the neighbouring parishes affected the people of Tunbridge Wells in many ways and these are recorded as well.

Nobody under the age of 64 in 2009 can have any direct memory of the War; and nobody under the age of 56 can have any direct memory of the Years of Austerity. Most readers therefore will be too young to have experienced it.

So, before detailing the situation and developments in Tunbridge Wells during the Second World War and the Years of Austerity, it seems relevant to provide the reader (particularly those aged under 56!) with background information about the wartime situation in the whole of the UK; and how the War changed everyone's world and affected everybody's Quality of Life. In this respect, Tunbridge Wells was little different from most other towns in Britain, except that it was possibly slightly nearer the Front Line than most.

My research for this monograph has been extensive and has taken me to the National Archive, the British Library, the Centre for Kentish Studies and the East Sussex Records Office. But probably and not surprisingly, the most extensive archive is here in Tunbridge Wells in the Museum and Reference Library and particularly in the basement of the Town Hall, where are kept the Minutes, papers and correspondence of various Committees concerned with the

1

War, which have not existed for about 60 years and whose existence is now largely unknown, even by those people who work there.

Reading the Minutes of the monthly meetings of the Borough Council and its Committees, and particularly those of the Emergency Committee which at the beginning of the War met every morning, one is astonished at the many subjects connected to the war on which they had to make decisions on a daily basis, particularly in the early years; and also at the number of directives and regulations coming to them from Central Government.

Because Tunbridge Wells was a seat of Regional Government covering the whole of Kent, Sussex and Surrey, it had many important visitors. Some were already well known because of their careers in previous years in politics, industry and the armed forces. Others were not well known at the time, but were later to become leading figures during the War and in the development of Britain after the War.

It is not possible to pay tribute to all the men, women and children who died, were wounded, or received awards during the War. But I hope the ones whom I have mentioned will give some idea of just one Town's contribution to the War effort, and not least the contribution of the civilians who stayed at home.

Many events were reported in the local press, although often the locality was not named because of the censorship regulations in force at the time. Some events in fact were not told until much later, and there may be some which are still to be told.

I am sure that many of you who read this short history will have your own memories of the War and the post-war years. I hope that it will inspire further research and recording of the events, before the memories are lost.

I would like to thank my fellow-Committee members of the Local History Group for their support, help and encouragement, and particularly Dr. Ian Beavis of the Tunbridge Wells Museum and Art Gallery, and especially John Cunningham, the Chairman of the Group, who has been the sympathetic but stern Editor of all that I have written, and whose advice and comments have been invaluable.

The Author, aged 11.

Ann Bates, 6th. May, 2009

PRE- SECOND WORLD WAR CHRONOLOGY

1918	11th. November Armistice Day. End of World War I.
1919	Germany signs Treaty of Versailles.
1919–1933	Weimar Republic rules in Germany.
1920	Establishment of League of Nations, forerunner of the United Nations. Germany admitted in 1926, Soviet Union joins 1934. USA refuses to join League.
1921	Germany agrees levels of reparation at Versailles Conference.
1922	Mussolini appointed Prime Minister of Italy.
1923–1925	Hyper-inflation in Germany.
1924	Re-scheduling of German reparations (Dawes Plan).
1926	General Strike in Britain.
1929	Re-scheduling of German reparations (Young Plan). 29th.October. Wall Street Crash.
1929–1939	The Great Economic Depression worldwide.
1931	Banks collapse in Germany and Austria. Japan occupies Manchuria.
1932	Lausanne Conference finally suspends German reparations.
1933	January. Hitler appointed Chancellor of Germany. Roosevelt launches 'New Deal' in USA. World Economic Conference fails.
1935–1936	Italy attacks and seizes Abyssinia (Ethiopia).
1935	Saarland returned to Germany, after plebiscite in January.
1936	Re-armament starts in Germany, France and Britain. March 7th. Rhineland re-occupied by Germany.
1936	July. Civil War breaks out in Spain.
1937	November. Sino-Japanese War breaks out.
1938	March. 'Die Anschluss' – annexation of Austria by Germany. September. Munich 'Crisis' and Pact between Germany, France and UK over Czechoslovakia.
1939	March. Germany occupies Czechoslovakia. March 31st. End of Spanish Civil War. Franco enters Madrid. Italy invades Albania. Britain informally guarantees Polish independence. August 23rd. German-Soviet Pact secures Soviet neutrality. August 24th. UK Parliament recalled. Reservists 'called up.' August 25th. Britain signs Treaty of Alliance with Poland. September 1st. 4.15 am. Germany invades Poland. September 3rd. France and Britain declare war on Germany.

PART 1 INTRODUCTORY BACKGROUND

CHAPTER 1

THE WORLD FROM 1914 TO 1939

The First World War, which was expected by its participants to be over in a matter of months, dragged on for nearly four and a half years and descended at least on the Western Front into a stalemate of static trench warfare, in which half of each Army - the cavalry - could not be used in their conventional role and the other half - the infantry - were subjected to intolerable casualties from artillery bombardment, machine-guns, gas and barbed-wire.

The War eventually ended through exhaustion - human, material, economic and financial - on all sides; through the development of new weapons - aircraft and tanks; through the collapse of Russia on the Eastern Front into Communist revolution in 1917; and through the entry late in 1917 of a new participant, the United States of America, which did not have time to play a very large military part in the War, but whose entry tipped the balance psychologically and logistically in favour of the Franco-British allies.

Peace of Versailles

The ensuing 'peace', perpetuated in the Treaty of Versailles of 1919 and subsequent treaties, needs to be viewed in the context of bitter French memories of the German victory in the Franco-Prussian War of 1871 and its ensuing humiliation for France, as well as the understandably self-righteous feeling of justification by the victors, who had suffered four years of 'hell'.

This 'peace' saw:

* ❖ the break-up of the Hapsburg Austro-Hungarian Empire into a number of new independent states – Austria, Hungary, Czechoslovakia, and Yugoslavia;

* ❖ the dismantlement of the Ottoman Empire in the Middle East into a new and separate state, Saudi-Arabia, and a number of new states which were set up under French (Syria and Lebanon) and British (Palestine, Trans-Jordan and Iraq) mandates;

* ❖ the restoration of independence to former European states – Poland (partitioned by Prussia, Russia and Austria in 1795), Finland (ceded by Sweden to Russia in 1809),and Latvia and Lithuania (absorbed by

Russia in 1795); the restitution to France of Alsace-Lorraine (taken by Prussia in 1871); and

❖ the demilitarisation of the Rhineland, the 'buffer-zone' between Germany on the east and Belgium, France and the Netherlands on the west.

Even more important, the Treaty laid down that Germany in particular should make what would prove to be punitive financial and economic reparations to the Allies, which would be a source of great discontent to Germans over the ensuing years, and a cause of what would follow.

Consequences

The political, economic and social consequences of both the War and the Peace were enormous and some of them are still with us to this very day.

The First World War created a dramatic increase in world productivity and productive capacity, but without a continuing and corresponding increase in demand after the War had ended. With increased productivity but lower demand, food and raw material prices fell and this worsened the ability of all countries, *whether industrial or agricultural*, to buy and to trade with each other.

International finance never fully recovered from the dislocations of the War and the pre-War system of fixed exchange rates and free convertibility was replaced by the Gold Exchange Standard which was a compromise. This undermined many economies throughout the world and was to lead to the world-wide Great Depression of 1929-1939.

It particularly affected Germany, whose post-War government, the Weimar Republic (1919-1933), suffered unbelievable rates of inflation in the early 1920s, due in part to the cost of the reparations they were committed to make to the 'victors'. It was this environment, coupled with the strong German feeling that they had been badly treated in the Peace Settlement, which was to lead to the rise of Nazism in Germany, under the *Austrian* soldier, Adolf Hitler, who had fought in a German regiment on the Western Front. Hitler was appointed Chancellor of Germany in 1933, becoming its President in 1934, after the death of its incumbent President, Field Marshal Hindenburg, who had been the German Commander-in-Chief from 1916.

In some ways, World War II seems to be an extension of the World War I. There was after all less than 21 years between them - equivalent in 2009 to 1988, which does not seem very far away.

Many people who were to play an important part in the years from 1939 in Tunbridge Wells, had had distinguished records during the war twenty years earlier. Not least Churchill who, in August 1933 in a speech to his parliamentary constituents, referred to German rearmament with these words:

> ... *there is grave reason to believe that Germany is arming herself or seeking to arm herself, contrary to the solemn treaties extracted from her in her hour of defeat* ...

Revival of German nationalism

In the years up to 1939:

❖ Germany reoccupied in 1935 the Saar, a region which had historically belonged to France, but was German-speaking. It had been administered by the League of Nations since 1919. The re-occupation followed a plebiscite which showed that the inhabitants wanted to belong to Germany.

❖ Germany entered the demilitarised Rhineland with military forces in 1936, an act which was 'condoned' by the Allies and encouraged Hitler to be bolder.

❖ By 1938 there were 300,000 men in the German Army, when they were welcomed into Austria at the annexation (or in German, 'Anschluss') of that country by Germany in March 1938.

❖ The 'Munich Crisis' over Sudetenland, a German-speaking part of Czechoslovakia, was ostensibly averted by Neville Chamberlain in September 1938, but that did not stop the German Army from entering Czechoslovakia and occupying Prague, with little resistance, the following March.

❖ It was at this point that Neville Chamberlain guaranteed Polish independence which was to prove the trigger, *although not the cause,* of the Second World War.

It is also perhaps indicative of the somewhat unreal world of international politics as it then was (and how different, one may ask, is it today?) that Chamberlain at the height of the Munich Crisis could say in a BBC radio broadcast on 27th. September:

Chamberlain and Hitler.

6

'How horrible, fantastic, incredible it is that we should be digging trenches and trying on gas masks here because of some quarrel in a far-away country between people of whom we know nothing.'

Despite this somewhat incredulous and dismissive statement, Chamberlain did achieve another year of 'peace' in which British and French preparations for the inevitable war could be advanced, without actually having to fight.

Re-armament

Britain had already embarked on rearmament in 1937. There had also been an expansion of air defences since 1936, when the effects of air attacks on Guernica and elsewhere in the Spanish Civil War had struck home. In France, 14 Army Divisions were mobilised in 1938. As we now know, Hitler had not planned to go to war with the Western Powers until 1942, but circumstances dictated otherwise. It is worth recording that in 1939 Roosevelt requested Hitler not to attack European and Middle Eastern countries for the next 10-25 years.

World Unrest

At Christmas 1935, King George V gave his last Christmas broadcast in which he recognised that:

King George V.

'In Europe and many parts of the world anxieties surround us'

In other countries there was also unrest. Italy was under Mussolini's Fascist rule from 1922 and invaded Abyssinia (now Ethiopia) in 1935-6 and Albania in 1939. In Spain, there was a Civil War from 1936-9 in which Hitler supported General Franco and by October 1936, had supplied him with 95 aircraft and some 5,000 – 6,000 troops.

There were other disturbances: China and Japan were at war; and there was unrest in Palestine (which was a British mandate from 1919-1948) and the West Indies (which were British colonies until the 1950s). Later in 1939, Russia invaded Finland.

So the World, not just the West, was in turmoil.

At home, 1936 saw the death of George V and the constitutional crisis which led to the abdication of Edward VIII and the accession of George VI.

On Christmas Day 1937, King George VI gave his first Christmas message in which he said:

King George VI – Christmas Day, 1937.

'As we look back on the year now closing, we see over parts of the world the shadows of enmity and fear.'

While these shadows were clearly known and recognised, no one was sure how prepared they were to meet them, or knew how much time they had to prepare.

CHAPTER 2

HOW THE WAR AFFECTED THE BRITISH

All War changes all lives, dramatically. This chapter seeks to provide information on the changes in the lives, lifestyles and quality of life of the British during the Second World War.

POPULATION

Great Britain started the War with a population of 47,762,000, of whom only 41% (or 19,473.000) were the working population, that is those in civilian employ, or the Armed Forces, or registered unemployed. The breakdown of these figures at June 1939 was:

	1939		
	Total **'000**	**Men** **'000**	**Women** **'000**
Total Population	47,762	22,962	24,799
Total Working Population	19,750	14,656	5,094
in civilian employ	18,000	13,163	4,837
in Armed Forces	480	480	-
registered unemployed	1,270	1,013	257

By the peak of the War in 1943, these figures had changed dramatically. The total population had gone up by about 1 million, the working population had gone up by $2^{1}/_{2}$ million and were now 46% of the population, and the Armed Forces had gone up by $4^{1}/_{4}$ million. But those in civilian employ had declined by over $^{1}/_{2}$ million and the registered unemployed had declined by over 1 million to virtually none.

A prime factor in these changes was an increase of well over 2 million *women* in the working population, mostly in civilian employ, and also an increase from what was zero to just under $^{1}/_{2}$ million in the number of women in the Armed Forces. The breakdown of these figures in 1943 was:

	1943		
	Total **'000**	**Men** **'000**	**Women** **'000**
Total Population	48,789	23,574	25,215
Total Working Population	22,285	15,032	7,253
in civilian employ	17,444	10,675	6,769
in Armed Forces	4,761	4,300	461
registered unemployed	60	44	16

Source: Fighting with Figures. A Statistical Digest of the Second World War. CSO. 1995

9

QUALITY OF LIFE

Any war is bound to make life much more uncomfortable and living conditions much worse. There are shortages; there are restrictions; there is more regulation and more control by government; there is the need for everyone to have more personal protection; there is the need for local defence systems, in case of attack or invasion; and there is the need for conscription of Armed Forces to fight that war. All of these constraints on normal living generally last throughout a war and often for a considerable time afterwards.

But the Second World War was also the first war, apart from those fought centuries ago between Englishmen and in England, in which the British population *living in Britain* was at risk of life and limb from its enemies.

There had been some risk of this in the First World War. Germany had mounted 103 air-raids (fifty-one by Zeppelin airships), mostly on London; and a total of 300 tons of bombs had killed 1,413 people, but it was *relatively* slight.

"AM I AN ISLAND?"
Punch, 22 May 1940

Wartime cartoon.

Since then, the nature of war had changed even further. There was the continued rise of air power, with its ability to attack and bomb wherever it wanted, as was witnessed in the 1930s in both Abyssinia and at Guernica in Catalonia in Spain. There was the development of new weapons, such as gas, which seemed to threaten to asphyxiate everyone indiscriminately, and also the tank, which made cavalry, which had been the dominant factor in almost every battle in the previous 2,000 years, redundant in less than 25 years, and made a 'Blitzkrieg' (literally a 'Lightning War') possible. In all, the speed of war had accelerated considerably and this brought home to a marked degree, the fears of war to a British-resident population.

The Second World War was also the first War in which British women were involved in a *major and direct* way as semi-combatants, through the

Auxiliary Forces and the other voluntary organisations which were created to serve the War effort.

Shortages, and the consequent need for rationing of food, clothes, petrol and even furniture, were inevitable when we live on an island and the delivery of our needs can be problematic, as would be demonstrated by the initial success of German U-boats in the North Atlantic in 1940-41. So an efficient *and fair* system of rationing was needed, and achieving this could be problematic.

Restrictions are also inevitable when an individual's behaviour (and even freedom, if necessary) needs to be restrained for the greater good and safety of the whole population. So blackout and even curfew restrictions become justified and are not necessarily an infringement of human liberties.

More regulation and control were also necessary if the war effort was to be coordinated, waste and unnecessary duplication of effort eliminated, and more direction applied to achieving results. So it was a question of *telling* people what they must do, rather than just *asking* them. Choice of employment was no longer possible – men *and women* needed to be directed into what the country wanted them to do.

The Battle of the Atlantic is being lost!

The reasons why:

1. German U-boats, German bombers and the German fleet sink and seriously damage between them every month a total of 700 000 to 1 million tons of British and allied shipping.
2. All attempts at finding a satisfactory means of defence against the German U-boats or the German bombers have failed disastrously.
3. Even President Roosevelt has openly stated that for every five ships sunk by Germany, Britain and America between them can only build two new ones. All attempts to launch a larger shipbuilding programme in America have failed.
4. Britain is no longer in a position to secure her avenues of supply. The population of Britain has to do with about half the ration that the population of Germany gets. Britain, herself, can only support 40% of her population from her own resources in spite of the attempts made to increase the amount of land under cultivation. If the war is continued until 1942, 60% of the population of Britain will starve!

All this means that starvation in Britain is not to be staved off. At the most it can be postponed, but whether starvation comes this year or at the beginning of next doesn't make a ha'porth of difference. Britain must starve because she is being cut off from her supplies.

Britain's losing the Battle of the Atlantic means Britain's losing the war!

Leaflet dropped by Luftwaffe on Britain in 1941.

There was also the need for conscription – a very specific form of job-direction, about which for certain age groups there was no choice. But in this War, there was an additional consideration. For the first time, women were to take their place as *semi-combatants* in a war.

There was the necessity to provide more protection for the individual from bombs, gas, invasion and enemy attack. So there was a need for air-raid warning systems, shelters and gas masks for everyone, and defences to deter, hinder and delay potential invasion.

Volunteer local services and defence systems to deal with attacks from the air, or invasion by land were planned in Whitehall. This involved the creation of a number of different and differing organisations, at varying levels of sub-military performance.

Finally, there is the question of paying for all this *extra* expenditure, which calls for higher taxes, fund-raising and borrowing from individuals, corporations, institutions, both national and international, and from foreign countries.

Let us look in more detail at these seven considerations – Shortages, Restrictions, Regulation and Control, Conscription, Civilian Protection and Safety, Volunteer Local Services and Defence against attack or invasion, and Paying for the War – as they affected *and changed* everyday life and living conditions for everybody throughout Great Britain.

SHORTAGES

The experience of the First World War only 20 years earlier made everyone aware that some form of selective rationing would be necessary. This and the very British principle of ' fair shares for all' also made (almost) everyone accept it without too many objections.

'Black Markets'
Such acceptance did not, however, prevent the development of 'black markets', where goods in short supply commanded higher prices outside their usual or official channels of distribution. To be successful and to avoid official scrutiny, these 'black markets' needed to be relatively small, normally only open to a limited number of ' those in the know', very local in terms of both supply and demand, and probably were more successful, at least as far as the supply of food was concerned, in rural rather than urban areas.

Rationing
Rationing in case of war had been planned by the Government since 1936, but was not actually introduced until January 1940. A Ministry of Food had been set up in 1937, whose prime task was to oversee the fair distribution and rationing of food, and food rationing was to be controlled through some 1,300 local offices. As an indication of

Government foresight and planning, 50 million Ration Books had already been printed *before* Hitler invaded Poland in September 1939.

Food Rationing

Food rationing was introduced on the 8th. January 1940, with sugar, butter, ham and bacon being the first items to be rationed, followed by meat in March, and by tea, margarine, cooking fats and cheese in July. Spreads (jam, marmalade, treacle and syrup) were added to the list in March 1941 and eggs in June and milk in November. The last item of *wartime* food rationing was chocolate and sweets, which was introduced in July 1942. At the same time as meat was controlled, controls on the slaughter of fatstock were also very sensibly introduced.

It is ironic that other staple foods such as bread and potatoes which were not rationed during the War, had to be rationed in the post-War 'Austerity' years. During the War (as in the previous War), Government advertising urged people to eat less bread, for which the wheat had to be imported, and eat more potatoes, which were home-grown. The strategy seems to have worked as long as the sense of discipline created by the war lasted.

SAVE BREAD
and you save lives
SERVE
POTATOES
& you serve the country

Government advertising poster.

The weekly ration for an adult was (although a few special groups, such as pregnant women and children, received extra rations):

Sugar – 8 oz. (228 g)
Tea – 2 oz. (57 g.)
Butter – 2 oz. (57 g)
Margarine – 4 oz. (114 g.)
Cooking fat – 4 oz. (114 g.), although sometimes less was available
Cheese – 2 oz. (57 g.), although more was occasionally available
Spreads – 1 lb (454 g.) every two months
Milk – 3 pints (1.7 litres), sometimes dropping to 2 pints. Dried powdered milk also sometimes available – 1 tin every four weeks.
Eggs – 1 whole egg, if available, but sometimes only one every two weeks. Dried powdered egg also available – 1 packet every 4 weeks.
Ham and Bacon – 4 oz. (114 g.)
Meat – the quantity was defined by the price, which was 1s-2d (6p.) a week, of what was available. Sausages and offal were not rationed, but rarely appeared above the counter. Butchers kept them for their regulars.

Chocolate and sweets – 12 oz. (340 g.) every four weeks.
The last items to be de-rationed were meat and bacon in June 1954.

The public were also strongly encouraged to grow their own – in their gardens and their allotments – with the now-famous slogan 'Dig for Victory'. And this did work – the number of allotments peaked at 1.4 million in 1943, producing an estimated 1.3 million tonnes of vegetables. (By comparison, the number of allotments in 2009 is estimated to be about 300,000).

Dig for Victory poster.

The Rationing System

In due course, there were to be two rationing systems in parallel with each other, but integrated into the same Ration Book. The original individual ' flat-rate' ration of basic foods was followed in 1941 by the introduction of a 'points' rationing system for foodstuffs and goods, such as canned and processed foods, dried fruits, rice and biscuits, and soap in all forms – bars, powder and flakes. (Detergents, as we know them, did not exist until after the War.) Each Ration Book holder was allocated a number of 'points', and all products were given a points 'value' (which was periodically adjusted). Unlike the straight basic foods rationing system, people could choose on which goods to spend their 'points', and also choose between retailers.

This points system was somewhat surprisingly introduced in response to public demand. The continued ability of the richer sections of the population to buy up stocks of unrationed goods which were more expensive and in short supply, was seen particularly in the winter of 1940-1941 to be exacerbating class tension and creating widespread dissatisfaction; and it actually led to demands for an extension of rationing. At the time of the introduction of the points system, it was also ordered very sensibly that ration allocations were not tradable, although how this could be controlled was obviously problematic, but it did become legal to give a ration as a 'gift' to someone else.

Coal, which was then the principal fuel for heating and cooking, was also rationed, with a variable quantity depending how far north one lived. At that time, very few households had central heating.

Ration book.

Ration Books

Food rationing was controlled by the Ration Book. Every person had their own Ration Book, which had on its cover the same details as the individual's Identity Card in order to minimise fraud. Every Ration Book contained a number of pages of coupons, of differing 'points' values to cover standard basic foods, and also optional foods and products which were of variable points.

Every household had to 'register' with specific retailers and Ration Books could only be used at retailers who were listed in the individual's Ration Book. The number of registered customers controlled the supplies which the retailers received. With every transaction, every retailer then had to cut out the 'spent' coupons, which was a cumbersome process.

The administration of rationing was obviously very time-consuming because it was so 'fiddly' – coupons had to be cut out, stored and recorded – and this certainly increased the length of queues, even if it did not create them. It also gave retailers more power over their customers, particularly in the context of giving small favours, since every retailer would have some customers who did not take up their full allocation, which could therefore be 'redistributed'.

Other Rationing

Rationing did not apply only to food, but potentially to anything which was both in demand and in short supply. It was applied to petrol from 3rd. September 1939, allowing a notional 200 miles a month, a restriction which continued until May 1950. It was then applied progressively to other products, such as soap, coal, and clothing and footwear (rationed from 1st June 1941) and also rather surprisingly, furniture, which continued to be rationed until June 1948.

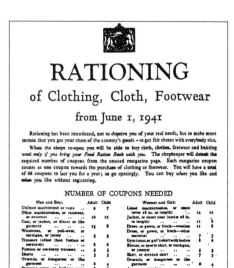

In doing so, a new 'quality' standard was created, which was officially called 'Utility' and had its own special symbol, the CC41 mark, which can still be seen on 'antique' furniture to this day.

CC41 symbol.

These categories were in some respects less complicated to administer and ration. Clothes are not bought every day or even every week, but this lower frequency of purchase is offset by the range and type of clothing being very varied and somewhat complicated. Clothing was rationed through a 'points' system, starting with 66 points in 1941, reducing to 48 in 1942 and 36 in 1943 and 24 in 1945. Clothing was in short supply which created a second-hand market for clothing which could not be controlled or 'rationed', and which consequently acted as a cushion or buffer for the first-hand market. But in all markets which were rationed, shortages led to some form of 'black market' and also a willingness by frustrated purchasers 'to make do and mend'. I can remember that there was a considerable amount of handing down of children's clothes, often as many as 4-5 times.

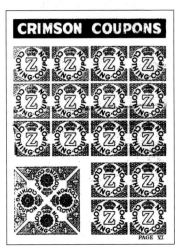

Example of clothing coupons.

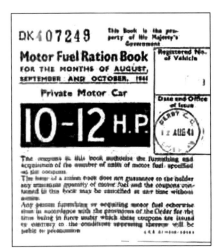

Petrol rationing coupon.

Petrol
Petrol was a relatively limited market, insofar as it was not purchased by most of the population, since at the beginning of the War only about 10% of households owned a car. There were 2,034,000 private cars registered in 1939, which declined with rationing to 1,503,000 in 1940 and to 713,000 by 1943. Even so, there did exist a market for 'black market' petrol coupons, mainly created by commercial van and lorry distribution, for which a variable margin of fuel consumption had to be allowed, and this could be manipulated into the black market.

Eating Out
Restaurants were exempt from rationing, probably because they were too difficult to ration, either fairly or effectively; and also because there was both a practical and a 'morale' justification for the minimum of control. This led to some resentment as the richer classes could eat out more frequently and initially, more expensively. So rules were introduced in 1940 to restrict this inequality: no meal could cost more than five shillings (25p, or £7.40 at 2009 values); or consist of more than three courses; and meat and fish could not be served as two courses in the same individual meal.

But there were also developed popular restaurants for the people, run by Local Authorities on a notionally non-profit basis. Initially they were called Communal Feeding Centres, but Churchill preferred the title 'British Restaurants' which is what they became. Local Authorities set them up in a variety of different premises, such as schools and church halls and some (including two in Tunbridge Wells) were even purpose-built. They evolved from the LCC's Londoners' Meals Service which originated in September 1940 as a temporary, emergency system for feeding those who had been bombed out. They developed with the encouragement of the Ministry of Food's Wartime Meals Division, which encouraged the setting up of industrial canteens, and lent Local Authorities money to start their own British Restaurants.

By November 1942, there were 1,899 British Restaurants in the UK. Although set up to be non-profit-making, this objective proved difficult to achieve and and at the end of the war, 546 Local Authorities found that they had made a profit and 203 a loss.

A three-course meal at a British Restaurant cost only 9d (3^3/$_4$p, equivalent to £1.10 in 2009). Standards varied, but the best were greatly appreciated and had a large, regular clientele. British Restaurants were open to all, but mainly served the workers - office and industrial.

Inflation
Inflation was also another factor which was encouraged by rationing. The overall Cost-of-Living Index between 1st September 1939 and the end of the War in 1945 increased by 31% (an average of just over 5% a year), but there were significant variation between categories of expenditure. Over the period, rent and rates only went up 2%, food went up a below-average 23%, while fuel and light went up 49% and clothing went up 67%.

Shortages always encourage price-rises, but workers did not suffer too much, since incomes increased more than prices. The average weekly wage of workers in manufacturing went up from 53s-3d in October 1938 (£2-66p, or £103.72 at 2009 values) to 96s-1d in July 1945 (£4.80p, or £143.62 at 2009 values), an increase of 80% at 1938 values, but only 38% at 2009 values. At the same time, the average weekly hours worked only increased by less than one hour from 46.5 hours in 1938 to 47.4 hours in 1945, although it should be recorded that at the peak of the War effort in July 1943, it had risen to 50.0 hours.[1] However, when talking of hours worked, it should not be forgotten that many people were also 'working' without any pay for probably about 12 hours a week in the ARP, Home Guard or other volunteer services.

❖❖❖❖❖

RESTRICTIONS

It was inevitable that war would bring restrictions of all kinds. These were particularly related to security, and to night-time security, and were extremely difficult for the 'freedom-loving' British.

Blackout

A 'blackout' operation was introduced on 1st September 1939 which would continue until VE Day on 8th May 1945. This required that all owners of buildings and all householders had to ensure, under pain of prosecution, that no light could be seen from any building after dusk. Initially, this required a massive purchase of blackout curtains or blackout, not just ordinary, curtain lining, by almost every household in the land. It also required daily vigilance by all concerned to ensure that no

Black-out poster

sliver, let alone a shaft of light, could be seen from the air. Control of this was maintained, principally, by ARP Wardens who were regarded by some (or was it many?) as being unnecessarily officious, and also by the Home Guard to a lesser degree. 'Put that light out' became a familiar shout after dark. Obviously the degree of enforcement depended on location and the particular character of the ARP Warden involved, and it

---

[1] *Source for all these statistics: Fighting with Figures, A Statistical Digest of the Second World War: CSO: 1995.*

18

could be argued that light visible on the ground was not necessarily visible 5,000 ft. up in the air, but it was better to be safe than sorry; and if the ARP erred on the side of being officious, it was for the common good and reluctantly accepted.

The regulation was strictly enforced as is shown by the initially increasing and subsequently decreasing number of successful prosecutions, most of which were dealt with a fine from the local magistrates:

Lighting offences against Defence Regulations

Year	England & Wales	Scotland	N. Ireland
1939	59,798	-	5,060
1940	299,260	31,290	15,589
1941	210,934	25,637	18,420
1942	154,080	17,285	12,584
1943	109,757	11,516	11,254
1944	73,831	6,390	9,405
1945	17,594	-	3,606

Source: Fighting with Figures: A Statistical Digest of WWII: CSO 1995

Masked headlights.

The blackout also applied to all shop fascias and shop windows – in fact, anything which emitted light. So most street lighting was switched off and only 'key' lamps, with their beams masked and pointing downwards, were permitted. Train, tram and bus windows were blacked out. Traffic lights were also masked with only a '+-shaped slit' of light showing on the red/amber/green lights, and car headlamps were treated similarly with an up-to-three ' – -shaped' slit (see photo above). To provide some degree of reflective light, the edges of many pavement curbs were painted white, particularly at corners, as well as 1-3 feet of lamp-posts and the trunks of roadside trees. Car owners were also encouraged to paint their front and back wheels, mudguards and fenders white, although this was not widely done.

Not surprisingly, the blackout led to a sharp increase in night-time road accidents and deaths and it was widely commented that it was not

19

enemy bombs, but the blackout, that caused the first casualties.

From 28th June 1940, just after Dunkirk, all owners of cars and vehicles also had to be willing *and able*, if and when instructed to do so by a *'proper authority'*, to immobilize *completely* their vehicles by removing the distributor head and leads, emptying the tank or removing the carburettor; and hiding the removed parts well away from the vehicle.

Curfews

Curfews were also imposed initially in southern areas, matching the 'blackout' times but these seem to have faded away. The same was also true for theatres, cinemas, pubs and other entertainment, but these restrictions were quickly removed, as counter-productive to public morale. But, at a time when few people had cars and even they had a petrol ration, curfews were in effect created by the restricted bus and train services which kept people from staying out, except within walking distance of their home.

IS YOUR JOURNEY REALLY NECESSARY?

TICKETS

RAILWAY EXECUTIVE COMMITTEE

Government poster.

Travel

Travel was discouraged by Government advertising (Is your journey really necessary?) and certainly the idea of anybody going on holiday outside of their immediate area, was no longer acceptable.

One restriction which lasted until the end of the War was access to and travel *within* parts of southern coastal regions. On certain routes and to certain destinations, permission to travel had to be obtained in advance. This restriction became particularly important with the build-up to D-Day in 1944.

Television

One victim of the War was the fledgling BBC TV service.

It had been launched from Alexandra Palace in November 1936 with 405-line definition, but technical limitations restricted its transmission range to a radius of about 30 miles and so there were only about 25,000 sets receiving the signal in 1939. Needless to say, it was only in black-and-white.

A typical set available in 1939 is shown right, at a price of 48 *guineas*, the superior (and apparently cost-reducing) form of pricing in those days, which was actually £52-8s-0d (£52.40, or £1,550 at 2009 values)

The BBC TV service was sensibly shut down on 1st September 'for the duration'.

It was resumed in June 1946 and a combined television and radio licence (for one TV channel and four radio programmes) was then introduced at a price of £2 (equivalent to approximately £60 at 2009 values. The current BBC licence fee for considerably more channels and programmes is £142.50).

A pre-war advertisement.

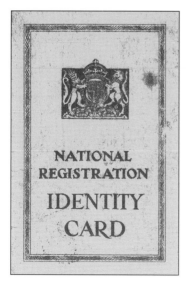

National Identity Card.

REGULATION AND CONTROL

War inevitably saw a huge increase in Government regulation and control, but this was accepted as 'inevitable' and without any undue public protest.

Identity Cards

The National Registration Act 1939 received the Royal Assent on 5th. September 1939 and set up a National Register 'for the duration of the present emergency', containing details of all citizens. National Identity Cards were then issued to all civilians on the Register and everyone was obliged to carry them.

The rationale for the Act was that it was to enable the co-ordination of national service, national security and the administration of rationing, in circumstances:

❖ where there had been major dislocation of the population caused by mobilisation and mass evacuation;

❖ where there was the wartime need for complete manpower control and planning;

❖ and where the likelihood of rationing required the need for an up-to-date system of standardised registration;

❖ all of this in the context that the last Census had been held in 1931 and the next was not due until 1941. (In the event, the 1941 Census was cancelled.)

It took a very short six weeks from the Royal Assent to implement the individual Registration system and by 20th October the public were invited through advertising to register for their Identity Cards and their Ration Books.

Identity Cards, as such, continued in force until 1952. In the interval, the individual Registration Number system had also been converted into an individual's National Insurance and National Health Service number, which exist to this day.

Civil Defence Regions
Twelve Civil Defence Regions capable of taking independent action if necessary, and covering the whole of England, Wales and Scotland, were created by the Government in April 1939 and the appointments of the 12 Regional Commissioners was confirmed on 19th April.[2]

The regions were the same as those established during the General Strike of 1926, when Britain's principal channels of communication and distribution were paralysed.

The South-Eastern Region, which covered Kent, Sussex and Surrey, was to have its HQ at Tunbridge Wells, with Sir Auckland Geddes. as Controller and Viscount Knollys as his Deputy.

---

[2] *The Times 19 April 1939*

CONSCRIPTION

Unlike Germany and France which had a long history of conscription stretching back well into the late 18th-early 19th century, Britain did not experience conscription until the 20th century. Conscription has also always been felt to go against the grain of British 'democracy' and 'the liberty of the subject'.

Conscription in the First World War and after

1914 Recruitment poster.

At the beginning of the First World War, the British Army was too small and although there was a large increase in the number of volunteers, it was not enough. So universal conscription was introduced in April 1916, when the War was almost two years old.

But the dislike of the *idea* of conscription was such that it was abolished in 1919 and it was not reintroduced until April 1939. It remained throughout the Second World War and afterwards during the so-called Cold War, until it was abolished in 1961.

The conscription re-introduced in April 1939 related only to men. But there was one new factor which had not been applied before to any significant degree.

Female Conscription

There had been a relatively small number of about 25,000 women in the three women's services which had been created in 1916 during the First World War, but these services had been disbanded about 1920. In the late 1930s, it was proposed that they should be re-formed and this happened during 1938-1939.

Women were to be recruited on an entirely *voluntary* basis and in a *non-combatant* role, into special all-women branches of the Armed Forces – the WRNS (Women's Royal Navy Service, known familiarly as Wrens); the ATS (Auxiliary Territorial Service, known as Ats) and the WAAF (Women's Auxiliary Air Force, known as Waafs). The use of the word 'Auxiliary' in two of their titles is indicative of the nature of their intended role.

The ATS was formed in 1938, the WRNS early in 1939 and the WAAF in June 1939. Only 4,000 had been recruited in total by the end of 1939, but this increased by the end of 1940 to 57,000 and to 116,000 by the end of 1941.

23

What changed the situation dramatically was the decision in 1941 to *conscript* women of a 'certain age', although they were given a small option - of either joining the women's Auxiliary Armed Forces or the Land Army, or of being '*directed*' to do essential factory work. The National Service (No.2) Act of 1941 laid down that this compulsory call-up applied to all unmarried women aged 20-30.

The result was that the number of women in the Armed and related Forces increased nearly 200% in one year, to 308,000 in 1942. It would increase by 1944 by another 177% to a maximum of 545,000. The ATS was the largest service with 199,000 in 1944, followed by the WAAF with 174,000, the Land Army with 80,000, the WRNS with 73,000 and Nursing Services with 19,000.

Male Conscription

Conscription for men was of all able-bodied men aged 18-45 and had been set initially and somewhat unrealistically in April 1939 for those aged 20-22 and for six months, but this was quickly changed to 'for the duration of the war', however long that might be. There were allowances or exemptions made for special skills, poor health or issues of genuine conscience. Some men, such as coal-miners and skilled factory workers and others whose jobs were considered 'essential', were exempted from conscription, but they were the exception rather than the rule. Male conscription essentially applied to the Armed Forces, but it was also

possible to be conscripted into other essential activities, such as coal-mining. Conscripted coal-miners were known by the familiar nickname of 'Bevin Boy', named after Ernest Bevin, then the Minister of Labour, (although subsequently the Foreign Secretary), who had been a miner in his youth.

My father had served in the Army in the First World War. He was aged 42 in 1939 and would have been liable for 'call up', but probably as the director of a building firm in the Town, this was considered essential work in view of the need to build ARP Posts and shelters and repair bomb damage. Later in 1942, when he was 45, he was conscripted into the Home Guard.

My father in Home Guard uniform.

Post-War

When the Second World War ended, those men who had been conscripted, were released to civilian life (the popular word for this was 'demobbed', an abbreviation of 'demobilised') over a period of about 18 months. But there was still considered to be the need for substantial Armed Forces and for a reserve of trained men who could be 'called up', if necessary. So conscription was continued for all men reaching the age of 18, but the period of conscription was limited - initially it was only for 12 months, but soon it was increased to 18 months and fairly quickly afterwards to two years. It remained two years until it was abolished in 1961, which was surprisingly early in view of the tensions continuing in the World.[3]

---

[3] *By comparison, most European countries in 2009 still have some form of conscription, although the period has been reducing steadily and for most it is now only about a year.*

VOLUNTEER SERVICES AND LOCAL DEFENCE

War calls for many contributions and sacrifices by civilians, freely given and freely made; and by 'freely' we mean not only voluntarily, but also without pay or reward.

A number of voluntary organizations relating to the defence of Britain developed in the inter-War years – the first was the Observer Corps (OC) in 1925, then the Air Raid Precaution Service (ARP) in 1937, the Women's Voluntary Service (WVS) in 1938, the Women's Land Army (WLA) in June 1939, the Auxiliary Fire Service (AFS) and the Air Transport Auxiliary (ATA) in September 1939, and finally at the beginning of the War, the Home Guard (HG), but initially called the Local Defence Volunteers (LDV), in 1940.

The emphasis up to the beginning of the war was on defence from attack from the air, which was the greatest fear, not helped by the popularity of 'futuristic' films, such as the Alexander Korda/H.G.Wells's 'Things to Come' (1936) which forecast World War II starting in 1940 and lasting for 20 years, then a 'Wandering Sickness' devastating the world in 1966, but all of this leading to the 'City of the Future' in 2036. (We're still waiting.)

London bombed, as depicted in the 1936 Alexander Korda film 'Things to Come'.

26

Observer Corps (later The Royal Observer Corps)

The Observer Corps (made Royal in 1941, in recognition of its services, particularly in the Battle of Britain and the 'Blitz') was a

ROC badge.

civil defence organisation operating in the United Kingdom from 1925 up to 1995. The OC operated a network of Observation Posts linked to Control Centres, which were linked to fighter and anti-aircraft artillery and to the ARP, for air-raid warnings. During the War, the ROC operated with about 28-33,000 members, mostly male and mostly part-time.

The ROC can trace its roots to World War I when there was a need for a warning system to bolster UK defences against bombing raids by Zeppelin airships. Initially it was a unique service, observing, identifying, and tracking potential enemy aircraft. When it was assisted by the development in the late 1930s of a new 'secret weapon' called RADAR (**RA**dio **D**etection **A**nd **R**anging), the OC played an entirely complementary role, since the radar defence system which was very rudimentary compared to what it is today, was only able to warn of enemy aircraft approaching the British coast. Once having crossed the coastline, the Observer Corps provided the only means of tracking their position and so was a crucial part of the Defence system.

ARP badge.

Air Raid Precautions (ARP)

As far back as September 1935, the Government had advised all local councils that they should start to consider Air Raid Precautions for their locality. This led eighteen months later to the formation of an ARP Service in April 1937, to which volunteers were recruited on a mainly part-time basis as Air Raid Wardens. By the end of 1937, some 200,000 had volunteered. By June 1940, the ARP had grown to 960,000, going over the million in 1941.

The role of the ARP Warden was to patrol the streets ensuring that the blackout was maintained, to warn the public about impending air-raids and get them to take shelter, and to assist in any 'clear-up' after a raid.

ARP helmet.

The Warden operated at least theoretically as a member of a team of six Wardens who staffed an ARP Post responsible for an area of about 500 houses. So there were about ten Posts per (urban) square mile.

Most wardens did not wear any uniform, except for an ARP armband and a steel helmet with the letter 'W' on it. Their role expanded as they were always first on the scene as the bombs fell.

Women's Voluntary Service (WVS)

The response to the call for ARP volunteers in 1937 was almost entirely men and since it was felt that women should be encouraged to volunteer as well, the Home Office asked the Dowager Marchioness of Reading in 1938 if she would be willing to form an organization to help local councils encourage women to join the ARP. She agreed and the WVS was born in June 1938 and by September 1939, it had 165,000 volunteer members. The WVS quickly outgrew its recruiting role.

WVS badge.

It became an auxiliary service to the ARP and to local councils, undertaking a wide variety of jobs, ranging from coping with child evacuees in September 1939, organizing canteen services for military personnel and the AFS, running rest-centres for the 'bombed-out', organizing 'salvage' campaigns, running clothing exchanges, and generally providing help, advice and information wherever it was needed. By 1943, the WVS had over one million members. It continues to this day as the Women's Royal Voluntary Service (WRVS).

Women's Land Army (WLA)

The Women's Land Army (WLA) was a civilian organization, first created

Women's Land Army poster.

in the World War I and reformed in June 1939, for women to work in agriculture, replacing men called up for military service. Women who worked for the WLA were familiarly known as Land Girls. The WLA was under the aegis of of the Ministry of Agriculture and Fisheries. At first, it was a voluntary organisation and by May 1941, only 11,000 had joined, but its membership increased to over 80,000 when women could be conscripted into it, following the National Service (No.2) Act of 1941. Land Girls, many of whom came from the city, quickly learnt to do every job on the farm and soon earned the praise of even the most sceptical farmer. They had a uniform (see poster on left) and their wage was 32/- [£1.60] for a 48-50 hour week. (The average for a male agricultural worker in 1939 was 38/- [£1.90]). The WLA was disbanded in October 1950.

Auxiliary Fire Service (AFS)

The Auxiliary Fire Service (AFS) was formed from volunteers in September 1939, and comprised initially 89,000 men and 6,000 women, to assist regular fire brigades. This had a great impact on the existing service, which comprised less than 5,000 professional fire-fighters and approximately 50,000 volunteers, and caused tension between the professional and auxiliary fire-fighters, especially over the latter's lower standards of training. For the part-time fire fighters, men were on duty every fourth night and women every sixth night. In order that one town or area could supply assistance more easily to another, all 1,443 local Fire Brigades and their AFS were merged into one National Fire Service (NFS) in August 1941, and this organisation would remain in existence until 1948.

AFS badge.

Home Guard (HG)

On 13th. May 1940, Anthony Eden, the Secretary of State for War, appealed for men to come forward to form a Local Defence Volunteer force [LDV], which later was renamed the Home Guard. The response was astonishingly quick. Within 6 weeks (by 30th. June), it had 1,456,000 *male* recruits and this total then increased slowly to its peak of 1,784,000 by June 1943. It was in effect a citizen army, for which no organization, no uniforms and no arms initially existed.

The role of the Home Guard, although voluntary, was distinctly military, unlike the other organizations which were civilian or at best, semi-military. They would all, in due course, be issued with uniforms and firearms; they would be subject to military discipline; and their role was to be an *additional and local* army to resist any invasion. While awaiting this invasion, they would naturally carry out a number of other relevant security duties. And yet, they were still volunteers and part-time – during the rest of the day, they carried on with their normal jobs.

"I thought I'd better patrol the links for a bit."
Norman Mansbridge cartoon – Punch.

The Home Guard remained almost exclusively male, even after the National Service (No.2) Act of 1941, probably because, unlike the other organisations,

29

they were expected to fight to the death, if necessary, and that was not considered in those days a job for women. It is indicative of their precise, clearly defined and specific role, that when the need for them had vanished (by D-Day in June 1944), that they were the first organization to be 'stood down' i.e. disbanded (before December 1944). Membership of the Home Guard had a distinct bias to those over 40, which may have encouraged its somewhat comical 'Dad's Army' image, but it should be remembered that if you were over 40, you almost certainly had fought in the trenches in the First World War, and if so, you *really* knew what war was about. Which was certainly true for my father and his two brothers.

Although, as events turned out, the Home Guard never had to be tested *in action*, their value to the defence of Britain cannot be disputed. Had it not been for their existence, the pressure and strain which would have been placed on conventional forces if they had not been there, would have been intolerable.[4]

Air Transport Auxiliary (ATA)
The Air Transport Auxiliary (ATA) was a civilian organisation set up in 1939 to ferry new, repaired and damaged military aircraft from UK factories, assembly plants and transatlantic delivery points to RAF and Fleet Air Arm airfields.

ATA wings

During the war, the service flew 415,000 hours and delivered over 308,000 aircraft of 130 types including Spitfires, Hawker Hurricanes, Mosquitoes, Mustangs, Lancasters, Halifaxes and Fortresses. The organisation recruited pilots who were considered to be unsuitable, for reasons of age or fitness (for either the Royal Air Force or the Fleet Air Arm); pilots from neutral countries; and, notably, women pilots. (They were consequently nicknamed "Ancient and Tattered Airmen" after the initials of their Service).

In late 1939, Pauline Gower, who was a pioneer woman aviator and the daughter of Sir Robert Gower, a Mayor of Tunbridge Wells and also for 15 years an MP (for Gillingham), was given the task of organising the women's section of the ATA.[5] There were 166 women pilots, one in eight of the entire service. Fifteen lost their lives in the air, including the British pioneer aviator, Amy Johnson, who vanished over the Thames estuary.

---

[4] *The Home Guard was reactivated in 1952 as a precaution against Cold War threats. It was disbanded in 1956 and since then, is no more.*
[5] *Spitfire Women of World War II by Giles Whittell, Harper Press, 2007.*

The Nature of these Organisations

With the exception of the WVS and the WLA, all these roles were mainly for men, although each organisation had their female members – the ARP had about 14%, and the NFS about 20%, mainly but not exclusively, in administrative roles. The Home Guard, however, did not have any women until 1943 and even then, they were never more than about 1% of the force.

What is probably a more significant distinction is the proportions of these organisations whose members were full- or part-time. All of these organisations were essentially volunteer, part-time (generally committed up to 12 hours a week), and needless to say, unpaid. (Those who were full-time, were of course paid.)

The overall membership figure for all these voluntary organisations was 4.4 million which matches fairly closely the 4.8 million men and women who were in the Armed Forces. But the voluntary organisations were only 70% men, compared with 90% of the Armed Forces, and they were overwhelmingly part-time (90%).

Some 4.4 million was 25% of the working population in civilian employ - a significant proportion to be doing a second *voluntary* job.

At their peak of employment in 1943, the breakdown between male and female, and full- and part-time workers was as follows:

Organisation	No. involved '000	Men %	Women %	Full-time %	Part-time %
Home Guard	1,793	99	1	1	99
ARP	1,030	86	14	8	92
NFS	371	80	20	34	66
Casualty Services*	184	30	70	26	74
ROC	33	88	12	26	74
WVS	1,000	–	100	5?	95?
WLA	80	–	100	100	–
Total No.('000)	4411	3071	1340	463	3948
Total %	100	70	30	10	90

Source: Fighting with Figures – A Statistical Digest of the Second World War, CSO, 1995
* Ambulance & First-Aid

CIVILIAN PROTECTION AND SAFETY

The principal danger for civilians was initially thought to be gas attacks, which were seen to affect pervasively and lethally whole neighbourhoods, while a bomb could only destroy a few houses and people.

Hitler will send no warning –

so always carry your gas mask

Government 'gas mask' poster.

Gas Masks

The threat and fear of 'poison gas' attack proved, but only over time, to be a total ' false alarm'.

Gas had been used as a weapon for the first time on the Western Front in the First World War, and by both sides, with a certain amount of unpredictable/unreliable success. Having been introduced, it was assumed that its use would be extended to civilian situations, particularly since the main aircraft development post-WW1 was in the development of bomber aircraft, which had not existed as such, in WW1.

As a result, some 39 million gas masks were issued in 1939, in three different sizes. The public were instructed to take their gas masks with them at all times, which most did. However, the quietness of the so-called 'Phoney War' from September 1939 to April 1940 gave people false courage and many stopped carrying them. As things turned out, they were quite right and there was nothing to fear.

The standard gas mask (see photo right) was uncomfortable, claustrophobic, smelt of rubber and steamed up very easily. It was only the greater fear of the alternative, that persuaded anybody to carry one. That fear would prove eventually to be unfounded, but it would take up to two years for most people to realise it.

The real danger for the public was from explosive bombs, and while this was appreciated from the beginning, the emotive fear of 'invisible' gas was initially

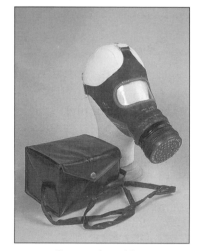

Gas mask and box.

32

dominant. But it was understood from the beginning that there was a need for suitable 'bomb' shelters. There were to be three types of shelter – the Anderson and the Morrison which were for a single household, while the ARP shelters were public, open to all who could get there and they took as many people as each shelter could cram in.

Anderson Shelter.

The Anderson Shelter

The Anderson shelter (named after Rt. Hon. Sir John Anderson MP, PC, the then-Home Secretary) was an outdoor shelter designed to be dug, ideally 4-6 feet down, in one's garden and was the first shelter to be offered to the British public in 1939. It consisted of overlapping curved sheets of corrugated iron, with corrugated end–walls, which with wooden supports, some bricks, a concrete floor and a door (frequently wooden), normally took 4-6 people, but could take more if the design was larger. Arrangements were made for the distribution of Anderson shelters both nationally and regionally to areas likely to be raided. They were to be free to families with an income of less than £250 per annum [£9,580 at 2009 values], otherwise they cost £7 (£270 at 2009 values)

The Morrison Shelter

The Morrison shelter (named after Rt. Hon. Herbert Morrison MP, PC, the then Minister of Supply), was an indoor shelter, essentially a steel frame 2'6" high, 6'6" long and 4 ft. wide, with a steel plate roof and wire-mesh sides and was introduced in March/April 1941 for those without a garden in which to put an Anderson shelter. It was

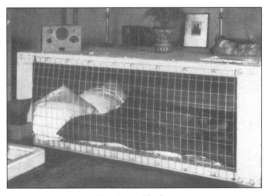

Morrison Shelter.

designed to go inside the house, in the largest space available and could take 2 people, with some discomfort. It was available in one and two-tier versions. The principal protection it gave was from above, against ceilings or rafters collapsing.

ARP Shelters

ARP Shelters were shelters for all the public and were located mainly in large public buildings. Most could hold hundreds of people. They were often underground in basements or cellars and were generally conversions of existing sites, although some were purpose-built. The London Underground was used as a shelter, particularly overnight when the trains had stopped. Caves were also used as shelters, although the availability and suitability of caves was somewhat limited in most areas. Tunbridge Wells did have some caves, but they were not really suitable.

Air Raid Warnings

An Air Raid Warning system was devised very early on, which consisted of a chain of sirens covering a defined area, which broadcast very loudly for about a minute, two very distinctive wailing noises – one for 'Take Cover', the other for 'All Clear'. The sirens which were located about 400 yards apart, could be heard by everybody except the very deaf; and everybody soon learned to distinguish between the two. What was true was that many warnings proved to be 'false', since the specific target was generally unknown or was at least unpredictable, but the warning had to be given to everybody 'just in case'. So Tunbridge Wells which was on the flight-path for London had many 'false' alarms, although later with experience, the Royal Observer Corps and the RAF radar system (which was still notionally a 'secret weapon' unknown to the enemy) which tracked incoming enemy aircraft, learned to judge from the height of the aircraft, what was their intended target.

Air raid warning siren.

Other Precautions

Other precautions, which were fairly standard, were to have buckets of sand and of water and a stirrup-pump, on every corridor of every office

Anti-blast precautions.

or works, in order to put out the incendiary bombs which were expected; and also to criss-cross all glass windows with adhesive tape, in order to minimise the risk of flying shards of glass. I remember these strips as the brown paper strips which one had previously used to wrap and seal parcels, which had adhesive on the back and which had to be licked. It didn't taste nice.

PAYING FOR THE WAR

The final but unavoidable necessity was having to pay for the War, which would obviously be considerably more expensive than maintaining the Peace.

This called for higher taxes; the raising of long-term loans from the public in the form of War Bonds and National Savings; and international loans and extended credit from other countries and financial institutions, an area which was then nowhere near as developed as it is today. A major loan/delivery scheme for essential supplies was agreed with the USA, called 'Lend-Lease', and started in 1941. It was to take Britain over 50 years before the last repayment under this scheme was made to the US Government in the late 1990s.

A remarkable feature in Tunbridge Wells and also nationally in many towns throughout the War, was the enthusiastic public response to a series of fund-raising campaigns which were organised to generate War Savings to pay for the war.

National Savings certificate.

35

Spitfire named 'Royal Tunbridge Wells'

The first National War Savings campaign was launched by the Mayor in Tunbridge Wells on 9th. August 1940. It was a **'Spitfire Fund'**, to buy a Spitfire for the R.A.F. When it closed on 29th. September, it had raised £5,031 [equivalent to about £165,000 at 2009 values) which was more than enough to 'buy' a Spitfire; and a Spitfire was actually named 'Royal Tunbridge Wells'. In February the following year a plaque was presented to the Mayor, which is now in the Borough Archives.

The second campaign was **'War Weapons Week'** which was held from 13th. - 20th. December 1940. There was an opening ceremony and an exhibition, which included a German Messerschmidt 109 which had been shot down near Brighton. It was put on show in the new Library and Museum building which was not yet in use (it would not actually be opened formally until 1950).

Bombers and Shells from Tunbridge Wells

TUNBRIDGE WELLS

WAR WEAPONS WEEK

Begins To-morrow (Saturday)

•

WE WANT

TWO BOMBER SQUADRONS

COSTING

£500,000

This can only be realised by YOUR help

£250,000, our original aim, has already been promised

•

Do your bit and invest every penny you can in

WAR BONDS · DEFENCE BONDS · SAVINGS CERTIFICATES · DEPOSIT MORE IN P.O. SAVINGS BANKS

Issued by the Tunbridge Wells Savings Committee

'War Weapons Week' appeal.

The target was to raise £500,000, which was said to be the cost of two bomber squadrons. The target was exceeded – actually £510,224 was raised - *in just one week*, an enormous amount for just one town, particularly when it is converted at 2009 values to approximately £15,500,000. Nationally, £124 million was raised (£4.05 billion in 2009).

Shot-down Me109 going on display in Tunbridge Wells Library.

HMS Brilliant.

'**Warship Week**' was held from 28th. February- 7th. March 1942 when it was hoped that £450,000, or more, would be raised for a destroyer. This was successfully achieved with £651,000 and as a result, H.M.S. Brilliant which had already been commissioned as long ago as 1930, was 'adopted' by Tunbridge Wells. £17 - 4 - 0d per head, equivalent to £525 at today's values, was given by the people of Tunbridge Wells, the highest in Kent. The Mayor requested that all schools should have an additional day's holiday in recognition of the effort put in by children during the week.

'**Wings for Victory**' **Week** was held in May 1943 when, on average, £12 - 5 - 0d per head was raised (£380 equivalent today).

'**Salute the Soldier**' **Week** was held in June 1944 for which a full programme of events were planned. The aim was to raise £450,000.

National Savings Thanksgiving Week, was held from 10th.-17th. November 1945 - the fifth such week held since 1940. A formal opening ceremony was held in the Assembly Hall and the Week raised £645,000 [equivalent to £19.3 million at 2009 values].

Later a telegram was received from Hugh Dalton, Minister of Economic Warfare:

> *Thank you Tunbridge Wells for the splendid total of your savings in Thanksgivings Week. Your savers and voluntary workers have combined to bring about a notable success. Well Done - Hugh Dalton.*

It was announced later that the total of war savings raised in Tunbridge Wells to the end of 1944 amounted to £8,207,510 or £230 per head [approximately £249 million, or £7,100 per head, at 2009 values]. Later in 1945 this figure had grown to reach a total of £8,477,586, or £243 per head. These are truly astonishing figures and they suggest that Tunbridge Wells had an above average quotient of rich people, a fact which the history of the Town over the past 400 years supports.

PRISONER-OF-WAR CAMPS

A problem which grew as the War developed, was the containment and housing of a constantly increasing number of enemy prisoners-of-war (PoWs). Obviously at the beginning, there were few of them and they were principally Luftwaffe from the Battle of Britain and some Kriegsmarine (German Navy) personnel, particularly from U-boats. But with the beginning of the North African Campaign in 1941, there were an increasing flow of Italian PoWs, followed subsequently by German. This became a flood with the invasion of Italy in 1943 and the D-Day landings in 1944.

UK PoW camps.

By the end of the War, about 560,000 German and Italian prisoners-of-war (402,000 Germans, 157,000 Italians) were imprisoned in Britain, with a further 425,000 having been shipped to Canada and after 1942, the USA.[6] Those in Britain were equivalent to just over 1% of the British population and were housed in about 600 camps. The list of camps was numbered from 1-1,045, but not all numbers were used. All prisoners were screened and graded white or grey or black, according to their assessed security rating, with extremists, such as declared Nazis or Waffen SS, being graded black. All prisoners had to wear an appropriate white/grey/ black patch on their uniform and prisoners were largely segregated by their colour coding.

For obvious reasons, most camps were north of London with many in the North and Scotland. The most extreme prisoners were placed as far away as possible, to deter escape attempts and reduce the likelihood of any success. As far as is known, no German escapee ever got back to Germany from Britain.

---

[6] *For the record, the number of British Armed Forces taken prisoner by the enemy in the Second World War was 172,592 – 135,009 in the War against Germany and 37,583 in the War against Japan.*

There were 19 PoW camps in Kent and 8 in Sussex. Two – Mabledon and Somerhill – lie within the current boundary of the Tunbridge Wells Borough Council and a further six are within a ten mile radius of Royal Tunbridge Wells:

Camp No.	Name/Location
40	Somerhill, nr. Tonbridge, Kent
629*	Mabledon Park, Tonbridge, Kent
267	Mereworth Castle, nr. Maidstone, Kent
629*	Borough Green, nr. Sevenoaks, Kent
631	Bearsted, nr. Maidstone, Kent
566	The Grove, Worth, Sussex
238	Ardingly, Sussex
1017	Sheffield Park, nr. Uckfield, Sussex

* These numbers are inexplicably duplicated, which was not an uncommon occurrence.

As can be inferred from its number, Somerhill was one of the earlier camps. When the International Red Cross visited it on 15th. July 1942, they found it contained 575 Italian prisoners and by 1st. April 1943, this had increased to 750. However it subsequently held German prisoners.

It is worth recording that PoWs were given the same rations as British servicemen and so were better fed than British civilians. Most PoWs were put to work – the exception being officers and those with black patches – mainly in agriculture, but also in construction/reconstruction, for which they were modestly paid. It was estimated in 1946 that 169,000 were employed in agriculture and 22, 000 in construction.

After the end of the War in 1945, repatriation of German and Italian PoWs was a slow process. It did not start until 1946, the Italians were the first to be repatriated as they had become 'allies' in the meantime and repatriation did not end until November 1948, when the last German PoWs were returned home.

CHAPTER 3

THE MILITARY DEFENCE OF SOUTH-EAST ENGLAND

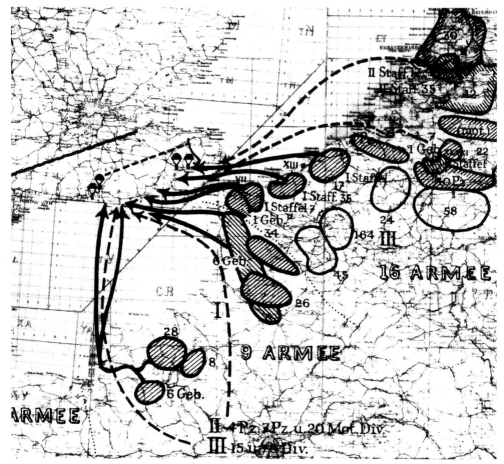

Map of German invasion plans.

XII CORPS

Following the defeat of, but 'miraculous' evacuation of 316,000 British and Allied troops from, Dunkirk, XII Corps was established in June 1940, to be responsible for the defence of the Kent and Sussex coast against German invasion, which was recognised by all as the next likely target.

Its HQ was to be Tunbridge Wells, which was a sensible and reasonably central position 20-25 miles from the coast, straddling the borders of Kent and Sussex and sharing its location with the HQ of Civil Defence Region 12.

Its first General Officer Commanding (GOC) was Lieutenant-General A.F.A.N. Thorne, CB, CMG, DSO, known to his friends as 'Bulgy' or Andrew (although the first A in his initials stood for Augustus). General Thorne was an Etonian and a Regular officer with a distinguished WWI record. Prior to being promoted to take command of XII Corps, he had been, as a Major-General[7], in command of the 48th. (South Midlands) Infantry Division in I Corps in the British Expeditionary Force (BEF) in France from 1939-40.

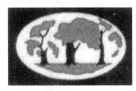

XII Corps badge.

The XII Corps badge was an oak, ash, and thorn in an oval. It was apparently chosen to link the name of its first commander, Thorne, with *The Oak, the Ash and the Thorn* featured in *Puck of Pook's Hill* by Rudyard Kipling, the Corps having being raised in Pook's Hill country (i.e. Kent/Sussex).

XII Corps consisted of three Divisions - **the 56th (London), the 43rd (Wessex) and the 44th (Home Counties)** – and these usually had three Infantry Brigades each, with three battalions in each Brigade – so it normally would have had a complement of 27 Infantry battalions, all of whom had regiments of Armoured, Artillery, Engineers and Signals in support.

The 56th Division was positioned on XII Corps's right flank, with its HQ at Tenterden, although this was subsequently moved further east to Wye, between Ashford and Canterbury, in June 1941.

The 43rd Division was on the Corps' left flank, with its HQ at Wye between Ashford and Canterbury. Subsequently, this was moved further back to Higham, just north of Rochester, in June 1941 when the 56th. Division HQ was moved to Wye.

The 44th Division had suffered fairly heavy losses at the end of May 1940 near Oudenarde and this may be why it was the reserve division for XII Corps, with its HQ much further from the coast at Harrietsham, just east of Maidstone on the A20.

---

[7] *Major-General is actually a lower rank than Lieutenant-General, because the original 17th century title for the rank was Sergeant-Major-General, but the first word has been dropped for a long time – hence the opportunity for confusion about apparent seniority.*

The 56th (London) Infantry Division was a British Territorial Army division of the First and Second World War and was part of XII Corps from June 1940 to November 1942. The Division's badge was the sword from the coat-of-arms of the City of London.

At the outbreak of war in September 1939, the Division was mobilised as motorised infantry under the title of the 1st London Division. The Division was not sent with the BEF to France but following Dunkirk, it was reorganised as an infantry division in XII Corps in June 1940 and was redesignated the 56th (London) Infantry Division on 18th. November 1940.

The Division had four Brigades with twelve battalions –three from the Queen's Royal (West Surrey) Regiment, two from the Royal Fusiliers (City of London Regiment), and one each from the Oxfordshire and Buckinghamshire Light Infantry, the London Scottish Regiment, the London Irish Rifles, the Royal Berkshire Regiment, the Welch Regiment, and the Coldstream and Grenadier Guards.

The Division remained in XII Corps until it was moved to the Middle East in November 1942, thereby missing the victory of El Alamein by only a month. It served in Iraq and Palestine before moving to Egypt in March 1943 and thence forward to Libya and the North African front, in April 1943. The division then went to Italy in September 1943 and fought at the Battle of Monte Cassino in January 1944, serving there until March 1944 when it was withdrawn to Egypt. It returned to Italy in July 1944, taking part in the battles along the Gothic Line and remained there until after VE Day.

 The 43rd. (Wessex) Infantry Division was a First Line Territorial Army Division which had served in WW1. In 1935 the Division adopted the "Wyvern" (a mythical creature which combined the ferocity of the dragon, with the cunning of the serpent, and the swift strike of the eagle) as its Divisional badge.

The 43rd (Wessex) Division landed in Normandy during the week-end of June 24-26th 1944, well-trained but so far untried in battle. From then until the German Armies pulled back across the Rhine early in March 1945, the 43rd Division took a leading role in every one of the major operations of the British Second Army - the Normandy battles, the advance in the Low Countries, Operation MARKET GARDEN (the offensive in September 1944 to cross the Meuse, Waal and Nederrijn Rivers, and which included the siege of a British Parachute Division at Arnhem), Operation VERITABLE (the British and Canadian offensive between the Meuse and the Rhine in February 1945) and the Rhine crossing.

 The 44th. (Home Counties) Infantry Division was also a First Line Territorial Army Division, which had been part of the BEF in France and Belgium in 1940.
The Division was composed of regiments from the Home and Southern Counties, with nine battalions in its three Brigades - three battalions of the Queen's Own Royal West Kent Regiment, three battalions of the Royal Sussex Regiment and two battalions of The Queen's Royal Regiment and one battalion of The Buffs (Royal East Kent Regiment).
In 1942 the Division was sent to Egypt, where it took part in the battles of Alam El Haifa and El Alamein. It was not thought to have performed well, which is presumably why it was disbanded in January 1943. It was however reformed in 1947 and finally disbanded in 1968.

THE SITUATION IN JUNE 1940

... must have been extremely worrying. Invasion seemed not only highly likely, but imminent, and following Dunkirk, British military forces must have been in considerable disarray. The BEF had had to leave behind nearly all their equipment at Dunkirk and so there was a severe shortage of arms, ammunition and vehicles of all kinds.

" Of course at the moment it's still just a suspicion." 31.iii.41

Cartoon by Osbert Lancaster.

The organization of XII Corps must have been done in great haste, since two of its three Divisions had returned from Dunkirk only days before. Organisations do not suddenly appear fully developed. They grow, they develop, they evolve. This is apparent with XII Corps. The War Diaries of the different units in the Corps, now held at the National Archive in Kew, all start at different times – none before June 1940, many in June, some in July and even some in August, including quite interestingly, that of the Corps's GHQ. We will return to these War Diaries later.

In June 1940, the fear of invasion was paranoiac, which was very understandable. Suspicion and credulity went hand-in-hand. The quite unfounded fear of a Fifth Column was almost universal. The nation was obsessed with the related fears of treachery and airborne attack; and what in hindsight, were undue, unnecessary and unacceptable precautions, were nonetheless accepted by everybody.

There was however absolutely no question that Germany was preparing to invade Britain. On 16th July, 1940, Hitler issued his Directive No.16 which gave the code name SEA LION to the operation and required that preparations for the invasion be completed by mid-August. A pre-requisite for invasion was that Germany needed air- and sea superiority to ensure success. The original plan was to land 25-40 highly-mechanised Divisions, initially confirmed as 40, but which was subsequently reduced to just 13. The Directive called for 'a surprise attack on a broad front extending approximately from Ramsgate to a point west of the Isle of Wight.' This was amended to a narrower front when the number of Divisions was reduced. But a fallacy which seemed to persist in German thinking, was that SEA LION would be no more than a river-crossing writ large.

A LAST APPEAL TO REASON

BY

ADOLF HITLER

Speech before the Reichstag, 19th July, 1940

English housewives reading Hitlers' appeal.

On the night of 1st. August 1940, large numbers of a leaflet, entitled 'A Last Appeal to Reason' which was a translation of Hitler's 'peace offer' made in the Reichtag on 19th. July, were dropped by the Luftwaffe on many towns in England, including Tunbridge Wells. I remember my father picking one up and I have that copy to this day. It was treated by everyone as a joke, albeit a somewhat pointless and obscure one. But why was it done? A gross misunderstanding of the British character? The belief that the British could be made to come to their senses and sue for Peace? It was a deliberate act, which clearly shows that Hitler thought it would work, since it was repeated for the next 3-4 nights.

THE BATTLE OF BRITAIN

Hawker Hurricanes.

On 30th July, Hitler had ordered Marshal Goering, the Commander of the Luftwaffe, to start 'the great battle of the Luftwaffe against England'. Goering's directive for what would be called OPERATION EAGLE was issued on 2nd August, effective 3rd. But the weather was unkind and the Luftwaffe were not able to strike in force until 12th August.

In the course of the Battle of Britain, the Luftwaffe changed their strategy twice. Initially from 12th-24th August, they concentrated their attacks on forward RAF stations (such as Manston, and West Malling, some 10 miles from Tunbridge Wells), on radar stations[9] on the South Coast and on aircraft factories, all in the South and South-East of England.

Then from 24th August – 6th September, they turned their attention to the Sector Stations, such as Tangmere, Debden, Kenley, Biggin Hill, Hornchurch, North Weald and Northholt, which each controlled a number of RAF stations and were further inland; and whose importance had only belatedly been recognised by the Germans. On 24th, some German bombers targeted for Sector Stations went off-course

"Eglantine Cottage? Go down the lane past the Messerschmitt, bear left and keep on past the two Dorniers, then turn sharp right and it's just past the first Junkers." *Punch*, 4 September 1940.

and dropped their bombs on London. This was not apparently intentional, but it produced a swift reaction from Churchill, who ordered the bombing of Berlin by the RAF on the following two nights.

Then on 7th September, in retaliation and on Hitler's specific orders, the Luftwaffe started their first concentrated attacks on London, dropping incendiaries and high-explosive, for 57 consecutive nights. But, despite this, the *aerial* Battle of Britain was effectively over before the end of the month.

An important element in how the course of the Battle of Britain developed, was the ability by both sides (in all good faith) to under- or over-estimate, or to exaggerate/ minimise or misinterpret, the losses of aircraft and the remaining fighter strength of the other side. As a result, both sides were much nearer to final victory on paper, than they were ever in fact. In the end, it was like a game of poker – the first to blink

---

[9] *In 1940, radar, which both sides possessed, was a purely defensive device – it gave extremely accurate bearings, but was much less accurate about the height and number of the approaching planes. So it was indispensable to British defences but of less use to the attacking Germans. It was only in 1941 that the British developed airborne radar sets, which turned the night-fighter from being a blind hunter into a sniper with a night-vision 'scope.*

was the loser – and that was the Luftwaffe, as far as the 'Battle of Britain' was concerned.

Between 10th July and 31st October 1940, the claimed and actual number of destroyed aircraft were:

	Claimed	Actual	% overstated
RAF successes	2,698	1,733	55%
Luftwaffe successes	3,058	915	234%

Source: Denis Richards: The Royal Air Force 1939-1945 Vol.I

By 17th September, it would seem that Hitler had recognised that with the coming of winter, there could be no invasion of England in 1940, but it was not until 12th October that he ordered the elaborate invasion infrastructure – barges, troops etc. – to be dismantled 'as unobtrusively as possible' and it was not in fact until 13th February 1942 that German troops who had been allocated to the invasion, were *officially* released from this role.

It did not however prevent the Luftwaffe from keeping up their pressure subsequently in other ways, by changing tactics and targets; and by switching from mainly daylight fighting with the RAF to mainly night-time 'Blitz' bombing of Britain's biggest cities.

In hindsight, it can be seen that after September 1940 the chances of Britain being invaded were remote. *But at the time this was not apparent to the British.* The general and entirely reasonable assessment of the situation was that SEA LION was being postponed, not cancelled, and particularly for weather considerations. This was a great bluff which concealed what had become Hitler's next Grand Design - the conquest of Russia. The Directive for this - No.21 - was issued on 18th December with the original date for the start of OPERATION BARBAROSSA being set for 15th May 1941. It was eventually started five weeks late on 22nd June.

But until this happened, it had to be assumed by the Allies that the Soviet-German Friendship Pact of August 1939 still held and so the German invasion of Russia in June 1941 was for most people a surprise. After that, people began to have a new understanding - Germany could not fight on three fronts at the same time - Russia, North Africa and Britain - and so Britain was safe from invasion, *although not from attack.*

❖❖❖❖❖

This general situation for Britain leads us back to examine the more detailed situation in South-East England.

XII Corps was established as part of *Eastern* Command in June 1940 at the peak of the post-Dunkirk paranoia. Lt. General Andrew Thorne had been appointed GOC of XII Corps – a Corps of three Infantry Divisions which had *never* fought together before; and two of which, it can be inferred having escaped from Dunkirk *without any of their equipment*, were 'shell-shocked' from their experience as part of the BEF in France, literally less than four weeks previously. It was his job to 'whip them into shape'. It is difficult to gauge the Army 'politics' of the time from official reports which were by their nature brief and impersonal, reporting conclusions and decisions, rather than the discussion behind them. But the fact that he was replaced ten months later, suggests that it was felt that he was not performing adequately for whatever reason; and he was moved (technically he was promoted) in April 1941 to become GOC, Scottish Command, and Governor of Edinburgh Castle.

This may have been unfair, but in the hysteria of the times, it may be understandable – results were not expected tomorrow, or even today, *but yesterday*. South-East England was the centre-point of all military activity and everybody's performance was under the microscope. It should be recorded that Thorne is credited with creating the XII Corps 'Observation Units' – a euphemism for the highly-secret undercover 'guerilla' units which were intended to, and would, 'go underground' in the event of German invasion; and that he subsequently became Sir Andrew, which is usually a recognition of success rather than failure.

But there were also changes taking place in higher command, which must have had a 'knock-on' effect further down the line.

CHANGES IN HIGHER COMMAND

The Commander-in-Chief (C-in-C), Home Forces, up to May 1940 was General Sir Walter Kirke. He retired on 27th May 1940, obviously because a stronger Commander was deemed necessary in the event of the impending disaster at Dunkirk. He was succeeded by General Sir Edmund Ironside, who was the Chief of the Imperial General Staff (CIGS). This succession was not a promotion, but rather a sideways move, since the C-in-C was subordinate to the CIGS, but it may

Sir Edmund Ironside.

have been seen as a short-term necessity to cope with an immediate disaster situation. Ironside was to last only two months in the post, resigning at 2.45pm on 19th July, but being compensated by his Field-Marshal's baton on 28th August 1940 and his peerage on 29th January, 1941. However, he never held another official post.[10]

Ironside's resignation is somewhat enigmatic, but it would seem that he was a casualty of:

❖ politics (Churchill who had been an ally, had been persuaded to turn against him);

❖ disagreements with, and lack of support for his proposals from, his military subordinates;

❖ and the paranoia and panic of the times.

General Sir Alan Brooke.

Ironside's successor was General Sir Alan Brooke (later Field-Marshal Lord Alanbrooke) who remained C-in-C, Home Forces, until he was promoted to be Chief of the General Staff (CIGS) in December 1941. He was succeeded by General Sir Bernard Paget, who up to that time was GOC, South-Eastern Command. This opened up the opportunity for Montgomery, by then GOC, XII Corps, to succeed him. For the record, General Paget remained C-in-C, Home Forces, until July 1943 when the structure of command was changed and he became GOC, 21 Army Group, which was formed to control the British Forces selected for the invasion of Europe. And General Paget was to be superseded in this role by Montgomery in January 1944. But we are now 'running slightly ahead of the game' – *so let us go back to 1941.*

---

[10] *Ironside, who had an adventurous early career, was considered by many to be the inspiration for John Buchan's character, Richard Hannay (The Thirty-Nine Steps [1915], Greenmantle [1916], Mr. Standfast [1918], and The Three Hostages [1924])*

Lines of Defence/ Nodal Points

The military thinking in 1940 on the defence against invasion rested on the idea of there being certain clearly-defined Lines of Defence, or Stop Lines, which could be defined as 'major' (Command, or Corps) or 'minor' (Divisional, Regimental) and were drawn across the whole of the south of England. They were coupled with what were called 'nodal points' which were particular points of either vulnerability for the defenders, or opportunity for the enemy, which needed therefore to be defended more heavily.

A Line of Defence was relatively broad and obviously took into account geographic/topographic factors, such as the North or South Downs, the location of towns, and major obstacles, such as rivers, railways and key roads.

A 'nodal point' (which was also often referred to as ' an anti-tank island') was much more local and would be a particular strategic point, such as the bridge over the Medway at Tonbridge, a strategic cross-road such as the A26/A21, or a particular road or rail junction, or a specific and direct route for enemy advance. In all, there were initially 43 defined 'nodal points' for Kent, although they were constantly being assessed and re-defined, and 28 were defined as Category A; and 15 as Category B. In Montgomery's view, the two key nodal points were Canterbury and Ashford. Nodal points for the Tunbridge Wells area, were Tunbridge Wells, Tonbridge and Penshurst. Tunbridge Wells started as being part of several nodal points, but eventually the whole of Tunbridge Wells was defined as one nodal point. It was stated that nodal points were expected to hold out under attack for up to 7 days.

In April 1941, Lt. General Thorne was succeeded by Lt. General Bernard Montgomery, CB, DSO,[11] who took over command of XII Corps on 26th. April 1941. But before that happened, there had been a change in the structure of command.

A new and what was thought to be a 'more-relevant-to-the-Invasion-situation' Command was created on 15th. February 1941. It was called 'Southern-Eastern Command' and was formed for operational and administrative purposes from the Aldershot Command

South Eastern Command badge. and that portion of the Eastern Command which lay south of the Thames. It took overall control of 'all forces in the counties of Kent, Sussex, Surrey, Hampshire and Berkshire, less those portions under the control of London District or Southern Command'. XII Corps was to leave Eastern Command and in doing so, it would shed some of its territorial responsibilities (for Sussex) to 4 Corps, which was also to be in South-Eastern Command. South-Eastern Command HQ was at Reigate. South-Eastern Command was to be renamed 'Army' by Montgomery but was to cease to exist at the end of 1944.

The various War Diaries reveal the sequence of events:

24th and 26th February 1941 "General Sir Bernard Paget, the GOC of South-East Command, visited XII Corps HQ." As a result, defence of Sussex passed from 12 Corps to 4 Corps on 25th. February.

5th March "Relief 12 Corps completed. 56 Div. Right, 43 Div. Left, 44 Div. in reserve" This probably refers to the defence of Sussex being passed to 4 Corps.

21st March "GOC visited 43 Div."

28th March "GOC visited 12 Corps."

General Sir Bernard Paget.

26th April "Lt.Gen. B.L. Montgomery, CB, DSO took over command of 12 Corps, vice Lt. Gen. A.F.A.N. Thorne, CB, CMG, DSO".

They also recorded that Exercise "Moriaty" started on 26th and finished on the 29th.

---

[11] *At the start of the Second World War, Montgomery was sent to France with the British Expeditionary Force, where he commanded 2nd Corps. He was forced to retreat to Dunkirk during Germany's Western Offensive and arrived back in England on 1st June, 1940. Montgomery was then placed in command of the 5th Corps (July 1940-April 1941), the 12th Corps (April 1941-December 1941) and the South-Eastern Command (renamed by him as Army) from December 1941-August 1942, before taking command of the 8th Army in North Africa.*

THE ARRIVAL OF MONTGOMERY

Lt. Gen. Bernard Montgomery.

Montgomery arrived in Tunbridge Wells in the middle of the Exercise and by all accounts was appalled by what he saw. Many officers had their wives with them as if they were on a peacetime posting; and he immediately ordered that all wives should leave what could well become a Battle Zone. He also thought most of the men were unfit and ordered PT (Physical Training) for everyone. On 12th May at Maidstone, Montgomery gave an address to all Divisional officers, which was also attended by Sir Bernard Paget, GOC, South-Eastern Command.

By 16th. May, Montgomery had published 'The XII Corps Plan to defeat Invasion" which indicated that XII Corps was 'responsible for defeating invasion in Kent'. Note that Sussex was no longer under 12 Corps, having been passed from 12 Corps to 4 Corps on 25th. February 1941. This is no doubt the explanation of why the three Divisional HQs were moved further east in June 1941.

In his Plan, he instructed that the phrase 'Defence Schemes' which was commonly used, was to be banned since it was 'liable to induce a defensive mentality' and was to be replaced by the phrase 'Plans to defeat Invasion'. He also went on to say 'Every Officer, or OR (Other Rank], must be able and mentally wishful, to take part in a real rough-house lasting for weeks. If they are to do this, they must be 100% fit; they must be more than merely fit, they must be 'hard'. They must be 100% enthusiastic for the battle. They must possess 100% binge."

'Binge' was a favourite word with Montgomery. It did not mean to him what the OED defines as a drinking bout or spree, but rather energy, drive, determination. He gave the name to three Corps exercises.

The first was Exercise 'Binge' held from 24th-26th June, 1941, during which quite a lot went wrong and Montgomery was very critical. After it, he wrote to the whole Corps saying "The Army is not a mutual congratulation society. Great issues are at stake, if we lose the battle in Kent, we may lose the war."

The second Exercise was called 'More Binge' and took place from 5th – 8th. August, for which his conclusion was that there must be 'no relaxing' on what they had achieved.

His final Exercise was called 'Great Binge' and took place from 24th – 27th November but by this time, Montgomery had actually been promoted to command the South-Eastern Command, succeeding General Sir Bernard Paget, who had been promoted to C-in-C, Home Forces.

THE SWING OF THE PENDULUM

By this time, the pendulum was beginning to swing in Britain's favour, although this is possibly only apparent in retrospect. Germany had invaded Russia in June 1941, an action which virtually guaranteed that Britain would not be invaded, although it took some time for this to be fully realised.

When Japan attacked Pearl Harbour in Hawaii on 7th December, 1941 and declared war on both the USA and Britain, and both Germany and Italy declared war on the USA on 11th. December, Britain and the Commonwealth were no longer alone in their struggle.

The USA had been sympathetic to Britain's position for a long time. The first 'Lend-Lease' shipment of goods and equipment had started to arrive in April 1941 and there was also cooperation and exchange of information. As a small example, Col. Haynes Kroner, the US Assistant Military Attaché is recorded as visiting various units of XII Corps on 23rd May, and no doubt he visited many others as well. But now with Pearl Harbour and the German-Italian Declaration of War, the USA was locked into 'the Cause' and it did wonders for British morale.

THE OUTCOME

The loosening of the defence system was a corollary of the diminishing risk of invasion and it would seem that XII Corps as a *defence* system had less and less relevance. That did not mean that it did not have a fighting role, but rather that the nature of that role had changed and therefore new structures and systems were required. It is indicative of changing priorities that two of XII Corps' divisions – the 56th and 44th – were detached in mid-1942 and sent to North Africa to fight in Montgomery's 8th Army against General Erhardt Rommel.

Such a detachment did not mean that the South East was left with a dearth of troops. Rather the reverse, in fact. There had been Canadian troops stationed in the South-East since December 1939. All of them were volunteers and by the summer of 1942, there were over 200,000 of them. To ease their frustration at doing little or nothing, some of them were to be given a major but what was to prove a highly punitive part in the Dieppe Raid of 19th August, 1942. Besides them, with the USA entering the War from December 1941, American troops started to arrive in 1942 with a huge build-up in numbers in 1943, in anticipation of Operation OVERLORD (D-Day) in 1944.

So it was not that the South-East was undermanned against any potential invasion, but more simply that the nature of the War had changed: the threat of invasion had vanished (although it took some time for everybody to appreciate this); and the increasingly large number of troops in Southern England were not there to defend it, but to be the spearhead of the Allied invasion of Europe.

PART 2 TUNBRIDGE WELLS IN THE SECOND WORLD WAR

CHAPTER 4

PREPARING FOR WAR 1930–1938

Tunbridge Wells in the Second World War would be in a very different position from the one it had held in the First World War.

It would find itself in the front-line of defence against the extremely serious risk of a German invasion, which had never been a possibility in

'Bredbury' on Mount Ephraim.

the previous War. Tunbridge Wells had been chosen as the Regional Centre of Government for the South East, in the event of invasion, and this was to be based at 'Bredbury' on Mount Ephraim. After Dunkirk, it would also be a Forward Defence Area and the Headquarters of XII Corps, with its HQ based in Broadwater Down, charged with the defence of Kent and Sussex against invasion.

In 1939, the town received thousands of child evacuees from London (while getting them out of London is understandable, it is somewhat puzzling that so many were sent *towards* the enemy, rather than *away* from him). Slightly later, in mid-1940, it witnessed the Battle of Britain being fought in the skies above and was surrounded throughout the War by RAF airfields (nearly all fighter airfields) which were in a constant state of alert. It was also a host to many of the Allied troops making preparations for D-Day in June 1944. Later in 1944, Tunbridge Wells witnessed the relatively-successful interception by the RAF of many of the German V-1 flying bombs – sadly the RAF were never able to catch up with the V-2 rocket. So Tunbridge Wells was really in the thick of it, as far as the Second World War was concerned.

And yet, it got off remarkably lightly, with little loss of life, or damage. Some 846 bombs fell on it, mostly in the summer and autumn of 1940, as well as 6 V1 'flying bombs' in 1944-5; but only 13 men and 2 women were killed and 31 seriously injured and 36 slightly injured; and 13

War Memorial, Civic Way.

houses were destroyed, and 113 severely damaged, with a further 5,488 slightly damaged (mostly broken windows). It also suffered less in another respect – only 166 names were subsequently added to the 776 already on its First World War Memorial in Civic Way.

War did not come as a surprise to anyone, although as a child, I was not aware that it was impending. It had been brewing for a number of years and while no British person wanted it, and hoped against hope that it would never occur, when it came, the nation rose to the challenge. Because it was no surprise, Britain and Tunbridge Wells were not entirely unprepared for a second War following the War which was supposed 'to end all Wars'.

As early as March 1930, there were discussions taking place regarding Air Raid Precautions (ARP) and four years before the outbreak of the War, the Home Office in July 1935 recommended that all local authorities '*which might be subjected to an attack by hostile aircraft*' should set up ARP committees and prepare plans to deal with the effects of Air Raids. The Tunbridge Wells Council in their July 1935 meeting discussed the issues raised in the letter and decided that the letter should be referred to the Watch Committee, *[the Committee then responsible for 'policing' in the Borough]*. At their next meeting, they resolved that the Town Clerk be instructed to obtain from the KCC (Kent County Council) "particulars of any scheme proposed to be adopted by them in connection with 'Air Raid Precautions". It is thought that KCC may have been slow to react to this request.

But it is worth recording that during the four years up to the outbreak of War on 3rd. September 1939, the Council had been making plans for civil *defence*, even though Britain did not embark on *offensive* general rearmament programme until 1937.

In May 1935, there had been a passive defence exercise held over South East England, and on 26th. July *The Courier* reported that the St. John Ambulance Brigade was anxious to enlist persons to help in their scheme for training the local population in the use of gas masks in case

---

[12] *The Courier 26 July 1935 p 15.*

of gas attacks. One of the greatest fears at this time was that gas would be used in air-raids, a fear which was no doubt created by the extensive use of it on the Western Front by both sides during World War I. The Police Force started training in air raid precautions in 1936, with the emphasis on gas warfare.

The British Union of Fascists had been founded by Oswald Mosley in 1932, before Hitler actually came to power, but it was to be particularly associated with Nazism[13]. Fascism[14] was the 'umbrella' word to describe a belief in firm, controlled and directed government in which the rights of the individual would be subjugated to the needs of the State, as would be exemplified by the rule of Mussolini in Italy from 1922 and Hitler in Germany from 1933.

Oswald Mosley.

Mosley had had a varied political career and was described by some as one of the most impressive Fascist leaders in Europe. The members of the British Union of Fascists were known as 'Black Shirts' because of the black shirts which they wore as uniform. A Public Order Act had been passed in 1936 banning the wearing of political uniforms in public.

Tunbridge Wells was to witness an anti-Black Shirt rally in the autumn of 1936. The Black Shirts' local HQ was in Tonbridge, from where propaganda leaflets were distributed. On the evening of Saturday, 10th October, between 30 and 40 Black Shirts arrived in Tunbridge Wells and were greeted in the Five Ways area by huge crowds which became unruly, with many 'missiles' being thrown. There were no serious casualties and the Police were able to escort the demonstrators away. No arrests were made and on the following Monday, the Police were congratulated by the Mayor, Mr E. B. Weeks, at the Borough Police Court. In a long report, *The Courier*[15] describes the turbulent scenes. Arrangements had been made for a further meeting to take place at High Brooms Station where over 2000 local people gathered, but they were to be disappointed when only two Blackshirts turned up.

---

[13] *A word derived from **NA**tional So**Z**ialismus Parte**I**, the name of Hitler's political party.*
[14] *A word with Latin roots: fasces, the bundle of rods, bound up around an axe, which was the symbol of the power and authority of the Roman Imperial State.*
[15] *The Courier October 16 1936 p 8. See also Council's Watch Committee minutes.*

October 1936 saw other more peaceful meetings. Sir John Marriott gave a course of lectures, entitled 'Democracy and Dictatorship', which were held in the Parish Hall of King Charles the Martyr in Warwick Park and filled the Hall.[16] And at a luncheon held by the Rotary Club, the future development of the Town was discussed, with Mr Strange as speaker.[17]

Rusthall Beacon.

The Spanish Civil War had started in July 1936 and in late May 1937, 60 Basque child refugees arrived at Rusthall Beacon [now The Beacon Hotel], which had been bought for that purpose by Miss Payne, the owner of St. Christopher's Nursing Training College in Pembury Road. After a short while, these children were able to return home. But they were soon to be replaced in 1938 by 50 Jewish children who had come from Austria and Czechoslovakia on the Kindertransport[18] in 1938-9.[19] In the summer of 1944 these children were evacuated to Scotland because of the V1 and V2 attacks. They returned to Tunbridge Wells in 1945, and the hostel finally closed in the early 1950s.[20]

In February 1937, local authorities were asked by the Home Office to turn their attention to the fire risks in their area, suggesting that the peacetime fire brigades would not be able to cope with the fires which experts were predicting would be caused by enemy bombers. From the beginning of 1938, men and women aged between 25 to 50 years were urged to enrol in the newly formed Auxiliary Fire Service [AFS] and by September 1939 there had been a good response in Tunbridge Wells.

Amongst the premises used in Tunbridge Wells by the AFS were 46a The Pantiles, and 6a Lower Green Road, Rusthall. The premises of the Baltic Saw Mills, Meadow Road were used for the parking of Fire Brigade vehicles. 'Holly Bank' in Crescent Road became a billet for the NFS [National Fire Service] at a later date.

---

[16] The Courier, October 9 1936.
[17] The Courier, October 9 1936, p 10.
[18] The name (literally Childrens' Transport) given to a humanitarian endeavour which in 1938-9 brought around 10,000 children, mostly Jewish, and without their parents, out of Austria, Germany, Poland and Czechoslovakia by train to Britain.
[19] The Courier 13 March 1942. One of these refugees, Margot Pagina, was killed in a road accident involving an army truck.
[20] See' The Beacon' by Erica Prean, published privately 2006.

One somewhat surprising incident was reported in May 1937, when it was learnt that *The Courier* had been banned in Italy by Mussolini and copies of the paper were being returned to this country.[21] Study of the January-March 1937 issues of *The Courier* suggests that this might be due to a general anti-Fascist editorial approach, coupled with specific reports of Lord Hardinge speaking to the Tonbridge Division of the Conservative Secretaries Guild(!) on 'The Danger Spots of Europe' which obviously included Italy; and Sir Adrian Baillie of Leeds Castle, who was the Conservative candidate in a Parliamentary bye-election in March, speaking on re-armament and fascism.

In March 1938 the Home Office issued a leaflet setting out the choices which were open to citizens who wished to volunteer for a new body, called Air Raid Precautions or more familiarly the ARP, the duties of which were described as 'passive defence'. At the same time the Home Secretary, Sir Samuel Hoare, spoke on the radio, on 14th March 1938, calling for a million volunteers, as air raid wardens, first aid workers, drivers, gas decontamination squads, and rescue squads. A Government leaflet 'What You Can Do' was issued to every household.

Staff of Thomas Bates & Sons Ltd. ready for a gas attack!

The Government also issued no less than eight Air Raid Precautions Handbooks for the public, priced between 3d and 6d. It is indicative of the overwhelming preoccupation with the likelihood of a gas attack, that the first five handbooks were entirely concerned with gas – Personal Protection against Gas; First Aid and Nursing for Gas Casualties; Medical Treatment of Gas Casualties; Decontamination of Materials; and Structural Precautions against Bombs and Gas.

There were also a further nine so-called Memoranda, priced between 2d and 6d, which covered Organisation of Air Raid Casualties Services; Rescue Parties and the Clearance of Debris; Organisation of Decontamination Services; Air Raid Wardens; Anti-Gas Training; Local Communications and Reporting of Air Raid Damage; Personnel Requirements for Air Raid General and Fire Precautions Services, and

---

[21] *The Courier 21 May 1937 page 9.*

the Police Service; the Air Raid Warning System; and the Protection of Foodstuffs against Poison Gas. So it cannot be said that the Government, or the Public, were unaware of the potential dangers.

Neville Chamberlain.

The international political situation continued to deteriorate during 1938, and reached its climax in September when the Prime Minister, Neville Chamberlain, flew three times to Munich (an unprecedented act in those days) to negotiate with Hitler over the Sudetenland (i.e. Czechoslovakian) situation.

Tunbridge Wells continued to take precautions against war. In July, the Education Committee had received a letter from Kent County Council proposing a conference of all local education authorities regarding ARP in Schools. Heads of Elementary (the then-word for Primary) Schools were advised:-

'that in the event of hostilities schools in the Borough should be closed if this happened during school hours, and the children should return home as soon as possible'.

In September 1938, the Education Committee arranged a survey of ARP provisions for shelters in Elementary Schools in the Borough. Schools listed the number of pupils and their methods of protection and the likely cost. The total estimated cost was £5,089, and the Borough Surveyor was instructed to proceed.

Miss E. Hope-Paley, the Commandant of Kent 94 V.A.D. (Voluntary Aid Detachments)[22] wrote to The Courier of 30th September calling for volunteers to join the local detachment of the British Red Cross Society, stating that she would interview volunteers on Friday and Saturday either at 9, Broadwater Down or Arlington House, Carlton Road, which was the boarding house of a boys' school.[23]

Arlington House.

---

[22] *VADs had been established by the British Red Cross Society in 1910 to run auxiliary military hospitals in houses, church halls and schools. Kent VAD ran over 80 such hospitals in Kent during the First World War, caring for over 125,000 wounded.*
[23] *Later Miss Hope-Paley was also to be involved with the War Comforts Association.*

On Monday 26th September, all Local Councils received a telegram from the Home Office giving instructions to issue respirators (which was the original name for what would commonly be called 'gas masks') and dig trenches immediately. Note that it was a telegram rather than a letter, which implies a high degree of urgency, which is not surprising, since this was the middle of the 'Munich' Crisis.

On the night of Wednesday 28th.September, the Home Secretary, Sir Samuel Hoare, in a message to all Local Authorities urged them to push rapidly to complete the distribution of gas masks, trench digging, and First Aid. He added that:

> 'it would be unwise to relax the spirit of activity shown during
> the past weeks, for taking precautionary measures'

The 30th September issue of 'The Courier' reported in some detail on the preparations that were being made. Notices appeared on Tuesday 27th, advising the public where they could attend for the issue of gas masks.

The gas masks were delivered in kit form (they came in four pieces) to the old hospital building in Goods Station Road where they were assembled by hundreds of volunteers (including boys from The Skinners' School who assembled 8,000) and then issued to 17 centres, which were mainly Parish Halls.[24] Some 32,000 gas masks were ready for issue by the Wednesday and a further 9,000 arrived on the Thursday. At the time, the population of Tunbridge Wells was less than 36,000.

Mr H. T. Taylor of the Town's Public Health Department had previously received instruction on a course organised by the Government, and held at a civilian Anti-Gas School, on decontamination in the event of a gas attack. He was responsible for training others in the local area.

Advice was available from the Borough Surveyor's Office for those with cellars, on how to strengthen them to act as air raid shelters. Detailed plans of a garden trench shelter for six persons were also published in *The Courier*.

At this time, the Chief ARP Officer was Mr A.B.H. Read, with Major G.L. Parker and Inspector Morgan being responsible for general ARP training, and Dr. F.C. Linton, the Town's Medical Officer of Health, for casualty services. Some 300 ARP Wardens had been enrolled, and many were already fully trained.

---

[24] *The Courier 30 September 1938 p 18.*

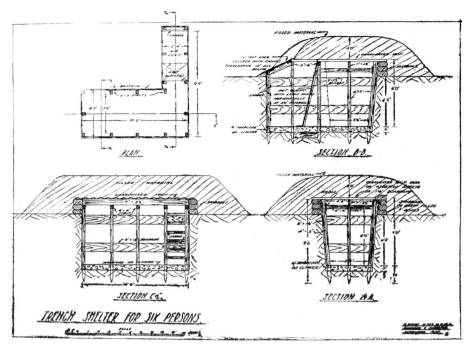

Garden trench shelter for six persons, as featured in The Courier.

Two hundred men from the local Labour Exchange started digging air-raid trenches in open spaces such as Calverley Grounds, St. John's Recreation Ground, the Hilbert Recreation Ground, the Common (between the Inner and Main London Road near Church Road), Still Green and the Mary Caley Recreation Ground in Rusthall. The trenches were said to have been 7 feet deep and 5 feet wide covered with corrugated iron, with 2 feet of soil on top, but they were to prove liable to flooding. Schools also had similar trenches dug in the schoolyards.

All the main stores in the Town reported customers stocking up with extra food, candles, and batteries and many items were quickly sold out. At a meeting, demands were made for adequate bomb proof shelters to be provided for the public.

Radio bulletins on Monday 26th September 1938, announced that Territorial Army Units were to be mobilised. The Town's Unit, the 163rd Battery of the 5th Kent Anti-Aircraft Brigade R.A. [TA] assembled at the new Drill Hall[25] in St. John's Road.

---

[25] *The Hall had only been opened earlier in September with the opening ceremony being performed by Col John Egginton O.B.E. T.D. D.L., Honorary Colonel of the Brigade, and attended by Sir Robert Gower.*

TA Drill Hall in St John's Road.

The TA units dispersed the following morning (27th) to their stations, leaving in buses provided by the Maidstone and District Bus Company.

Maidstone and District Bus, used by the TA.

WVS

The recently-formed Women's Voluntary Service (WVS) were responsible in 1938 and 1939 for organising the billeting of evacuees. They were also responsible for furniture and clothing distribution in Tunbridge Wells. No.22, Church Road became their main emergency clothing store, but later this was moved to No. 16, The Pantiles.

No. 81, London Road became the Civil Defence HQ of the WVS in Tunbridge Wells with Miss Muriel Wells as the local Tunbridge Wells organiser.[26] They provided meals and hot drinks in many situations during the war years, particularly in the aftermath of bombing. Their work continued throughout the following years, and up to the present day.

Miss Luard making camouflage nets.

Another task organised and coordinated by the voluntary services was the making of camouflage nets, known as 'netting', and one Tunbridge Wells inhabitant remembers it 'as the filthiest job I have ever known. We use to wear overalls, a scarf round our hair, and a mask something like a surgical mask, it was such a dusty job we drank as many cups of tea as the ration would allow'.[27]

---

[26] *Miss Wells later became the first female Mayor of the Borough, in 1949.*
[27] *'How we lived then' by Norman Longmate, Hutchinson, 1971.*

The WVS also set up a Communal Centre for the elderly at The Assembly Hall, which operated throughout the War.

After all the frantic activity during the last week of September 1938, it was ironic that the Prime Minister, Mr Neville Chamberlain, returned from Munich and fooled himself *and the whole country* by declaring that the Agreement which he had signed, would mean:

"*Peace in Our Time*".

In the euphoria which accompanied this declaration, Sunday 2nd October was declared *National Thanksgiving Day for Peace.*

Chamberlain with his 'piece of paper', returning from Munich.

After the Munich Agreement, there was some relaxation of the measures which had been prepared – for example, the evacuation of children. So for another year there was an uneasy peace, life in Tunbridge Wells carried on as usual, with people having summer holidays and the annual events of the Town taking place - Cricket Week, Tennis and Bowls Tournaments and the Agricultural Show were amongst the big attractions at the time.

There was to be no Christmas Day broadcast by King George VI in 1938.

CHAPTER 5

TUNBRIDGE WELLS IN 1939

On 1st January 1939, The Archbishop of Canterbury in a broadcast New Year's Sermon said that the nation should:

'hope for the best and prepare for the worst'.

And later on 29th June 1939, Lord Halifax said:-

'All Britain's might behind her pledges
– unchallengeable Navy: Air Force to fear none.'

By the start of 1939, further defensive measures were being put in place. Arrangements were made for the distribution of Anderson shelters both nationally and regionally to areas likely to be bombed. They were to be free to families with an income of less than £250 per annum. [£9,580 at 2009 values]

Civil Defence Regions
Civil Defence Regions were introduced by the Government in April 1939 and the appointment of Regional Commissioners was confirmed on 19th. April.[28]

No 12 [South Eastern] Civil Defence Region which covered the counties of Surrey, Sussex and Kent was established with its HQ in Tunbridge Wells. These Regions were the same as those established at the time of the General Strike in 1926, but it is possible that the choice of Tunbridge Wells as the HQ may have been influenced by defence considerations, since all the major towns in the area were essentially coastal towns - Chatham, Margate, Canterbury, Dover, Folkestone, Hastings, Brighton – and it would not make sense to have the HQ on what would be the front-line of invasion.

Tunbridge Wells was suitably central – 20–25 miles from the coast, 35 miles from the centre of London – and on the Kent-Sussex border and near to Surrey. It would also fit in with the subsequent military organization of the defence of South East England. XII Corps, which was not to be created until June 1940 i.e. after Dunkirk, was to be responsible for the military defence of the Kent-Sussex coast, and very sensibly chose Tunbridge Wells as its HQ. So the HQs of both military and civil defence would be in the same place.

---

[28] *The Times 19 April 1939.*

Sir Auckland Geddes.

The actual HQ of No.12 Region was established at 'Bredbury', No.78, Mount Ephraim, which had been requisitioned by the Home Office on 10th February 1939. Sir Auckland Geddes, (later Lord Geddes) was appointed Regional Commissioner.[29] He continued as Regional Commissioner until July 1941 when he resigned, due to failing eye sight.

Geddes' deputy was Viscount Knollys[30] who was appointed shortly before the outbreak of war. In June 1941, Knollys resigned to become the Governor of Bermuda. Geddes's legal advisor was Mr Hartley Shawcross K.C.[31] who took over from Knollys as Deputy Regional Commissioner.

When Geddes retired, he was succeeded by Lord Monsell [1881-1969] who remained Regional Commissioner until the summer of 1945, when he retired as the War was ended.[32]

Lord Monsell.

Amongst their many duties, Regional Commissioners were to act for the Government in the event of a breakdown of central control through invasion or any other disaster. Tunbridge Wells was located on what was called both the forward 'Stop Line' and the Newhaven-Hoo Peninsular GHQ line, which was planned to protect London and the Midlands. It was also a Class 'A' Nodal Point, which in the event of an invasion was expected to hold out for seven days. These defence plans were not completed until 1940 by General [later Field-Marshal] Sir Edmund Ironside.

---

[29] *Geddes [1879–1954] was born in Scotland and had had a distinguished career in medicine. During the First World War he had become Director of Recruiting, later Minister of National Service and President of the Board of Trade.   In 1920 he became British Ambassador to the U.S.A.*

[30] *Knollys [1895-1966] was the son of the Private Secretary of both King Edward VII and George V. He had a distinguished record during the First World War and a successful business career in Barclays, BOAC and Vickers. His appointment to Bermuda may have been a 'diplomatic/political' move, connected with the Duke of Windsor, (who was a 'family' friend, but somewhat of a political ' loose cannon'), being 'exiled' to be Governor of the neighbouring Bahamas, for the duration of the War.*

[31] *Later to be Sir Hartley Shawcross, the Attorney-General, who lead the British prosecution team at the Nuremburg Trials of 1945-6, and subsequently to be Lord Shawcross.*

[32] *Monsell (1881-1969) had a naval background and had been a successful MP (Conservative Chief Whip from 1923-1931 and First Lord of the Admiralty from 1931-1936), retiring from the House of Commons in 1935 upon his elevation to the peerage. He had entertained the Mitford sisters and Ribbentrop at Dumbleton Hall in Yorkshire and met with Hitler in 1936, at the request of Stanley Baldwin.*

National GHQ Line.

[1880 - 1952],[33] but by August 1940 the GHQ line was declared out of date by the newly appointed Commander-in-Chief of Home Forces, General Alan Brooke [later Field-Marshal Lord Alanbrooke], and it was abandoned in 1941.

Premises used by various departments of the Civil Defence Region included Mount Ephraim House as South Eastern Divisional Food HQ office, with Mr Postlethwaite as food officer; and 81, London Road as the ARP HQ with Mr A.B.H. Read as Chief ARP Officer. Amongst the many other buildings requisitioned at this time were 40a Camden Road; 15, High Street; Culverden Hall; and the basement of The Great Hall. They were used as ARP posts, and public Air Raid shelters.

The Borough Civil Defence Centre was situated at the Town Hall and the Council had made plans for Aultmore, Kingswood Road, to be an alternative Civic HQ. [See Appendix 1 for a list of properties requisitioned by the Army and the Civil Defence.]

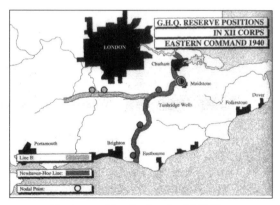

Newhaven–Hoo Peninsular GHQ Line.

---

[33] 'Ironside's Line' by Colin Alexander, Historic Military Press, 1999.

In Tunbridge Wells, the WVS which was already well-established, became part of Civil Defence Region 12, and the regional administrator from 1938-1946 was Lady Worsley.[34]

Also in April 1939, the Prime Minister announced the introduction of conscription for men over 20 years of age, who would have to serve with the army for a period of six months. In the light of the experience of the First World War, such a term of service was unrealistic. But probably the Government felt that to announce a more realistic period of service, would produce too much opposition.

A circular was issued by the Home Office asking for the stepping up of ARP precautions against air raids.

The Council held a meeting a meeting on 5th. April 1939 to appoint an Emergency Committee to deal with the day-to-day running of issues relating to the then-peacetime and subsequently-wartime situation.

It is therefore somewhat surprising that the first meeting of this Emergency Committee was not to be held until five months later on 1st September 1939 at the Town Hall. Initially the committee met every morning, later the meetings became less frequent, the last being held on 24th October 1945. The Committee was responsible for the day-to-day running of the Borough throughout the War years.

Alderman Westbrook.

Alderman Charles Westbrook was the Mayor for that year (and with the coming of war, he would remain Mayor for the next six years, only retiring when the War ended in 1945), so it was not surprising that he became and remained Chairman of the Emergency Committee. He was joined by Alderman Burslem and Councillors Harries and Hillman, with two to form a quorum. Alderman Westbrook also chaired other sub-committees during the war years. Not surprisingly, he did not seek re-election to the Council in the Borough elections of 1945. He was the first Skinners' School Old Boy to be elected Mayor.

---

[34] *Lady Worsley's husband had been killed in the first War, and in 1945 she was awarded the O.B.E. and later in 1954 the C.B.E. for her services to the WVS.*

The Jubilee Celebrations

In the middle of all this tension, the Borough of Royal Tunbridge Wells was also celebrating an important anniversary – the 50th Anniversary of it receiving its Charter as an independent Borough in 1889. *The Courier* listed ten days of celebrations starting with the Charter Jubilee Day of Saturday 20th May and continuing through to the following Monday, which was Whit-Monday and in those days, a Bank Holiday.

Charter Jubilee Day – opening of the Assembly Hall.

The busiest day was the Wednesday which was also Empire Day. This started at 8 am with the Ringing of Peals of Bells at St. Peter's and St. Luke's, followed at 10.45 am by a Thanksgiving and Empire Day Service in Calverley Grounds, led by the Bishop of Rochester. At 1pm, there was Lunch for visiting Mayors 'and other distinguished visitors' at the Calverley Hotel (*now the Hotel du Vin*). At 2pm, there were Sports for the elementary school children at the Higher Ground on the Common. At 3pm, the Marchioness Camden, accompanied by her husband who was also Lord-Lieutenant of Kent, opened the new Assembly Hall, with music by the Tunbridge Wells Symphony Orchestra. At 4pm on the Pantiles, there was the Coronation of the Charter Queen, Miss Meryl Maldwyn Jones, by Miss June Duprez, the Star of London Film Productions' latest film, 'The Four Feathers'. At 5.45pm, there was a Grand Carnival Procession, followed at 6.30pm by the opening of the Pea-Nut Funfair by the Mayor. Finally at 8pm, there was a Band Concert in the Calverley Grounds.

On the other days, there were Band Concerts (usually Military) every day in the morning in the Pantiles and in the evening in Calverley

24th May 1939 – Charter Jubilee Day – the Charter Queen in procession in the Pantiles.

Grounds; a Parade of 'HM Forces and local Civil Defence Services'; a Grand Fireworks Display; three performances of ' The Pageant of the Pantiles'; a Charter Dance; a Hospital Ball; a Cricket Match on the Higher Ground; as well as a Tea and Entertainment given by the Mayoress for 'Old Folk' in the Assembly Hall, several exhibitions and four performances of ' The Pirates of Penzance' by the Tunbridge Wells Amateur Operatic and Dramatic Society (TWODS) in the Assembly Hall. It must have been quite a celebration.

Saturday 8th July 1939 saw the whole of the ARP system tested in a major 'black-out' exercise held in Southern England, with the S.E. Region under the supervision of the Commissioner Sir Auckland Geddes, his Deputy, and Home Office officials. The exercise involved the black-out of 15 counties, with an area of 18,000 square miles, from midnight to 4 am. *The Courier* reported the exercise as:

THE BIG BLACK-OUT
The Largest Air-Raid Test Yet Attempted In the Country,
BUT RAF UNABLE TO CO-OPERATE OWING TO LOW CLOUDS:
Excellent work by ARP Services.

It was estimated that 30,000 ARP volunteers in Kent and Sussex were mobilized, but because 'cloud cover' was too low, 'hundreds of RAF planes never left the ground'. But the test was not apparently universally successful.

The Courier reported that 'what made Saturday night's blackout unreal to Crowborough inhabitants was, that while they had to have their lights extinguished by 9.30 pm, the street lights of Tunbridge Wells were plainly visible until about midnight.'.[35]

At the conclusion of the exercise, Geddes was able to say (possibly somewhat optimistically):

> *'The ARP machinery is well designed and able to meet any call made on it, but there is still the need to speed up the services.'*

As an indication of the understandably confused assessment of the situation, it was possible for Lord Hardinge to declare in a speech at a

[35] *The Courier 14 July 1939 p 13.*

meeting held at his home in Penshurst just a month before the outbreak of war, (and which *The Courier* described as 'a brilliant analysis of the current political situation'):

> *'I do not believe in the imminence of war while confidence in Mr Chamberlain and Lord Halifax remains unimpaired'*[36]

Given the political situation throughout the 1930's, this seems just a little optimistic.

War was declared on Sunday 3rd. September, at 11.00 am. I can remember listening with my father to the Prime Minister, Neville Chamberlain, speaking to 'the Nation' on the radio from the Cabinet Room at 10 Downing Street:-

> *'This morning the British Ambassador in Berlin handed the German Government a final note, stating that, unless we heard from them by eleven o'clock, that they were prepared at once to withdraw their troops from Poland, a state of war would exist between us. I have to tell you now that no such undertaking has been received, and consequently this country is now at war with Germany'.*

Although I can remember the speech clearly, I do not think that I appreciated the significance of it, although clearly my parents did.

The first air-raid siren sounded in Tunbridge Wells and elsewhere shortly after the broadcast, at about 11.20 am. Thinking we were about to be 'raided', my parents and I, somewhat illogically, went outside. The alarm was caused by a light aircraft returning from France which had failed to report its movements to the authorities and had been presumed to be hostile.

In the evening, King George VI broadcast to 'the British Empire':

> *'Stand calm, firm and united ... over and over again we have tried to find a peaceful way out of our differences between ourselves and those who are now our enemies. But it has been in vain, we have been forced into a conflict. For we are called, with our Allies, to meet the challenge of principle which, if it were to prevail, would be fatal to any civilized order in the world.'*

---

[36] *The Courier 11 August 1939 p 12.*

Also on 3rd.September, the Regional Commissioner received a message from the Secretary of State for the Home Department, on behalf of H. M. King George VI:

> *'Now that the emergency has come I wish to express to all civil defence volunteers, my appreciation of the way they have responded to the call, and of the fine spirit in which they are facing the long hours and discomfort inseparable from the performance of their duties.*
>
> *The Queen and I have seen for ourselves something of your organisation, and we have no doubt whatever that the courage of the volunteers, coupled with patience during times of inaction, will be equal to tasks may be in store for them'*

George R. I.[37]

Two weeks after the outbreak of war, the WAAF [Women's Auxiliary Air Force] which had only been formed in June 1939, started a recruiting campaign with centres at Maidstone and Brighton.[38]

On 27th September, a War Budget was announced by Sir John Simon, the Chancellor of the Exchequer, with a 36% increase in the standard rate of income tax from 5/6d (27$\frac{1}{2}$p) to 7/6d (37$\frac{1}{2}$p) in the £. Surtax was raised to a maximum of 9/6d (47$\frac{1}{2}$p) in the £, making the maximum tax on top-scale incomes 17/- (85p, or 85%) in the £. Beer was increased by 1d a pint, tobacco by 1$\frac{1}{2}$d an ounce, whisky by 1/3d a bottle and sugar by 1d a lb. The top rate of Death Duties (today's Inheritance Tax) was increased to 60% and excess profits of firms were to be taxed at 60%. A punitive scheme of taxing profiteers was also to be introduced. Most of these taxes were to be increased again in 1940.

Evacuees from London.

Evacuees and Education
In view of the expected air-raids, large-scale evacuation of children from London had been planned since early 1938. A Home Office circular which had been received by the KCC in March 1938 had allotted Tunbridge Wells Borough 5,598 evacuees, with 3,600 arriving at the

---

[37] *R.I. stands for Rex Imperator – King and Emperor – a title used until 1947.*
[38] *The Courier 15 September 1939 p 5.*

West Station and 1,998 at High Brooms station. This evacuation nearly took place at the time of the Munich Crisis in 1938, and provisional arrangements had been made for them to arrive by train on Friday 30th September 1938. However following Chamberlain's discussions in Munich and the apparent reduction of the threat of war, the evacuation was delayed until the end of August/beginning of September 1939.

Some 4,888 were eventually to be billeted in the Town and the rest in outlying areas. The billeting tribunal consisted of Sir Robert Gower, Mrs Lillian Burslem and Councillor John Crabtree. There was no compulsory billeting, but those willing to house a child were paid 10/6d a week for the first child (equivalent to £15.50 at 2009 values) and 8/6d (£12.50) a week for the second. The Town Clerk had obtained possession of 25, Frant Road to be used as a hostel for evacuees, bedding costs were reported to be £45 charged to the Council, and other costs were to be borne by the Government.[39]

The Pump Room.

The main reception point for children arriving from London, was the Pump Room on the Pantiles, no doubt because of its proximity to the West Station, where they were to be given a medical inspection before going to other dispersal sites. The number of evacuees allotted to Tunbridge Wells was in fact not reached; some never arrived, and many returned home after a short time. By January 1940, there were only 855 school children from London in the Borough.

Many schools were evacuated to Tunbridge Wells.

❖ They included Blackheath High School for Girls who joined up with the Tunbridge Wells High School for Girls, which was situated at the top of Grove Hill Road, in Camden Hill/Cambridge Gardens. The Blackheath High School rented No.24 Calverley Park which was nearby, as an annex, and equipment from Blackheath was brought down by road. Mr and Mrs Bishop became caretakers, and Mr and Mrs Gilroy from Blackheath looked after the buildings. I was a pupil of the Tunbridge Wells High School for Girls, but did not join until nearly two years later, in the Autumn Term of 1941.[40]

---

[39] *Later in 1948 this house was used as a petroleum office annex.*
[40] *Some of the Tunbridge Wells girls (including myself) returned to Blackheath as boarders after the War.*

- Colfe's Boys' School from Lewisham joined Skinners';
- The Greenwich Blue Coat School for Girls was at Culverden House (4 Culverden Park Road).

Among the London County Council (LCC) Schools evacuated:

- Randell Place Boys and Girls Infant Schools *[Greenwich]* shared premises with St Barnabas Church School. At first the two schools alternated class time, working a morning or afternoon shift, but by May 1940, the London school had been accommodated elsewhere.
- Deptford RC Boys School joined St. James's Senior Boys School, for half day working.[41]
- Clyde Street [London] Infants joined Rusthall Infants.
- Lee C.E. Infants School were placed with Down Lane Infants in Byng Hall.
- Invicta Mixed and Infant Schools merged with St. Stephens Mixed and Infant.
- Invicta Senior Girls joined Rusthall Girls School.
- Notting Hill Nursery School was housed at Hollyshaw in Camden Park.

Log Books of schools record the disruption that the war caused to the everyday running of schools in Tunbridge Wells. Initially with two schools sharing the same premises, the most common solution was to have one school take the morning 'shift' and the other the afternoon. But in due course, alternative accommodation was generally found.

By February 1940 the number of children, local and evacuated, attending public elementary schools in the Borough amounted to:-

	Resident	Evacuated	TOTAL
Full Time	1,717	652	2,369
Half Time	913	151	1,064
Total	**2,730**	**803**	**3,433**

On the 25th September 1939, the Local Education Committee decided that the Autumn Term scheduled to start on 1st. October should not start until placings and accommodation for all the evacuated children had been decided. Consequently it was not until 16th. October that the schools reopened. Later in 1940, the Committee advised that the number of children in school at any one time should be halved. It was

---

[41] *Oral history: Jane Dickson. Two Deptford schoolboys were billeted on a family in Prospect Road. They were sons of a greengrocer and at weekends, their father would arrive to see his sons with a crate of beer in the back of his van. Later they were replaced by two girls.*

also recommended that children should not leave their schools during an air raid.

Whilst many schools were being evacuated to Tunbridge Wells, some pupils of Tunbridge Wells schools were going to other parts of the country. They included the Sacred Heart School in Pembury Road, (now Beechwood Sacred Heart School)[42] which in 1940 went to Albrighton Hall near Shrewsbury until 1945. The vacant building was then used to house nurses who had been evacuated from Guy's Hospital.

Air Raid and Defence Precautions and Restrictions

WHAT GERMAN TROOP CARRIERS ARE LIKE

Recognition Silhouettes in The Courier.

During the last four months of 1939, *The Courier* reported every week on what actions should be taken by the people of Tunbridge Wells. On the 8th September there was a full page report published, giving advice and instructions of what to do and not to do. Interestingly, the list contained 18 Don'ts and only 8 Do's. Also published were the silhouettes of German planes, to educate the public in recognizing them.

Other information published included emergency bus and train times (there would be no buses after 9pm and their frequency was lowered), and restrictions on postal services and shop hours. The postal restrictions introduced actually provided a better service than exists today in 2009 – deliveries were cut to two a day, collections were reduced to *five* a day with the last at 7.45pm (10.45pm at the Head Post Office in Vale Road), and the Head Post Office in Vale Road and the Sub-Head Post Office at Fiveways would close earlier at 6.30 pm, and sub-Post Offices at 6pm.

There were reports on the preparations which the Council had been making, and in particular the Borough Surveyor had been

---

[42] *'Calm Amidst the Waves', Chapter 8 : Jane Bakowski, Gresham Books, 2004.*

active in making the Town as safe as possible:

'the first steps taken at the commencement of the present crisis, on 23rd August, were to provide facilities for the movement of traffic under black-out conditions.'

Despite the Borough Surveyor's efforts, the movement of traffic under blackout conditions was causing problems. In October 1939, Kent County Council (KCC) reported that there had been a 73% increase in road traffic accidents in September compared to the same month in 1938. Somewhat ironically, one of those involved was Sir Auckland Geddes, who had been run down by a lady cyclist while inspecting ARP measures in Hastings.

The Ministry of Transport reported that nationally the number killed in road accidents in Britain in September 1939 had more than doubled - to 1,130, compared to 554 in 1938.[43]

Other measures were suggested. In October, Sir Auckland Geddes considered that prominent buildings in the town should be camouflaged, including The Opera House, but this suggestion was not pursued.

Sandbags at 'Hell Fire Corner' (the Municipal offices) in Tunbridge Wells.

Defence measures included the resumption of the construction of the concrete lined trenches in Calverley Grounds. Tank obstructions known as 'Dragon's Teeth' were built at strategic road junctions, and in the countryside, pole and wire obstacles were constructed to prevent glider landings. Other measures included the filling of sand bags to protect public buildings, and there were advertisements in the press advising on the methods which could be used to stop the sand bags rotting.

Orders were placed with local builders for 22 Air Raid Warden's Posts to be constructed. Air Raid Shelters were established under the New Civic Centre, opened in 1939. The caves beneath the rocks on the Common opposite Dudley Road would be opened if necessary, but these were later closed because of the damp conditions.

---

[43] *In 1939, there were 2,034,000 private cars on the road in the UK. With petrol rationing, this dropped to 1,423,000 in 1940 and to 755,000 by 1944. It may be relevant to record that in 2008 there were 34.2 million vehicles (28.4 million cars) on the roads in Britain and road deaths were 2,538.*

Air Raid shelter under the Common, drawn by E. Owen Jennings, Principal of the Art School.

Decontamination stations were established at the Kent & Sussex Hospital, and at the Fonthill Rest Rooms on the Common *[Fonthill was newly built in 1939[44], and today's reader will know it as The Forum].*

Decontamination Squads, as well as Rescue Parties and Repair Services were also set up, based at the Council depots in Quarry Road and Rusthall. Ambulances were also based at the Assembly Hall, Fonthill and the two Corporation depots.

First Aid Posts were established at the Kent & Sussex Hospital and St Mark's Parish Hall and two mobile First Aid Posts were based at The Homeopathic Hospital in Church Road.

Mobile First Aid Post No.2 in Tunbridge Wells.
(Photo: Ruth Wakefield)

[44] *The Courier 19 May 1939.*

Amongst the subjects which the Council considered at their meetings during October were the protection of children during air raids, and in particular the 'trench scheme' to be dug in the grounds and playgrounds of local schools which was estimated would cost approx £5,000, and the 'boarding-up' of school windows with sandbags.

In the first months of the War, daily Air Raid drills were held and gas masks were worn by the children during these drills. School timetables were disorganised not because of air raids as such, which were very few, but because of air raid warnings in the form of a wailing siren, which sounded whenever enemy aircraft

A school trench scheme: a posed photograph.

approached. The Observer Corps who set off these sirens, did not know what was the target for these planes and so had to warn everybody 'just in case', with the children (and adults) having to go to the shelters every time there was an alarm. There were a large number of what were for

Children in St. Mark's Primary School Air Raid Shelter

Tunbridge Wells 'false alarms'. It was reported by St. Barnabas's School that in one week alone, the children had spent sixteen and a half hours in the shelters. Night raid alarms also took their toll, with many children being absent from school because of lack of sleep.

There were also practical problems about gasmasks – they were lost, mislaid, damaged and in the case of children, they outgrew their masks and needed larger ones. Repair and replacement was in due course to be undertaken by the WVS. Previously an ARP Warden had been responsible for inspecting the gas masks and those needing to be replaced or repaired, were taken to the Town Hall free of charge, but in following years a charge was made for this.

Guy's Hospital Medical School was evacuated and situated at Sherwood

Park in Pembury Road, with the students being housed at Hurstmead, and two other houses in Sandrock Road. Lectures were held in the basement of the newly built Baptist Tabernacle in Upper Grosvenor Road, and qualified Doctors and Nurses joined Pembury Hospital.

KCC had earlier made arrangements for aged, infirm and chronically sick members

Sherwood Park.

of the civil population to be evacuated from coastal areas in the South East. Until the Ministry of Health could arrange transfer to other parts of the country, approximately 1000 persons were transferred for a short period to Pembury Hospital by motor coach and ambulances. There had been a review by the Ministry of Health in the Spring of 1939 and instructions had been given that additional wooden EMS (Emergency Medical Service) hutments should be erected at Pembury Hospital to accommodate 36 beds in each, allowing for a total of 400 extra beds. David Salomons' House, now Broomhill, which had been given to the KCC before the war became a large County Store/Depot of medical equipment of all types.

Queueing for ration books outside Crabb Hall, Tunbridge Wells.

On 5th September 1939, the National Registration Act had been passed to create a National Register of all citizens, with a view to managing an integrated system which could control not only the issue of individual Identity Cards and Ration Cards, but also control the requirements of labour direction and con-scription (principally to the Armed Forces). This took a little time to implement and organise and it was not until 20th October that advertisements appeared advising the public where they could go to register, to receive their Identity Cards and Ration Books. Food rationing started on 7th January 1940.

Rusthall ARP on parade. Left to right: E. Burtenshaw, E. Lawrence, Mrs B. Taylor, J.H. Barnes, R. Gunnis, P. Putting, Mrs E. McFarlane, R.J. Dixon, Col. Woulfe-Flanagan, H. Smith and R. Ellis.

The ARP held in July, October and December 1939 a series of demonstrations and exercises preparing for the expected air raids, including an incendiary bomb demonstration. The exercise on the morning of Sunday 2nd December involved settling alight and extinguishing a derelict house, White Lodge, in St. John's Road. *The Courier* reported it under the headlines:

MOCK AIR RAID ON TUNBRIDGE WELLS
DARING RESCUES FROM BLAZING BUILDINGS
SUCCESSFUL ARP EXERCISE

The only problem seemed to be that, as *The Courier* reported, there was only one operational telephone line in the Control Centre in Quarry Road and this not surprisingly led to long delays in orders being given and reports being received. To compound the problem, the telephone in the second depot in St. John's Road 'broke down for over an hour'. Despite all this, the organisers deemed the exercise 'a success'.

Other civil defence exercises were to follow in 1940 and 1941.

ARP Locations in Tunbridge Wells

The ARP HQ was at 81, London Road, with a sub-HQ at 15/17 Grange Road, Rusthall.

There were 21 ARP Wardens' Posts in the Borough, with an initial complement of one Chief Warden, five Head Wardens and 42 Wardens (subsequently enlarged). These Posts were at:

Blackhurst Corner
Birling Road
17, Broadwater Down, adjoining St, Mark's Church
49 Claremont Road
Culverden Park and Culverden Farm
Earl's Road
Forest Road
Gas Works
Linden Park
Mary Caley Recreation Ground, Rusthall
Meadow Road
Oak Road
Post Office, St. John's Road
Royal Chase
Rusthall Open Air School
St. John's Road
St. Mark's Road

Other Support Locations in Tunbridge Wells

Ambulances	Assembly Hall
	Corporation Yard, Quarry Road
	Corporation Yard, Rusthall
	Fonthill, The Common (now The Forum)
Decontamination Units:	Kent & Sussex Hospital and Fonthill
First Aid Posts	Kent and Sussex Hospital
	St. Mark's Parish Room
	Mobile Units – Homeopathic Hospital (2)
First Aid Points	Bretlands, Rusthall
	21 Molyneux Park
	74 Warwick Park
First Aid Parties	Corporation Yard, Quarry Road
	Corporation Yard at Rusthall
Rescue Parties	at both Corporation Yards
Repair Services	Gas Works, Clifton Road

Air Raid Shelters

There were 53 public ARP Shelters in the Borough, of varying sizes. Most were in basements or cellars, very few were purpose-built. They were at:

Rock, Thorpe & Watson, 88 Grosvenor Rd., with a capacity for 350 persons, (230 with gas protection)
Great Hall (an unspecified number)
Civic Centre and Assembly Hall (an unspecified number)
Culverden Hall basement (200 persons)
Old Market, Camden Road (200)
Christian Science Church, St. John's Rd. *(now the Freight Transport Assoc.)* (150)
St. James' Rd (100)
Nevill Bakery & Spicer's Shop, St. John's Rd (75)
Pantiles Information Centre (50) *(not the current Fishmarket site.)*
Cadogan Playing Fields (50)
Mr. Bridge, East Ward – Nissen Hut (50)
Portland House, 3 Frant Rd. (50)
2, Cromwell Rd. (33)

as well as other shelters with unspecified numbers at:

Calverley Rd:	*50/- Tailors*	*and Sibthorpe's (10,12,14)*
Camden Rd:	*Friendly Societies Hall*	*John Tester & Co. & 114*
Prospect Rd	Cambrian Rd	Silverdale Rd
Oak Rd	Clifton Rd	Caley Rd
Brook Rd	Rochdale Rd	South Grove
Chandos Rd	Mount Sion	Goods Station Rd
The Pantiles	St. Luke's Hall	St. Peter's
St. John's	59-60 St. John's Rd	14, John St.
Down Lane School	County School	Christchurch School
Hilbert Recreation Ground	Brighton Lake	Hawkenbury
Rusthall	Wards, London Rd	Sandhurst, Pembury Rd
The Mitre, St. James' Rd		Ferrars Estate
Albion Rd Electricity Yard		22, Church Rd
T/Wells District Maternity Home		14 Little Mount Sion

There were also at least nine ' Trench' shelters in:

Calverley Grounds – Upper and Lower	Hilbert Recreation Ground
Bayhall Road Works dept. depot	St. James' Road
Rochdale Road vacant land (75)	

Rusthall: Mary Caley Recreation Ground, Congregational Church and 125 Rusthall High Street.

In October 1941, the Borough Surveyor reported that in relation to possible invasion, it had been planned to provide Public Air Raid Shelters for 30,000 (out of a then-population of about 36,000). However by October 1941, provision had only been made for 9,575, leaving approximately 20,000 places unprovided. However by that time, the threat of invasion and the consequent need for everyone to be provided with a place in a Public Shelter, had diminished considerably.

The Council decided to suspend the Tunbridge Wells and South Eastern Counties Agricultural Show, Cricket Week, Tennis Week and Bowls Week, for the duration of the war. Other regular events were also cancelled or suspended and none were to be restored until the summer of 1946. This was a necessary decision which must have had a big effect on the Town, which had grown used to creating and having its 'own entertainment' throughout the year, but particularly in summer months.

On October 21st, all men aged 20-22 had to register for National Service and in South-West Kent, 619 signed on, 240 of them in Tunbridge Wells. About 2% declared themselves to be conscientious objectors and one of them is reported as saying "The last War was fought to put an end to Prussian militarism; it produced Hitler. This War may finish off Nazism, but it will probably put militant Communism in its place. War is morally wrong in itself; but worse than that, its effects are always evil". How right he proved to be.

By the beginning of December 1939, the first reports appeared of local servicemen, members of the BEF [British Expeditionary Force] in France and Belgium, being wounded or killed.

The winter of 1939/1940 was very cold, not only in Britain but all over Europe. The severe weather at that time was not reported, because it was thought that this information could be useful to the enemy. It was only later that such weather reports were permitted.

As a result of the War, a surprisingly large number of welfare and other war-related organizations and funds were created in the Town. They included:

❖ The Tunbridge Wells War Comforts Association, which was probably the earliest and was formed in November 1939. The objectives of this Association were to co-ordinate all the various efforts in the Borough for the provision of comforts in Tunbridge Wells to members of the armed forces. The first meeting was held on Wednesday 22nd. November 1939 when the Officers and Committee were appointed. The Chairman was the Mayor, Alderman Charles Westbrook, the Hon. Secretary H. S. Whiting and the Hon. Treasurer W. Reeve, of Lloyds Bank. A list of all men and women serving with the forces was proposed. And by February 1945 the Association had the names and addresses of 2,269 Tunbridge Wells men and women serving in the forces, not counting those who were prisoners-of-war. Of the many parcels sent to those serving, most contained cigarettes amounting to over 750,000 in total (an average of 330 per recipient), of which just under half (327,500) were sent out in 1944 alone.

❖ The Tunbridge Wells War Savings Association formed in December 1939, which masterminded the Spitfire Fund (1940), War Weapons Week (1940), Warship Week (1942), Wings for Victory (1943), Salute the Soldier Week (June 1944), as well as Savings Weeks every year.

❖ The National War Savings Movement

❖ The Tunbridge Wells Knitting Society over the years produced thousands of garments for the services and bombed out families, providing over 35,000 garments by 1944.

❖ Tunbridge Wells PoWs Next-of-Kin Depot

❖ Tunbridge Wells PoWs Service Depot

❖ Tunbridge Wells Coop Society Pals Away Fund

❖ Waste Paper Recovery Association

❖ Merchant Navy Ship Adoption Society

❖ Aid to Russia Fund

❖ Aid to China Week (1943)

❖ Prisoner-of War Fund (1943)

❖ Russia Week (1944)

❖ Welcome Home Fund (1945)

Besides these, there were a number of Drives – for Salvage, for Metal, for Books, for Paper – as well as Campaigns – for Fuel-Saving (1940), Road Safety (1940) and Anti-Waste (1940). There were also all the national campaigns – such as Dig for Victory; Careless Talk Costs Lives; Save Bread, Eat Potatoes; Is Your Journey Really Necessary?

❖❖❖❖❖

The Tunbridge Wells Chamber of Trade held an informal luncheon at the end of November at The Spa Hotel[46] at which Sir Alexander Geddes was guest of honour. In his speech he gave the following warning :-

'that we were passing into a grave and great crisis. I am aware that many people are speaking and even thinking that the risk has passed. Nothing could be more disastrous than the spread of that idea'.

On Christmas Day 1939, the King broadcast his Christmas Message in which he quoted the now famous lines from Miss M.L. Haskins' poem,[47] The Gate of the Year:

'I said to the man who stood at the Gate of the Year,
Give me light that I may tread safely into the unknown'

Blackout material advertisement.

As 1939 drew to a close amidst all the preparations for war, life for the people of Tunbridge Wells seemed relatively normal. They went about their business as usual, with the local shops advertising their wares for Christmas. But some items on sale were not conventional Christmas presents: blackout material; gas mask *cases*, which were not supplied with the gas masks;[48] Identity Card cases; buckets and shovels for fire fighting; and low powered electric light bulbs. It was relatively a quiet Christmas, apart from when the medical students from Guy's Hospital held a Rag Week, unheard of in Tunbridge Wells, in support of the Army Comfort Fund.

Tickets for the Mayor's Christmas Treat on 28th December were distributed to children

---

[46] *The Courier, 1st. December 1939, p.2.*
[47] *Minnie Louise Haskins (1875-1957) studied and taught at the London School of Economics. She wrote ' The Gate of the Year ' in 1908. She died in Crowborough , aged 82, in 1957. A friend wrote to The Courier early in January 1940 , objecting to the media portraying Miss Haskins as a 'Village Girl Poetess'.*
[48] *The Courier offered readers a pattern for making your own.*

in local schools. The Pantomime at the Opera House was 'Cinderella' – twice daily at 2.15pm and 7.30 pm, but for only two weeks, beginning on Boxing Day. At the Assembly Hall the Christmas attraction was "When Knights Were Bold", with a matinée every day. This was followed on 1st January, by a 'Christmas Ghost' story entitled 'A Murder has been Announced' for just one week. The Ritz Cinema was showing Katherine Hepburn and Cary Grant in 'Free to Live', coupled with "The Gracie Allen Murder Case", and the Kosmos and the Great Hall were each showing two 'double-bill' programmes during the week.

After Christmas, the Winter Sales commenced as usual. In those days Sales were usually held only twice a year, summer and winter. It all seemed relatively normal and 'peaceful'.

But the 'Phoney War' (as the relatively quiet first seven months from September 1939 – April 1940 were called) would soon be coming to an end.

1939–1940 CHRONOLOGY

1939 January 5th   Germany demands return of Danzig by
                                      Poland.
      March   Germany occupies Czechoslovakia.
      March 31st   End of Spanish Civil War. Franco enters
                                      Madrid.
                                      Italy invades Albania.
      April   Civil Defence Regions created by UK
                                      Government.
      April 19th   Appointment of Regional Commissioners.
      August 24th   German-Soviet Pact secures Soviet neutrality.
      September 1st   Germany invades Poland.
      September 3rd   France and Britain declare war on Germany.
      September 16th   USSR invades Poland.
      September 29th   British War Budget announced.
      November 30th   USSR invades Finland.

1939 Sept–April 1940   The so-called ' Phoney War'. British
                                      Expeditionary Force in France and
                                      Belgium.

1940 January 8th   Food rationing begins in UK.
      April 9th   German invasion of Denmark and Norway ends
                                      the 'Phoney War'.
      April 30th   Britain suffer its first civilian casualties at
                                      Clacton, Essex.
      May 10th   Churchill replaces Chamberlain as Prime
                                      Minister.
      May 10th   Germany invades France and Benelux.
      May 15th   Netherlands surrenders to Germany
      May 20th   German Army reaches English Channel
      May 28th   Belgium surrenders to Germany.
      End May–early June   Battle of Dunkirk and Evacuation.
      June 22nd   France signs Armistice with Germany.
      August 12th-Sept 15th   Battle of Britain
      August 24th   German bombers off-course bomb London.
      August 25th   RAF bomb Berlin in retaliation.

1940 7 Sept–10 May 1941   The 'Blitz' principally on London (76 consecutive
                                      nights), but also Birmingham, Coventry,
                                      Manchester and other major cities.
                                      Casualties: 60,595 killed (29,890 in London),
                                      and 86,182 wounded (50,507 in London)

CHAPTER 6

TUNBRIDGE WELLS IN THE DARKEST YEARS 1940–1942

1940

As 1940 started, the Emergency Committee of the Borough Council reported that the revenue and capital expenditure on the ARP for the nine months to 31st December 1939 had been £38,127, much of which was covered by Government grants, but this still left £6,229 to be found by the Council through the rates.

Food rationing, which had been planned for since 1936, was introduced on the 8th of January 1940, with sugar, butter and bacon being the first items to be rationed, followed in March by meat, tea, margarine, and cooking fats, and in July by many other items such as dried milk and eggs and the introduction of a points system for 'goods which were not specifically rationed'. Controls on the slaughter of fatstock were also introduced.

Towards the end of January and into the beginning of February, there were heavy snowfalls in the area, disrupting traffic. The following winters of 1941 and 1942 also had severe winter weather.

The cold weather affected schools, with class rooms being too cold at the very beginning of the morning. Often the children were sent home until later in the day.

Neville Chamberlain and Sir Auckland Geddes, March 1940.

The first 3-4 months of the year were quiet – part of the first six-seven months which were dubbed 'The Phoney War'.

In March 1940, the Prime Minister Neville Chamberlain, together with the Home Secretary Sir John Anderson, paid a visit to 'Bredbury', where they were greeted by Sir Auckland Geddes, the Regional Controller, and his deputy Lord Knollys, Mr Guy Carlton the Chief Constable of Tunbridge Wells, Inspector Sly, Sergeant Crossman, and other officials. They inspected the HQ building and met many members of staff. Sir John, accompanied by Lord Knollys, inspected the cave on the

87

Attlee inspecting the Home Guard at the Assembly Hall.

Common which had been adapted as a public shelter and later he visited the Borough Control Room in the Civic Centre where he met the Mayor, Alderman Westbrook, and the Town Clerk, Mr. Whitehead, and saw the new police station and police court. Many other Ministerial visits to the Town followed throughout the war, including one from Clement Attlee, the Deputy Prime Minister.

On 13th. May 1940, Anthony Eden, the Secretary of State for War, appealed for men to come forward to form a Local Defence Volunteer force [LDV], which later was renamed the Home Guard. About 500 men volunteered in Tunbridge Wells. Lt. General Sir Cecil Romer G.C.B. [1869 - 1962] was the Officer in charge of the South East Region Home Guard, which took in Kent, all of Sussex and part of Surrey, and his HQ was in Tunbridge Wells. Brigadier H.O. Knox commanded the Tunbridge Wells area units, which were:

22nd (Tunbridge Wells) Kent Home Guard Battalion;
21st (Southhborough) Kent Home Guard Battalion;
23rd (Goudhurst) Kent Home Guard Battalion;
and 18th Sussex Home Guard Battalion (Eridge, Frant, Lye Green)

Tunbridge Wells Home Guard machine-gun crew.

These Battalions manned a large part of the defensive area known as the 'Ironside Line', which included pillboxes built at strategic locations in the local countryside, many of which can still seen today.[49] Other defences included road blocks, anti-tank ditches, 'dragon's teeth', 'booby traps' and the 'amazing and totally unexpected' Fougasse which was an oil 'and other incendiary' device, to be exploded without warning on the advancing enemy.

[49] *See map in Kent Defences, page 44, and 'Ironside's Line'.*

First Award For Bravery

In early May 1940, the first local man to win a medal for bravery was Pilot Officer J. P. S. Smyth RAF, son of Richard and Lena Smyth of Culverden Down. He was awarded the DFC (Distinguished Flying Cross).[50] In October 1942, he was killed in North Africa and is buried in the Heliopolis War Cemetery outside Cairo.[51]

He was the first of many local men to be recognized for their bravery in the following years. (See Appendix 2 for other Awards)

Dunkirk

In the last days of May and in early June 1940, reports of the BEF retreat in France were appearing in the British Press. An 'armada' of boats – large, small, naval, commercial and private, in total over 600 craft – carried out a daring rescue operation called Operation Dynamo, which brought between 316-338,000 mainly British evacuees (even the official statistics do not agree) from Dunkirk back to England. The original estimates in planning Operation Dynamo were that it would rescue 'up to 45,000 of the BEF'.[52] What is generally overlooked in reporting the 'miracle' of Dunkirk is that while about a third of a million men escaped, virtually all their equipment had to be left behind.

Part of the Dunkirk 'armada'.

Tunbridge Wells suffered particularly. 'D' company of the 4th Battalion, The Queen's Own Royal West Kent Regiment was the local Tunbridge Wells Territorial Army unit. At Morbecque near Dunkirk on the 28th May, 'D' Company saw action and of 122 men, only nine returned home, 43 were killed, others died of wounds, and the rest were taken prisoner.[53]

---

[50] *The Courier 10 May p. 3.*
[51] *The Courier 30 Oct 1942 p 6 for 'obit'.*
[52] *Admiral Ramsay: Dover Report 18 June 1940: NA/PRO ADM 199/792.*
[53] *See R.Gosling's file, T/Wells Ref. Library and Battalion History 'From Kent to Kohima'.*

On the 7th June, *The Courier* under the headline:

HOME FROM THE DUNKIRK INFERNO

listed the names of local men involved in the evacuation from Dunkirk, and many of those killed, wounded and taken prisoners.

Trains carrying hundreds of men rescued from Dunkirk travelled through Kent from the coast, and teams of local men and women served food and drink when the trains stopped at stations along the line, many working twelve hour shifts. In the early years of the war, special ambulance and evacuation trains were kept in the extensive goods yards at the West Station [now Sainsbury's]. These trains were later moved to Sevenoaks.

Rescued Dunkirk men being refreshed at Paddock Wood Station.

After Dunkirk, the BBC set up a national chain of local radio stations to enable broadcasts to be made to people living within a small radius. This was in case national communications were cut in the event of an invasion. In Tunbridge Wells, there was a small BBC studio situated on the left hand side of Upper Grosvenor Road towards High Brooms, which is recalled in oral history records as having a staff of about 12 persons.[54]

Another radio station of great importance not far from Tunbridge Wells, was the transmitter on the B2188 road at King's Standing, which is possibly the highest point in the Ashdown Forest.[55] A large, underground and secret radio station had been built there early in 1940 by a road building team of the Canadian Army; and it was used initially by the Political Warfare Executive for propaganda broadcasts to Europe during the War: and particularly for 'black broadcasting' – the transmission of

King's Standing transmitter.

[54] *Oral history: Pam Edmonton, whose brother and future husband worked at the studio.*
[55] *Subterranea Britannica research and pictures by Nick Catford.*

ostensibly genuine German radio programmes broadcasting to Germany, which subtly made a whole series of statements/admissions which undermined the German case and cause. In 1942, the BBC obtained partial use of the site for its European service, whose message would be more direct/less oblique.[56]

The Fifth Column And Internment

There was also great concern about both English people and foreigners who might be 'Fifth Columnists',[57] about whom there was a great deal of paranoia and panic. On 11th May at 10 am, 175 aliens were arrested in Kent, twenty of them in Tunbridge Wells alone. It was done quietly and without fuss, as was demonstrated by the fact that two men were removed from St. Augustine's Catholic Church, without the officiating priest, Canon Edward Fennessey, being aware of what had happened until after the service.[58]

You never know who's listening

CARELESS TALK COSTS LIVES

Government poster campaign.

It is clear in retrospect that there was in this period a great degree of paranoia, suspicion and general fear, to which everybody could respond, and it is evident that, helped by the media, they did. The times were without doubt desperate, but not in retrospect, as desperate as they seemed at the time. Hindsight, which by definition puts everything into a more objective perspective, diminishes everything and gives a more balanced assessment.

Local Defence

On 27th May 1940, the Commander-in-Chief (C-in-C), Home Forces, General Edmund Ironside drove down in the late afternoon from Kneller Hall, Twickenham[59] to Tunbridge Wells with his ADC, Capt. Ralph Arnold.

---

[56] *After the war, it was operated for many years by the Foreign Office's Diplomatic Wireless Service and hired by the BBC for its World Service. For many years, its tall masts were a landmark visible over a wide area. It was closed by the Home Office in 1992, since when it has been used by the Sussex Police.*

[57] *The expression ' 5th Column' dates from the Spanish Civil War when, with four columns advancing on Madrid, one of Franco's aides said that they already had a Fifth Column inside Madrid. The expression caught on, to describe secret agents or traitors inside, and this led to much suspicion of any stranger, or any unfamiliar face.*

[58] *'Gentlemen at War' by Roy Ingleton (Cranbourne, 1994), although this incident is not mentioned in the 222-page Parish history, 'One Cog'. (1995)*

[59] *The then-HQ of the C-in-C, which would subsequently move to St. Paul's School, Hammersmith.*

Later that evening they dined with the Regional Commissioner, Sir Auckland Geddes. Arnold, in his book 'A Very Quiet War', describes Geddes as a brilliant talker. Next morning they left for the South Coast to inspect Territorials building coastal defences. What they discussed that evening, is not stated or even known, but it could only be the military defence of the area, its structure and its organization.

No doubt as a result, General A.F.A.N. Thorne, who had escaped from Dunkirk, was four weeks later to be appointed Commander of XII Corps, which had just been created as part of Eastern Command.

General Thorne.

XII Corps consisted of three divisions - the 56th (London) Division, the 43rd (Wessex) Division and the 44th (Home Counties) Division - in total some 50,000 men, each with 3 Infantry Brigades divided into 4 Infantry Battalions with supporting cavalry [i.e. Armoured] and artillery regiments - who had been designated to defend the Kent and Sussex coast line against a possible invasion; and sensibly Tunbridge Wells which was on the border of Kent and Sussex, was chosen as the Corps HQ.

On the 25th. June, shortly after his arrival, Thorne asked for a team of Officers from the 1st Canadian Division to report to his HQ to select sites for defensive posts and prepare camouflage for his GHQ in Broadwater Down. Later anti- tank officers arrived to select further sites for guns, pill boxes, road blocks and infantry positions. Other officers who were stationed on the South Coast with the 43rd Infantry Division reported to

Camouflaging GHQ, in Broadwater Down.

XII Corps HQ to position further road blocks and anti tank obstacles. Because of the isolation of XII Corps in Kent and Sussex from the rest of Eastern Command which was north of the Thames, their strategic plans and activity had to be completely separate and it would make sense *in due course* for a new Command – the South-Eastern Command – to be created.

In July 1940 following General Ironside's replacement as C-in-C by General Sir Alan Brooke, Ralph Arnold was appointed ADC to Thorne, the GOC of XII Corps. The GHQ mess at No. 10, Broadwater Down was run to a high standard by another ADC, Capt. Alan Perrins [of Worcester Sauce fame]. When not on duty, Arnold describes walking down Frant Road to Mr Pratley's Bookshop [now Hall's Bookshop in Chapel Place].

The following Spring, Lt. General Thorne was promoted to full General and to be GOC, Scottish Command and Governor of Edinburgh Castle, two posts which he held until the end of the War. Lt. General Montgomery succeeded him as GOC, XII Corps.

The Battle Of Britain

What is called 'The Battle of Britain' is generally thought of as an aerial battle, which primarily it was, but it had also territorial and maritime elements as well. It can be said to have begun with a miracle never expected - the evacuation against all the odds of 316,000 British and French and allied troops from Dunkirk at the end of May/beginning of June 1940. The Germans fully intended to invade Britain in 1940 – Operation SEA LION was their codename for the Invasion and its D-Day was first set for the 15th, and then subsequently 21st September, before it was postponed/cancelled.

" Come, come Harriet, remember Drake ! " 10.ix.40

Osbert Lancaster cartoon.

Before German troops could invade, the Germans recognised that the Luftwaffe had to have air control of the English Channel and hopefully most of Southern England, first to allow a mine-sweeping and mine-laying programme to be carried out before the invasion; and sub-sequently to permit an uninterrupted invasion. This was never achieved and as a result, SEA LION was cancelled, although thought for quite some time by the British and also most Germans under Hitler, to be just a postponement related to seasonal and weather considerations.

Throughout the battle, the RAF was commanded by Air Chief Marshal Sir Hugh Dowding, later Lord Dowding

Typical Pillbox.

Dragon's Teeth defences.

Removed roadsigns.

"I'll tell nobody where anywhere is."
Punch, 24 July 1940

[1882-1970], who after the war lived at No. 2, Calverley Park, until his death.

During the summer of 1940, anti-invasion preparations continued in Tunbridge Wells with more concrete-lined trenches being dug in many parts of the Town, with Tank obstructions known as 'Dragons' Teeth' being located at strategic road junctions, and with the construction of so-called 'pillboxes' (because they were shaped like them).

The Removal of Direction Signs Order [1940] was instigated in June 1940 by General Ironside when he was C-in-C, Home Forces. He ordered the removal of all road and directional signposts throughout Southern England. Town maps and even the names on council vehicles were removed. This was meant to deprive the invading forces of any indication of where they were, but probably it only confused everyone, except the locals. In any case, after the War, it was shown that the Germans had had very good maps of the planned area of invasion, so the action was unnecessary.[60]

Another precaution was the provision of obstructions on likely landing places by the enemy. The Town Clerk reported to the Emergency Committee[61] that he had received a '*secret letter*' from Regional HQ with regard to this matter. The Council instructed the Borough Surveyor to take all necessary steps on property belonging to the Corporation. Unfortunately, the sites are not named

[60] *'German Invasion Plans for the British Isles 1940'.*
[61] *Council minutes 24 July 1940 Vol 637.*

in the minutes. But it is recorded that the Borough Council ordered that the name 'Tunbridge Wells' should be expunged from all Council vehicles, properties and signs and that maps of Tunbridge Wells on display in the centre of the Town for the benefit of visitors, should be removed. It is easy to smile at this in 2009, but it does demonstrate the sheer fear and paranoia which existed at the time and affected everybody.

Calverley Grounds crater.

From the 13th June, there was a ban on the ringing of church bells, except in the event of an invasion. This ban was eventually lifted on 4th April 1943.

My memory of the summer of 1940 is one of sunshine and blue skies and watching the dog-fights over Tunbridge Wells. But I also remember, as we did not then have an air-raid shelter, spending the whole day of Sunday 15th September with my family in the basement of the offices of T. Bates & Sons in Nevill Terrace, with nothing to do except listen to the 'wireless'.

The second half of July saw the first real dog-fights in the skies over Kent. Through the later months of the fine summer, the Battle of Britain was at its height and a number of incidents were reported in the Borough. But it would seem that relatively few planes actually crashed in Tunbridge Wells. Records show that in just over 3 months between 15th August and 21st November 1940, only 11 planes crashed in Tunbridge Wells – 5 German (4 Messerschmidt 109 and 1 Dornier 215, of whom there were 4 dead and 2 captured); and 6 British (6 Hurricane, of whom 2 were killed).

Calverley Grounds crater.

Reports of air attacks appeared in *The Courier*, though the locality was never given, due to censorship. Among the first on the Town was a bomb which fell on 22nd August in the Calverley Grounds causing a large crater in a flower bed. Later on 29th September, an 'oil' bomb was dropped which totally destroyed the Pavilion in the Calverley Grounds.

The first Tunbridge Wells civilian to be killed by enemy action was Charles Pattenden, of Eridge Road. He was an engine driver and while driving between two (unspecified) South Coast towns on 3rd. July, his train was bombed and machined gunned by a German aircraft. He died later from his injuries.[62]

21 Windmill Street, with St. Peters' Church in the background.

On 28th August there was a direct hit on 21, Windmill Street. In this incident, the family had a miraculous escape. A little girl was trapped in her cot but was not seriously injured. She suffered from shock and spent some time in hospital, but the experience did not have any long-term effects. That 'little girl' later married and is still living in Tunbridge Wells.[63]

On 10th September, a house in Lansdowne Road was partly demolished and Mr Hubert Moon died from his injuries. But the worst incident of the whole war occurred on the 12th September at 5.10 pm, when a lone German bomber probably on its way from London, released, or more likely jettisoned 22 HE Bombs and 22 incendiaries (since it was a court-martial offence in the Luftwaffe to return with a bomb-load), in a path stretching from Connaught Way, Great Culverden Park, the Kent and Sussex Hospital, St. Augustine's Presbytery, and Grosvenor Road to Five Ways.

21 Windmill Street.

---

[62] *The Courier 2nd. Aug 1940 p 3.*
[63] *Oral history: Brenda Worsell.*

Twelve men and women were killed, two seriously injured and 14 slightly injured. Lincoln Redman, a paper boy aged 11 and son of a widow of Beulah Road,[64] who was only doing the paper round as a favour for a friend, was killed when the fifth bomb landed in the Hospital forecourt. Hetty Mills was killed at Basinghall Street, and seven were killed and 15 wounded at Wallis, Hollier and Lee, a wholesale grocers' warehouse in Basinghall Street, the site of which is now under the Royal Victoria Shopping Centre. Stanhays in Mount Ephraim was also hit.

In the same month, a 500 kg. D/A HE [Delayed Action High Explosive] bomb was dropped near the Hastings Railway line behind Forest Road in the stock nursery of Wallace Nurseries, causing the line to be closed for 10 days.

During the month of August alone, six German airmen were buried in the Borough Cemetery. In September 1940 the Burial Board received a Circular from the Ministry of Health[65] instructing them that it was the duty of local authorities to bury enemy airmen who had been killed, but obviously the Burial Board had anticipated this.[66]

A German Messerschmidt 109 crashed on 5th October on the Spa Golf Course, now the Tunbridge Wells Golf Club. The pilot was wounded and taken prisoner.

On the 6th November, an ARP Officer submitted particulars to the Borough Council concerning action taken by Kenneth Peck in rescuing the pilot from the crash; and it was recommended that he should receive a commendation for bravery. On 13th November, the Town Clerk reported to the Council the evidence he had obtained from the Manager of the Spa Hotel with regard to the conduct of Kenneth Peck, and the Council resolved that a letter of commendation be sent to Kenneth Peck.[67]

Up to November, twenty-one British aircraft were reported to have crashed around Tunbridge Wells (obviously a larger catchment area than the one recorded above, with only 5 British aircraft.) These included two at Little Bayhall Farm and one at High Brooms Viaduct, the pilot of which was Fl. Lt. Rhodes-Moorhouse, DFC. He was the son of Lt. William

---

[64] *'One Cog' by Ted Marchant, St. Augustine's Church history 1838-1995, 1995.*
[65] *Minutes of the Burial Board dated 19th September, 1940, page 6.*
[66] *In October 1962, the remains of these German airmen were exhumed under a Home Office licence and taken to the German Military Cemetery at Cannock Chase in Staffordshire. Two other German airmen who were buried later, were also taken to Cannock Chase.*
[67] *Council minutes Vol 637 TWB Archives.*

Rhodes-Moorhouse, the first airman to be awarded the VC, posthumously in 1915, and both father and son are buried at the family home, Parnham House, Beaminster, Dorset.[68]

War Weapons Week parade, Lord Camden taking the salute from Civic Way.

In August the Mayor inaugurated a 'Spitfire Fund' and by the end of September £5,031 had been raised, which more than was required to 'buy' a Spitfire. This was followed in November by a 'War Weapons Week' which raised £510,224.

From 21st September, the Regional Commissioner ordered that theatres, cinemas, public houses and restaurants were to close at 10 pm. Other restrictions and regulations imposed under the Defence Regulations Act included the wasting of food. The result of this was that in March the following year, a woman was fined for throwing away food, and in May, James Toop & Sons, Butchers of 25–27 Calverley Road were fined for contravening rationing orders.[69] Kite flying, the ringing of church bells, the use of rattles, hand bells, and police whistles were forbidden in June 1940. Other provisions were incorporated into the Official Secrets Act, one of which was that the taking of photographs of crashed aircraft was forbidden, which resulted in a man being arrested. The taking of souvenirs from aircraft was also prohibited, but many small boys managed to evade the police and army guarding the wreckage. This could be very dangerous as there might be unexploded bombs and shells in the wreckage.

A Home Office Pamphlet issued during 1940 advised on how to get advice if needed in the event of Air Raids. It recommended the many precautions that householders could take.

In September the nightly raids on London started which were to continue non-stop until May 1941 and which have become known as

---

[68] *The Courier 14. May 2004 for eye witness account.*
[69] *They were fined again in April 1941 – see The Courier, 25 Apr 1941, p 3.*

Air Raid Shelter
very similar to that at 20 Eridge Road.

'the Blitz'. I can remember seeing in the night sky from Rusthall Common, the red glow from the fires in London. By this time, we had an air-raid shelter, measuring about 14' by 7', in our garden. After 'high tea' at 6pm, my parents and I (and my pet dog) would retire about 7pm to the shelter, which had electricity, an electric fire and a 'wireless' (radio), but no window and only a small ventilation 'brick'. There we would stay until 7am the following morning, playing cards, Monopoly or other board games, and listening to the 'wireless' (particularly every week to Tommy Handley in ITMA [It's That Man Again] and occasionally to Lord Haw Haw[70]) and sleeping in three bunk beds.

As the air-raids died down in 1941, we returned to sleeping in the house but when the 'doodlebugs' (V1s) started in 1944, we returned to sleeping every night in the shelter.

Throughout the War, we lived at 20 Eridge Road. It was near the old West Station (*today the site of Sainsbury's*), which was a potential target for German bombers. While not many bombs actually fell during the 'Blitz' on Tunbridge Wells, we could judge how close they were, by how far the blackout curtain over the ventilation 'brick' blew out. We also had many broken windows, but fortunately no major damage.

On 13th October over 100 houses were damaged by bombs in Norman Road, Beech Street, Kirkdale Road, Camden Road, Springfield Gardens and Elim Cottages. On 18th October the Town was to suffer more bombs. No.5, Boyne Park was cut in half by a bomb and Miss Fanny Crossfield died from her injuries. Miss Dorothy Dennis, daughter of Albert Dennis who had been Mayor of Tunbridge Wells from 1930 to 1932, and who had been a VAD nurse in France during the First World War and was now in charge of the First Aid Post at the Homeopathic Hospital, Church Road, helped in the rescue of the casualties.[71]

---

[70] *William Joyce (1906-1946), nicknamed 'Lord Haw Haw' because of his drawl, was a British traitor who throughout World War II broadcast propaganda against Britain from Radio Hamburg. He was captured in 1945 and tried and executed in 1946.*
[71] *See ' Kentish Fire', by Hubert S. Banner, Hurst & Blackett, 1944.*

In October the Mayor paid tribute to the Civil Defence Services at a Council Meeting.

The cost of public shelters which were to be provided by the Corporation for 3,779 houses [13,272 occupants], was reported in August 1940 to be £29,862, of which £4,479 was to be paid for by the Council.[72]

 Alderman Westbrook was re-elected in November as Mayor for the third successive time. The Borough Council considered a scheme to provide accommodation for 1,000 more bunks in public Air-Raid Shelters.

Mr J.R.P. Postlethwaite was appointed Divisional Food Officer for the South East with his HQ in the locality. He was to hold the post for two years returning to London in 1942. In December, Lord Woolton, Minister of Food, made a visit to the Town. Earlier in the year, Lord De La Warr had been appointed Minister for *Food Production* in the South East.

The King, in his Christmas Day broadcast of 1940, summed up what so many felt:

> *'To the older people here and through out the world, I would say: In the last Great War, the flower of our youth was destroyed and the rest of the people saw little of the battle. This time we are all in the front line and the danger together; and I know that the older among us are proud that it should be so.'*

Secret Defence Projects
At least two secret defence projects, current in 1940-41, were not to come to light until well after the end of the Second World War.

The first was the XII Corps so-called 'Observation or Auxiliary Units', which were small resistance groups set up to fight a 'guerilla' war after any German invasion. Very little is known about these units, as few records have been released, or survive, but the GOC XII Corps, Lt. General Andrew Thorne, is generally credited with setting them up and they are thought to have remained in existence until 1942. They had a network of underground hideouts, constructed by the men themselves. Each man had to sign the Official Secrets Act and was issued with regular Home Guard uniforms and kit, and in addition they had explosives and other weapons not usually issued to the Home Guard. If

---

[72] *Emergency Committee minutes Vol 637 21 Aug 1940 and later minutes.*

attacked in their hide-outs, they were expected to hold out for up to seven days. The official battalion title was 203 GHQ [Reserve] Bn., Home Guard. The nature of their potential operation was essentially rural, rather than urban, so it is unlikely that there were any hide-outs in Tunbridge Wells. But they certainly existed further out in Kent and Sussex. More research, if it is possible, is needed on this fascinating subject.

'The Wilderness', Broadwater Down

There was another secret defence project taking place in the area, of which even Montgomery, then the GOC XII Corps, later denied any knowledge. Such a denial, however truthfully given, does not alter the fact that the project was being carried out, even if he was unaware of it.

"The Wilderness" on land in Hargate Forest, near Broadwater Down, [map ref TQ 575 375] had been requisitioned at the start of the war from the Abergavenny Eridge Estate, and was a complex of underground rooms and tunnels, which, it is thought, were planned to be used as a communications centre.

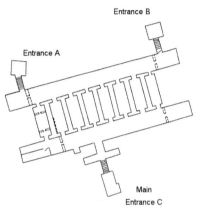

'The Wilderness' site plan

The tunnels were excavated by 20 men of the 172 Tunnelling Company, Royal Engineers, who were billeted at Mount Edgecombe and in other parts of the Town. Lt. J. Broadhead was in charge and among the others were Henry Blakeway, (who would later be Mayor of Tunbridge Wells), Herbert Taylor and Wally Churn[73] of the Borough Council Electricity

A tunnel in 'The Wilderness'

---

[73] *The Courier 9 Feb 2007.*

DANGER of INVASION

Last year all who could be spared from this town were asked to leave, not only for their own safety, but so as to ease the work of the Armed Forces in repelling an invasion.

The danger of invasion has increased and the Government requests all who can be spared, and have somewhere to go, to leave without delay.

This applies particularly to :—
SCHOOL CHILDREN
MOTHERS WITH YOUNG CHILDREN
AGED AND INFIRM PERSONS
PERSONS LIVING ON PENSIONS
PERSONS WITHOUT OCCUPATION
OR IN RETIREMENT

If you are one of these, you should arrange to go to some other part of the country. You should not go to the coastal area of East Anglia, Kent or Sussex.

School children can be registered to join school parties in the reception areas, and billets will be found for them.

If you are in need of help you can have your railway fare paid and a billeting allowance paid to any relative or friend with whom you stay.

If you are going, go quickly.

Take your
NATIONAL REGISTRATION IDENTITY CARD
RATION BOOK
GAS MASK

ALSO any bank book, pensions payment order book, insurance cards, unemployment book, military registration documents, passport, insurance policies, securities and any ready money.

If your house will be left unoccupied, turn off gas, electricity and water supplies and make provision for animals and birds. Lock your house securely. Blinds should be left up, and if there is a telephone line, ask the telephone exchange to disconnect it.

Apply at the Local Council Offices for further information.

Private Car and Motor Cycle owners who have not licensed their vehicles and have no petrol coupons may be allowed to use their cars unlicensed for one journey only and may apply to the Police for petrol coupons to enable them to secure sufficient petrol to journey to their destination.

ESSENTIAL WORKERS MUST STAY

particularly the following classes :—
Members of the Home Guard
Observer Corps
Coastguards, Coast Watchers and Lifeboat Crews
Police and Special Constabulary
Fire Brigade and Auxiliary Fire Service
A.R.P. and Casualty Services
Members of Local Authorities and their officials and employees
Workers on the land
Persons engaged on war work, and other essential services
Persons employed by contractors on defence work
Employees of water, sewerage, gas & electricity undertakings
Persons engaged in the supply and distribution of food
Workers on export trades
Doctors, Nurses and Chemists
Ministers of Religion
Government Employees
Employees of banks
Employees of transport undertakings,
namely railways, docks, canals, ferries,
and road transport (both passenger and goods).

When invasion is upon us it may be necessary to evacuate the remaining population of this and certain other towns. Evacuation would then be compulsory at short notice, in crowded trains, with scanty luggage, to destinations chosen by the Government. If you are not among the essential workers mentioned above, it is better to go now while the going is good.

AUCKLAND GEDDES,
REGIONAL COMMISSIONER FOR CIVIL DEFENCE,
TUNBRIDGE WELLS,
MARCH, 1941.

Department, Bob Blackford (a Post Office Engineer), Eric Woodruff and a Mr. Hayward. They started work in 1940 and finished the following year. It is certain that the centre was never used for any purpose, but why this was so, is unknown. It could be for as mundane and practical a reason as the site was prone to flooding. The land was returned to the Eridge Estate in 1945 and most of the records relating to it, are believed to have been destroyed.

The entrances to the tunnels are still visible, although the site, which is flooded, is too dangerous to visit. In 1996, the site was surveyed by the Subterranea Britannica Society. [*www.subterraneabritannica.com*]

1941
It is clear from the Danger of Invasion poster/leaflet shown left, which is dated March 1941 and signed by Auckland Geddes, that the fear of invasion was still very real. Indeed it seems to have increased, since the text says specifically 'The danger of invasion has increased and the Government requests all those who can be spared, and have somewhere to go, to leave without delay.' Note that the Government is still requesting, not ordering, but the threat of ordering is made in the last paragraph. The British Government did not know, what the USSR also did not know, that Hitler was about to attack Russia. What we now know in hindsight, was not known then.

The potential use of gas was still a major concern for the Civil Defence and an exercise was held at the beginning of May.

The other great concern was fires caused by incendiary bombs. The effect of these bombs had been clearly seen in the London Blitz and Tunbridge Wells had already had several hundred. During the whole War, Tunbridge Wells would be the target of 660 incendiary bombs, compared with only 186 HE (high-explosive) bombs and 6 Flying Bombs (V1s).

Initially there was a voluntary firewatching scheme in Tunbridge Wells with between 1,500–2,000 members, of whom about 80% were women. Firewatchers formed rotas to stay and sleep overnight in all unoccupied buildings, including business premises and the Town Council had to be notified in writing by firms. Firewatchers' recollections include that of a woman living near Tunbridge Wells who found the worst feature of firewatching in a Solicitor's Office where she worked, was trying to sleep among 'the rows of gloomy legal books'. Another on the middle watch (1 am–4 am) at a school was expected to chase the beetles from the school washroom.[74]

---

[74] *'How we lived then' by Norman Longmate, and local school log books.*

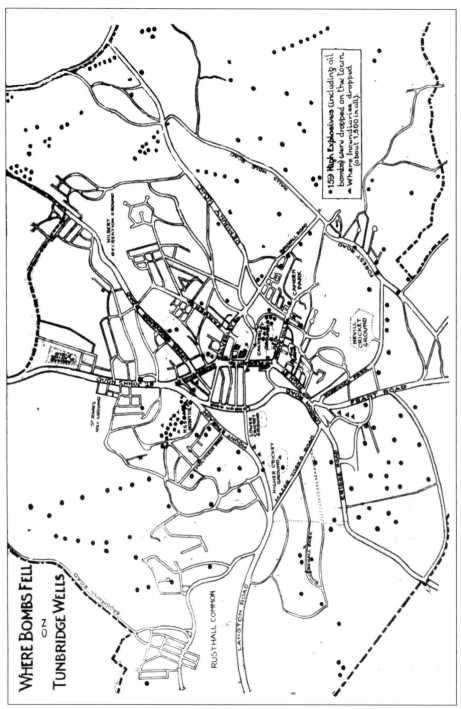

WHERE BOMBS FELL
on
TUNBRIDGE WELLS

- 159 High Explosives (including oil bombs) were dropped on the town.
▲ Where Incendiaries dropped (about 1,500 in all).

'Courier' map indicating where the bombs fell, fortunately, largely outside residential areas.

104

In 1940, men not already in the Services aged between 17–65 of age had been *asked to volunteer* at their local Town Hall, Police Station or Labour Exchange for Civil Defence and particularly as Local Defence Volunteers (Home Guard), and in two days over 500 had 'signed on' in Tunbridge Wells. But more were required for Civil Defence duties generally and only men could be made to enroll compulsorily for what could be a dangerous role. So a Civil Defence Duties (Compulsory Enrolment) Order was introduced in January 1941, making it obligatory for all men, aged 18–60, to register by 3rd May 1941.[75]

The results seem to have been a bit disappointing in Tunbridge Wells and possibly elsewhere. By that date only 5,750 men had 'signed on' and most of these were in any case exempt – 1,200 because they were already in the ARP or Home Guard; 3,000 because they were already engaged in firewatching duties, leaving only 1,550 as potential new recruits. There seemed to be no solution to the problem of non-registration – some men were prosecuted, but there always seemed to be some form of let-out for those who did not. This may have been a common problem for other areas as well.

Bernard Law Montgomery

Montgomery at El Alamein

On 7th May, 1941, Lt. General Andrew Thorne was replaced as GOC, XII Corps by the person who would become the Corps' most famous Commander, Lt. General Bernard Montgomery, better known at a later date as Field Marshal Viscount Montgomery of El Alamein. On taking Command of XII Corps, Montgomery was critical of Thorne and said in a letter to Kit Dawnay: 'I rather fancy I burst into Kent like a 15" shell, and it was needed!"[76]

King George VI visiting 10 Broadwater Down, Montgomery is on the right.

It was at No. 10 Broadwater Down, the XII Corps GHQ Officers' Mess, that King George VI paid a visit on the 13th June 1941. Later in the afternoon, the King visited the Mechanised Transport Corps unit in Birling Road, which was comprised of volunteer women drivers.

No. 69, Warwick Park had been requisitioned much earlier as the living quarters for the GOC and

[75] *Tunbridge Wells Advertiser, 14 June 1941.*
[76] *Letter 7 May 1941 to Maj. Christopher Dawnay, from 'The Full Monty: Montgomery of Alamein 1887–1942' by Nigel Hamilton, Allen Lane, 2001.*

Montgomery was to live there from April to November 1941, before being promoted to command for eight months the South-Eastern Command, defending most of the Southern coast of England. He was promoted yet again in August 1942 to command the Eight Army in North Africa, where he won an overwhelming victory over Rommel's forces at El Alamein in October-November 1942.

It is possible that Montgomery may have known Tunbridge Wells before the war, as his wife Betty was the widow of Captain Oliver Carver, who had been killed at Gallipoli in 1915. She was the daughter of Mr R. T. Hobart, JP [1840–1912], of Clarendon House, Ferndale, Tunbridge Wells. He had been a member of the Town Council and Chairman of the Watch Committee and before retirement had been in the Indian Civil Service. Montgomery and Betty Carver however did not meet until 1926, and they married the following summer. She had had two sons by her first husband, both of whom became regular army officers, and had a son, David, by Montgomery.[77] In 1937, Betty become seriously ill with septicaemia and died in October.

Another connection which Montgomery had with Tunbridge Wells, was that one of his confidential clerks, Lance-Corporal Joyce Walker, ATS, was the daughter of Bill Walker, the licensee of 'The Elephant and Castle' in Goods Station Road. She travelled around Britain on Montgomery's special train.

Montgomery was succeeded in the command of XII Corps by Maj.-General James A. H. Gammell, CB, MC, DSO (1892-1975) who was promoted to Lt. General on appointment on 25th. December, 1941.[78]

Dunorlan House.

Dunorlan
Mr Carteret Collins the last owner of Dunorlan, Pembury Road, died in February 1941

---

[77] *Montgomery's brother-in-law, Maj.Gen. Percy (Hobo) Hobart pioneered 'special tanks' such as flail mine-clearers, flame throwers, amphibian tanks and bridging tanks, with their bundles of 'fascines'. All made a major contribution to the Allied invasion, particularly in the 'bocage' of Normandy.*
[78] *Gammell was GOC, XII Corps for less than nine months when he was promoted to be GOC-in-C, Eastern Command in September 1942. He held this post until January 1944 when he became Chief-of-Staff to the Supreme Allied Commander, Mediterranean Theatre. He was made a Knight of the Bath (KB) in 1944.*

and the Borough Council decided to buy the estate. However, the purchase was not to be completed until June 1945[79] (and the Council would not take possession of the buildings until 1957). In the meantime, it was requisitioned in 1943 by the Army. It was initially occupied by troops who reputedly used the cornices, gables, statues and ornaments for target practice. Subsequently and somewhat ironically, it became the HQ of the War Damage Commission. It was also occupied as the HQ for the National Fire Service [NFS] and subsequently by the Ministry of Works.

April 1941 saw another increase in Income Tax, this time to 10/- [50p] in the pound.

In May, it was decided by the Council that the area in Hawkenbury known as Tutty's Farm was to be used for the burial of unexploded gas bombs, which clearly shows that they were still expected. However, no gas bombs ever fell and it was never used.

On 13th May 1941 Mr Herbert Morrison, the Home Secretary and Minister for Home Security, announced that all regular fire brigades and AFS [Auxiliary Fire Service] Units would be re-organised and amalgamated to form the National Fire Service (NFS). It was not until 1948 that local authorities resumed control of their Fire Services. A year later in 1949, the AFS was reformed and became part of the post-war Civil Defence Services until 1967, when all Civil Defence work ceased.

NFS badge.

Mr M. H. Bolt was appointed Chief Regional Fire Officer for the S. E. Region in September 1941. Prior to this, he had been the Chief Constable of the Dover area since 1935, and on his retirement in April 1943,[80] he became Assistant Chief Constable of the Tunbridge Wells area.

Royal and Ministerial visits to the Town continued during the year. Herbert Morrison, the Home Secretary, met Sir Auckland Geddes in

---

[79] *TWBC minute dated 6 June 1945 p 21.*
[80] *The Courier 30 April 1943.*

February 1941.[81] In May 1941, the Duke of Kent visited Bredbury and inspected the W.V.S. mobile canteens.[82] The Duke of Kent made another visit in June 1942, when he met Sir Hartley Shawcross who by then was Deputy Regional Commissioner. The Duchess of Kent also came to Tunbridge Wells when she inspected Civil Defence workers.

Duke of Kent meeting WVS – Geddes, on right.

Many ambulances, mobile first-aid posts and canteens were presented to the Civil Defence services in the Town. Some were given anonymously, others included one presented by Senora Jovita Mansilla de Bemberg of Buenos Aires.[83] Mobile kitchens were received by the WVS, one of which had been subscribed to by the Canadian Ladies Golf Union.[84]

St Christopher's Training College, Pembury Road, *(formerly Ravendale, subsequently Willicombe Park)* was transformed with the help of The American Air Raid Relief Committee, into a reception centre for babies who were victims of enemy bombing. In an article in *The Advertiser* dated 1st August 1941 there is a picture of the children with many named.

St Christopher's Training College.

Another Tunbridge Wells inhabitant became a victim of enemy action on 10th May[85] when Bernard J. Boorman was injured at Trafalgar Square, Woolwich Road, Greenwich in a heavy raid on London. He died the same day at St. Alfege's Hospital. He was doing relief work in the Greenwich area at the time. He was a member of the Quarry Road First Aid Post. Between 400 and 500 members of the Civil Defence Services from Greenwich and Tunbridge Wells attended his funeral.[86]

---

[81] *The Courier 7 February 1941(picture).*
[82] *The Courier 2 May 1941 p 5/6 [picture].*
[83] *See picture Courier 3 April 1942, p 2.*
[84] *The Courier 22 May 1942, p 2.*
[85] *Or 11 May 1941 according to CWGC records, which also say he is buried at Greenwich Metropolitan Cemetery. He is actually buried in Tunbridge Wells Borough Cemetery.*
[86] *Reports in The Courier 16 and 23 May 1941.*

It had been hoped that the Council would pay the funeral costs but this was refused, but later they agreed to pay J.Kempster & Sons, the undertakers, £5 - 5 - 0d, for the cost of the hearse from Greenwich. The family received no grant from the Government, despite the fact that the Ministry of Health had notified local authorities in March 1941 that a burial grant of £7-10-0d was payable in respect of privately arranged funerals of Civil Defence Workers killed by enemy action.[87]

In July 1941, Sir Auckland Geddes resigned as Regional Commissioner because of failing eyesight. Lord Monsell was appointed the new Commissioner.[88] He had had a distinguish career as a Member of Parliament before the war, retiring from the House in 1935. He was to remain as Commissioner until April 1945.[89]

In the Council Minutes of 30th July 1941, the Mayor called the attention of the Town Council to the award of the George Medal to Chief Petty Officer Arthur Holme RN who had been a meter reader in the Council's Electricity Department before the War. The Town Clerk was instructed to inform CPO Holme that the Council learnt with great satisfaction of the award of the George Medal to a member of staff and congratulated him on the recognition of his services and extended their Best Wishes to him for his safety while serving in the Royal Navy.[90] Although born in London, Holme had made his home in Tunbridge since the 1920's, living at 22, Hawkenbury Road; he continued to live in Hawkenbury until his death in March 1963.

 In November 1941, Alderman Westbrook was again elected Mayor for the sixth, but third successive, time.

Schoolboys throughout the war were always keen to get souvenirs from crashed aircraft and other military sites. One such event in November 1941, ended in tragedy when 12 year-old Richard Medhurst who had been evacuated from the Rochester area to Wren's Warren School near Hartfield, died in Pembury Hospital from serious injuries.

He and two other boys, Colin Caney and Herbert Willis, also from the Rochester area, found explosives in an area of the Ashdown Forest used by the military for training. They took the objects to school and the following day, while they were examining them, they exploded. At an

[87] *Burial Board minutes 5 March 1941 p1115/6 T/Wells archives.*
[88] *Report The Courier 25 July 1941. See also footnote no. 37.*
[89] *Letter from Monsell to TWB Council [minutes dated 4 April 1945 p 4] announcing his retirement.*
[90] *London Gazette 4th July 1941 and The Courier 18 July 1941 p 6.*

inquest held at Pembury Hospital, the Coroner Mr J. H. Soady said *'It is essential that everybody, grown ups as well as children, should realise the extreme danger and folly of picking up and playing with objects found lying about and which they do not know the nature of, or understand'.*[91] A verdict of 'Death by Misadventure' was returned.

It is interesting/revealing to see that, on 1st December, which was just before Pearl Harbour and the Japanese entry into the War, and which must have been about the nadir of Britain's wartime success, the traditional British way of encouraging team spirit through a competition with a trophy, is still thought to be both relevant and appropriate to what is a fairly desperate war situation. A circular (No. 125, dated 1st December 1941) was sent on behalf of the Regional Commissioner to all controllers and sub-controllers in the S. E. Region informing them that "it has been decided to hold a competition for the Civil Defence Casualty Services in this Region and a trophy to be won outright by the winning team will be presented by the Regional Commissioner". A trophy is definitively something which wins battles and even the war!

Japan entered the war on 8th December 1941 and many local men were taken prisoner as the Japanese Army captured Hongkong on 25th December, and Malaysia and Singapore in January/February 1942.[92] Their names were not reported until their release in 1945.

The King in his Christmas message of 1941 said:

> *'We are coming to the end of another hard fought year. During these months our people have been through many trials, and in that true humility which goes hand in hand with valour, have learnt once again to look for strength to God alone. So - I bid you all - be strong and of a good courage.'*

So another year had ended which had seen many more restrictions being imposed and shortages of numerous everyday goods.

1942

1942 was to be one of the worst years of the war with further restrictions being imposed on everyone. There was still concern that there could be an invasion and in April instructions[93] were published to that effect. However, it was not until November with the victory at El Alamein that there was some good news to report.

---

[91] *The Courier 12 Dec 1941 p 4.*
[92] *The Courier, for September 1945 lists the men returning.*
[93] *The Courier 10 April 1942 p 5.*

At the end of January 1942, there had been a serious fire at Rawson's Garage[94] in London Road, opposite Mount Sion.[95] It would seem that the fire was not handled well by the AFS and a letter was sent by the Tunbridge Wells Chamber of Trade to the Emergency Committee about the fire. The Committee resolved that the matter should be referred to the Borough Council for the Mayor and Town Clerk to draw to the attention of the Regional Commissioner, the apparently ineffective manner in which the AFS had dealt with the outbreak. Later a letter was received from the Commissioner regarding the matter. There was clearly serious concern about the Fire Service's ability to control fires in the event of incendiary bombs falling in the area.

It was at this time that the fire services were re-organised into the National Fire Service (NFS). It seems likely that this, together with the criticism of the handling of the Rawson Garage fire, may have lead to the resignation during 1942 of John W. Goodwin, Chief Fire Officer of the Tunbridge Wells Fire Brigade, who had been associated with the Brigade for 37 years and who had been appointed Chief Fire Officer in 1932. Goodwin was to die, suddenly and unexpectedly of a heart attack, in 1944 aged 58. There was a large congregation at his funeral including the Mayor, and members of the Council and the Fire Service.[96]

Queueing for the bus on Mount Pleasant, by Lonsdale Gardens c.1942.

The Mayor proposed[97] a draft of a local law for the formation of queues at bus stops. There were reports of scrambling at bus stops and the Town Clerk submitted the draft to the Minister of Health who with minor amendments gave his approval. The law came into force on 12th April 1942. There was a favourable reception for the new system by the public.

---

[94] *The Courier, 23 January 1942 p 6; 6 February 1942 p 6; 10 April 1942 p6.*
[95] *Rawsons also had a Showroom and workshop on Mount Pleasant, built in 1936 as part of the Ritz Cinema site by my father's firm. In 1940, with the decline of motor business, this site was turned into a machine-shop for munitions manufacture and over four million Bofors anti-aircraft shells were made there during the War, with staff working 24 hours a day and 7 days a week. Ref: The Courier, 4 February,1983 p5.*
[96] *The Courier 25 February 1944 p 6.*
[97] *The Courier 2 January 1942 p.6.*

A National Fuel campaign was launched to help war factories and plans for 'Warship Week' which was to be held from 28th Feb–7th Mar 1942 were announced. £450,000 or more had to be raised for the provision of a destroyer. Councillor McNab was Chairman of the Campaign Committee. After the opening ceremony, a procession moved off from Carr's Corner headed by the Band of the Royal Marines with many other contingents, which attracted large crowds. Two Grand Concerts at the Assembly Hall were arranged, and a naval exhibition at the Civic Centre.[98] The final amount raised during Warship Week was £651,000, £201,000 above the target and as a result, HMS Brilliant which had been commissioned in 1930, was adopted by the Town. Later in December 1942, a plaque was presented by the Lords Commissioner of the Admiralty to the Town, to commemorate the Town's adoption of H.M.S. Brilliant.

Many bus services were restricted with no services on a Sunday until 1pm and on weekdays there was a 9pm curfew. It was said that the new restrictions would make little material change as similar ones were already in force. Services were again curtailed in January 1943. Petrol had been in short supply and rationing had limited the use of cars to 200 miles per month. After March 1942, petrol for private cars was withdrawn completely, so travel for the general public was very limited. It should be remembered that there had been no street lighting since the beginning of the war, and no shop window lights: permission for restoration of these was not to be granted until April 1949. Because of the blackout, pedestrian casualties on roads in the Town were causing concern with many fatal accidents, and the Mayor asked the Emergency Committee to review the situation.[99]

Salvage
Salvage drives for metal, paper and glass (or recycling as we would now call it) were a regular feature of the Town's life throughout the War. In April 1941, at the instigation of Lord Beaverbrook, the Minister of Air Production, iron railings were compulsorily collected throughout the country. Exemption was given to historic examples and those where the removal would cause a danger to the public. In Tunbridge Wells, the Emergency Committee dealt with many appeals against removal, and in the minutes of the Committee, names and addresses are listed. Those removed included the Victorian drinking fountain in Grosvenor Grounds and the remains of the Grandstand in Calverley Grounds damaged earlier in the war. Others to disappear were the railings from Holy Trinity

---

[98] *The Courier 9 & 13 March 1942, p 3.*
[99] *The Courier 3 October 1941 and 6 February 1942.*

'Steam-rolling' tins, saucepans and other metal objects in Tunbridge Wells, 1941.

Church and the Church of King Charles the Martyr. Many were removed from houses throughout the Town and this was to change the appearance of the Town forever. Even today, it is possible to see where the railings were roughly sawn off, much to the displeasure of many residents.

Applications could be made to the Ministry of Supply, via the Town Clerk, for compensation which was 25/- per ton [£1.25p, or £37 at 2009 values]. Not only railings were salvaged, but metal of all kinds, including tin cans and saucepans, was collected. The irony was that much of the metal collected was unsuitable for reprocessing, but it certainly helped people to think that they were making a sacrifice for the War Effort.

In 1942, a salvage drive for waste paper was initiated by Alderman E. B. Weekes, Chairman of Weekes Department Store [now Hoopers since 1986], as Chairman of the Salvage Committee. He announced that children would be admitted free to a film show at the Opera House if they arrived with not less than 2lbs of paper. In the event, each child arrived with 6lbs on average, and by July, 4 tons 3cwt of paper had been collected.

Old Tunbridge Wells Rate Books, 1889-1913, going for salvage.

Amongst other paper sent for salvage were the old Tunbridge Wells Rate Books for the years 1889–1913, a matter of great subsequent regret for local and family historians.

With the ever increasing shortages, the public was asked to save what they had never considered saving before. Customers were asked in 1942 to return empty tooth paste tubes to the shops when buying a new one. (In those days, these tubes were mainly made of soft metal). Arrangements were made by the Ministry of Food and Local Authorities to collect kitchen waste for pig food. And when shopping, because of the lack of wrapping material, housewives would take their own paper bags and string to the shops. Older people can still recall ironing wrapping paper for re-use, especially at Christmas.

Those appointed to posts in the area during the year were Mr Arthur Bottomley [1907–1995] as Deputy Regional Commissioner, who later became well known as a Labour MP; and Rear Admiral H.P.W.G. Murray D.S.O. [1880–1958] as Divisional Petroleum Officer for the S.E. Region. Mr A.B.H.Read resigned as Chief Air Raid Warden and was succeeded by Police Sergeant F. C. Squirrell, who had been on ARP duties since March 1940, and in November 1942 he was promoted to temporary Inspector.

Visitors to the Town during 1942 included the Ambassador of the Republic of Argentina, who presented a mobile kitchen to the WVS, the gift from Senora Jovita Mansilla de Bemberg of Buenos Aires;[100] Lady Reading (the founder and Chair of the WVS); the Duke and Duchess of Kent on 19th March 1942; Princess Mary, the Princess Royal, who inspected the ATS HQ in Warwick Park in April ; Sir A. Baillie MP, who opened a fuel economy campaign; and Mr. Randolph Churchill.

British Restaurants

British Restaurants provided cheap and healthy meals for the public (at not more than 9d a meal – less than 4p, equivalent to £1.10 at 2009 values). *(See page 17 for further background information)*. Tunbridge Wells had two British Restaurants, both seemingly purpose-built – one in the Grosvenor Recreation Ground, the other in the Calverley Grounds. These restaurants continued to serve meals until 1945 when they finally closed and were transferred to the Education Committee in April of that year. The Grosvenor Recreation Ground Restaurant was then used by the children of St. Barnabas Mixed Junior School. The structure of the Calverley Grounds restaurant can still be seen as the café in today's Calverley Grounds.

The cost of building the two British Restaurants was announced by the Council in April 1942 as:

---

100 *The Courier 3 April 1942 p 5.*

	Grosvenor	Calverley
Building	£3,278 - 0 - 0	£3,312 - 0 - 0
Equipment	£565 - 0 - 0	£565 - 0 - 0
Refrigeration	£100 - 0 - 0	£100 - 0 - 0
Consumable Equipment	£250 - 0 - 0	£250 - 0 - 0
Total	£4,283 - 0 - 0	£4,227 - 0 - 0

Approximate cost of each at 2009 values: £130,000

In a speech given by Churchill in May, he paid tribute to the Police:

> *If I mention only one of them [the Civil Defence Services] tonight – namely the Police – it is because many tributes have been paid already to the others. But the Police have been in it everywhere all the time. And as a working-class woman wrote to me in a letter, What Gentlemen they are'.*[101]

In June a new defence regulation was passed authorising the employment of juveniles aged 12–15 during war time, and this was discussed by the Council.[102] In the previous month, Rachel Esther Ginsberg of Woodbury Park Road was fined £25 for not complying with a direction order by a National Service Officer to work as a machinist in Birmingham.

During October, the death of Wing Commander John Smyth D.F.C. R.A.F was announced. He was killed in action in North Africa and is buried outside Cairo. He was the first Tunbridge Wells man to be decorated in 1940.[103]

Also in October 1942, a mustard gas demonstration was held in Dartford and representatives from Tunbridge Wells attended. Surprisingly, it appears that there was still fears of a gas attack and invasion precaution plans were still been discussed. It was at this time that it was decided that the whole of the Borough should be treated as one Nodal Point. Prior to this date, parts of the Borough had fallen in different Nodal Point areas.

 Alderman Westbrook JP was re-elected Mayor, for the fourth successive time in November. During the war years there were no Borough Elections, and if a vacancy arose on the Council, an individual was nominated to serve.

---

[101] *See www.kent-police-museum.co.uk.*
[102] *Council minutes and The Courier 5 June 1942 p 5.*
[103] *The Courier 10 May 1940 p 3 and 30 October 1942 p 6 for obituary.*

In December, the Emergency Committee (whose membership was not directly elected) was criticized on the grounds of undemocratic representation and membership and this was reported in the Courier.[104]

Following the success of the waste paper campaign, a Prisoners of War Fund and a Book Drive were planned for 1943.

The King in his Christmas Message for 1942 said:

> 'We still have tasks ahead of us, perhaps harder even than those which we have already accomplished. We face these with confidence, for today we stand together, no longer alone, no longer ill-armed, but just as resolute as in the darkest hours, to do our duty whatever comes'.

So one of the darkest years of the War came to an end for the people of Tunbridge Wells.

---

[104] *The Courier 4 Dec 1942 p 5.*

1941-3 CHRONOLOGY

1941	Feb 14	German 'Afrika Korps' arrive in North Africa.
	Mar-Nov	Siege of Tobruk by Afrika Korps.
	May 20	German paratroopers invade Crete.
	May 27	'Bismarck' sunk by Royal Navy.
	June 22	Germany invades USSR – Operation Barbarossa.
	July	German 'Final Solution' initiated.
	Aug 20	Germans start siege of Leningrad (St. Petersburg).
	Nov 13	Aircraft carrier HMS Ark Royal sunk.
	Dec 7	Japan attacks Pearl Harbour in Hawaii.
	Dec 8	USA and Britain declare war on Japan.
	Dec 19–25	Japanese capture Hongkong.
1942	Jan 26	First US forces arrive in Britain.
	Feb 15	Singapore surrenders to Japanese.
	Apr 24	Luftwaffe begin 'Baedeker' raids on Britain
	May 30	First 1,000-bomber night raid on Cologne.
	June 3–6	Battle of the Midway: Japan defeated.
	June 21	Germans capture Tobruk
	June 24	Eisenhower appointed C-in-C, US Forces Europe.
	July 1-27	Stalemate first battle of El Alamein halted German advance.
	Aug 7	Montgomery takes command of 8th Army in North Africa.
	Aug 12	Churchill and Stalin meet in Moscow.
	Sept 13	Battle of Stalingrad (now Volgograd) begins, which lasted until February 1943.
	Oct 23–Nov 5	Second Battle of El Alamein – conclusive win
	Nov 13	Tobruk recaptured by British.
1943	Jan 14-24	Casablanca Conference – Roosevelt and Churchill.
	Jan 23	British 8th Army take Tripoli.
	Feb 2	Germans surrender at Stalingrad.
	Mar 20	8th Army win Battle of Mareth Line in Tunisia.
	Apr 19–May 16	Warsaw Ghetto uprising against Germans.
	May 13	German & Italian troops surrender in N. Africa.
	July 9	Allied Forces land in Sicily.
	July	Battle of Kursk: USSR defeats Germany.
	Sept 3	Invasion of Italy begins.
	Sept 8	Italian surrender announced.
	Sept 11	Germans occupy Rome and rescue Mussolini.
	Sept 23	Mussolini re-establishes Fascist government.
	Nov 22	Cairo Conference – Roosevelt, Churchill and Chiang Kai-shek.
	Nov 28	Teheran Conference – Roosevelt, Churchill & Stalin.

CHAPTER 7

TUNBRIDGE WELLS – TOWARDS VICTORY 1943-1945

1943

The planned book drive for 100,000 books, took place from the 9th - 23rd January. These were required to replace books lost in libraries which had been bombed, and for servicemen.

The Town's adopted ship HMS Brilliant had been in the news earlier when it was reported that she had been involved in the rescue of 250 men, women and children from a torpedoed merchant ship. A local member of the crew, Telegraphist Waldron, wrote to *The Courier*, giving a graphic description of the rescue.[105]

A Wings for Victory Week with an opening parade was held in May, when an average of £12-5-0d per head (£372 at 2009 values) was raised.

Home Guard parade past the Assembly Hall.

It was announced during April that £5 million (£258 million at 2009 values) had been saved in Tunbridge Wells since the beginning of the war, and a big rally was held in the Assembly Hall.

Chief Constable Guy Carlton who had been associated with the Borough for over 41 years, 16 as Chief Constable, retired when the Tunbridge Wells Police Force was merged with the County Force under the Amalgamation of Police Forces [Kent] Order, which was made on 1st April 1943.

Visitors to the Town during 1943 included Lord Woolton, Minister of Food, and the President of the British War Relief Society of the USA who visited in September St Christopher's Nursery School in Pembury Road (*now Willicombe Park*).

The Ministry of Pensions for the South East Region was established in 1943 at Hawkenbury in huts that had originally housed Italian prisoners of war.[106] In June 1942, Dr. Rankine had been appointed by the Minister

---

[105] *The Courier 22 Jan 1943, p 3.*
[106] *The Courier 24 Sept 1943 p 6.*

118

to represent RTWBC on the Maidstone and Tunbridge Wells District War Pensions Committee.

The Council estimated that in the coming year 1943/4, the total expenditure of the Emergency Committee for civil defence purposes would amount to £68,043 of which £44,425 would be payable in full by the Government, £16,270 receivable in grants, leaving £7,348 to be provided from local sources i.e. the rates.

The usual day-to-day announcements were made during the year, such as the issue of new ration books, and queueing points for regional transport. In June, it was reported that rubbish was being thrown into the Static Water Tanks in the Town. The Town had three Tanks - one of 22,000 gallons at Varney St., one of 11,000 gallons at Calverley Crescent and one of 5,000 gallons in Grover St, attached to the Victoria School, all of which had been installed in November/December 1939. These Tanks were vital stores of water for use in case of fires started by enemy action.

Blackheath and Tunbridge Wells High School for Girls received a 'Red Duster' from the British Ship Adoption Society in July. In the annual school report, there were accounts of various activities supporting the war effort by pupils, including gifts sent to the Adopted Ship, the SS Cormarsh, the number of items knitted and sent to the Merchant Navy, and the amount of savings collected weekly. Many of the older girls undertook work of National Service during the school holidays which included farming, fruit picking, hop picking and other similar work, but I was too young to do so.

During the later months of 1943,[107] the Allies were beginning to assemble troops and supplies for the invasion of Europe. The ban on travel without written authority was re-imposed on a large area of the South East of England, with residents being issued with passes. This security measure was accepted as a necessity by virtually everybody. A surprising feature of the War was how easily direction and regulation was imposed on the population.

Throughout the year there had been sporadic bombing attacks usually by single enemy aircraft, which suggests that they were not planned and were probably returning enemy planes which had been separated from their main force, offloading bombs which they had not dropped. In the Town, damage was caused to outbuildings at Rusthall Lodge on 8th

---

[107] *The Courier 13 Aug 1943 p 6.*

Rusthall Lodge bomb damage.

*A B17 Flying Fortress after crash landing
on a farm near Tunbridge Wells.*

May. There were no casualties, although the gardener had a lucky escape.

A number of aircraft crashed in the area south of the Borough mainly in Sussex, during the year. Many of these were damaged Allied bombers returning from raids over Germany. Fortunately all seemed to crash in open ground.

The Tunbridge Wells Home Guard planned an All Star Concert to be held in December. But because of intervention by the Lord's Day Society, it was cancelled and it was estimated that over £1,000 had been lost by the Red Cross who would have benefited.

The King closed his Annual Christmas message in 1943 with words from *'Memory Hold the Door'* by John Buchan:

> *'No experience can be too strange and no task too formidable,
> if a man can link it up with what he knows and loves'*

120

Army Camps

In the build-up to the D-Day invasion, when 850,000 Allied troops would be landed in Normandy in the first 24 days, nearly a million troops needed to be 'housed' in Southern England in preparation for it. Most of these, in view of their intended destination, were camped in Dorset, Hampshire and Sussex (and particularly West Sussex), but some were also located in Kent and around Tunbridge Wells.

Most camps were by definition 'temporary' – there were few existing barracks, there were some 'Nissen' and wooden hut camps, but the majority of the invading troops were 'housed' in tents, for up to nine months or even more. As a result of their temporary nature, there are few signs today of where these camps actually were.

While a relatively large number of troops were 'billeted' in houses in Tunbridge Wells, there were no camps as such in the Town. The Royal Signals were 'billeted' in Broadwater Down and Ferndale; the Royal Electrical and Mechanical Engineers (REME) in Calverley Park; a British hospital near Frant and an American hospital at Dornden, Langton Green; besides the XII Corps GHQ staff whose working 'offices' were in Broadwater Down, but who were 'billeted' at various houses which had been requisitioned in Broadwater Down, Eridge Road, Frant Road, Madeira Park, Nevill Gate, the Pantiles, Queen's Road, Roedean Road, Upper Cumberland Walk, Warwick Park, as well as various hotels (the Rosebank, Russell, Spa).

The following is a list of some 26 camps in the surrounding area, but it may not be comprehensive, since today the only evidence of their existence may be documentary.

Location	No. of Camps	Name(s), if known
Ashdown Forest	9	Camp Hill, Chuck Hatch, Forest Row, Kidbrook Park.
Black Hill	1	Green Wood Gate Camp
Burgess Hill	1	St. John's Common Camp
Crowborough	3	Warren Camp, West Camp, Golf Course.
Frant	1	Eridge Park
Hartfield	1	Marsh Green Camp
Ightham	1	Mote Park Camp
Lingfield	1	Hobbs Barracks
Maresfield	1	Maresfield Camp
Matfield	1	Sandhole Camp
Sevenoaks	1	Montreal Camp
Sheffield Park	2	Fletching Village & Lewes Rd. (6,000 Canadians)
Southborough	1	Great Bounds Camp
Tonbridge	2	Mabledon Camp, Mereworth Camp
Wych Cross	1	Pippingford Park Camp

1944

Night time bombing continued throughout the early months of 1944, and on 21st January incendiary bombs were dropped on Mount Ephraim and the Common and small fires were started which were quickly put out by the NFS. Eighteen properties were damaged, but there were no casualties. Other damage and casualties were reported in *The Courier* and pictures appeared regularly, but no names or addresses were given, but it can be assumed that they must have been in the local area. After the War, it was possible to identify many of these incidents from records.

Supplies of essential goods remained in short supply, coal was restricted, and the Council was still concerned about the use of water, and there were fears that water supplies would have to be limited.[108]

As in previous years, announcements were published advising the public on the use of electricity, food, the saving of fuel, allowances of coal and coke per household, and the distribution of new ration books. It was also reported that there was a 'Rat Menace' in the Town!

The public were 'asked' not to travel during the Easter and Whitsun holidays, and announcements were published to this effect. Given that there was little petrol and very few people had cars, and bus and train services were limited, there was no choice for people but to stay at home and attend local events and activities. But even these were limited as many of the usual annual events had been suspended since the early years of the war.

In March 1944, the Council Rate was announced for the coming year – 11/5d [57p] in the £, with the cost of Civil Defence 4d (under 2p.) in the £.

At the end of March 1944, the Regional Commissioner reported that:

> *during the quarter, the Region has become a civil defence training camp'.*

This seems to be an euphemism for all the military training which was being carried out.

During the early months of 1944, there was much military activity in the Town. Particularly in April and May, all of Southern England had become one large Army camp, and civilians were under strict security controls.

---

[108] *The Courier 23 June 1944, p 3.*

The build-up gained momentum, as D-Day 6th June 1944, approached. For lack of space, many army vehicles were parked permanently in residential roads around Tunbridge Wells.

During the period prior to 'D' Day, the Regional Commissioner was in constant communication with the GOC of South Eastern Command. The military prerogatives in the area at this time obviously took precedence over civilian requirements and included such issues as convoys en route to and from the coast, road communications, damage control, the prospective provision of casualty clearing stations, sites for AA guns, searchlights, and barrage balloons: and all these were understandably given priority.

In anticipation of D-Day, the 77th U.S. Army Evacuation Hospital was established at Dornden, Langton Green and today there are trees planted as a memorial on the site.

23 Calverley Park was requisitioned and used by the US and Canadian Armies prior to D-Day. During their stay, there was a fire in the house which damaged the balcony.

I have to confess that I (aged 12) have no particular memories of D-Day or its significance, apart from an awareness of a large number of planes going overhead on the night of 5/6th June. I was aware that great events were happening, but didn't really understand them. What struck home more at that age, was probably the news that my eldest cousin's husband had been wounded.

Women's Services Club, Mount Pleasant, Tunbridge Wells.

On the 17th June 1944, the opening ceremony for 'Salute the Soldier Week' was held.[109] Again, the WVS played an important part in coordinating the many services, setting up Welcome and Hospitality Clubs for the American troops, amongst others in the area. It seems strange that editions of *The Courier* published during the month of June made no mention of the invasion, presumably because of censorship. Reports of local men involved, only started to appear at a later date.

---

[108] *The Courier 23 June 1944, p 3.*

V1s and V2s

The V1[110] Flying Bomb and V2 Rocket attacks on London between June 1944 and March 1945 were the last German attacks on London and South East England. In today's world of guided missiles, they were distinctly 'unguided' – the Germans pointed them in an approximately correct direction and then hoped for the best, which depended on a number of variables, such as weather conditions (wind speed and direction; and barometric pressure); the precise trajectory (range and bearing) chosen; and (in the case of the V1 only) whatever opposition it met in the form of Anti-Aircraft fire, RAF fighter intervention and AA balloons.

V1 'Doodlebug'.

The V1 Flying Bomb (or Doodlebug, as it was soon nicknamed by the British public) was a small, jet-powered pilot-less plane that flew low at 350mph, before delivering its 1 tonne warhead. It was the forerunner of the modern Cruise missile.

V2 missile ready to launch.

The V2 Rocket, was the first ballistic missile and the forerunner of the technology that would put Man on the Moon. It weighed 13 tons and arrived at its target via the stratosphere at 3,000 miles an hour. There could be no warning of its arrival, as there was with the V1.

An estimated 2,419 V1's and over 500 V2 Rockets were to fall on Southern England, but principally on London. In total, 8,938 people were killed and approximately 25,000 seriously injured.

The original Luftwaffe plan was to fire 200 Flying Bombs **an hour** at London. Because of the efforts of the Allies, the maximum achieved was only ever 200 in one day.

The first V1 fell in Grove Road, London E4 at 4.25am on 13th June 1944. The last was to fall at Swanscombe on 28th March 1945, less than six weeks before the end of the War. On the 8th September, 1944, the first V2 landed in Staveley Road, Chiswick, adjacent to Chiswick House.

---

[110] *The V description was taken from the German designation for them as vengeance weapons – VERGELTUNGSWAFFE. Hence the V1 and V2. There was even a V3, which never flew.*

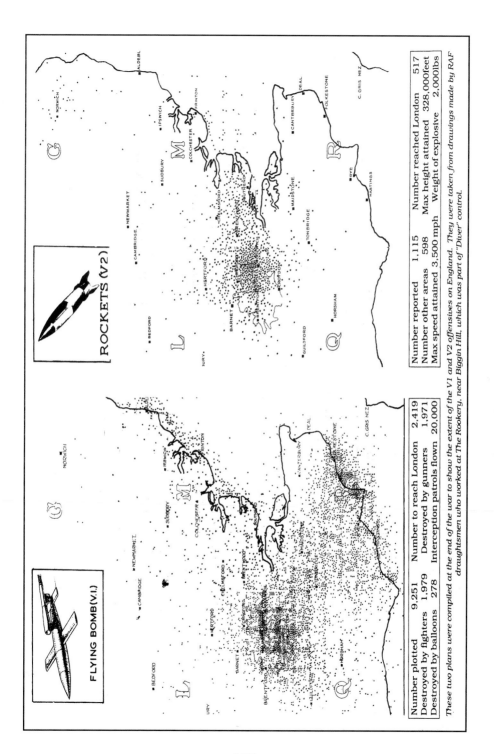

FLYING BOMB(V.1.)

ROCKETS (V2)

Number plotted	9,251	Number to reach London	2,419
Destroyed by fighters	1,979	Destroyed by gunners	1,971
Destroyed by balloons	278	Interception patrols flown	20,000

Number reported	1,115	Number reached London	517
Number other areas	598	Max height attained	328,000feet
Max speed attained	3,500 mph	Weight of explosive	2,000lbs

These two plans were compiled at the end of the war to show the extent of the V1 and V2 offensives on England. They were taken from drawings made by RAF draughtsmen who worked at The Rookery, near Biggin Hill, which was part of "Diver" control.

125

The last landed in Court Road, Orpington on 27th March, 1945.

It should be recognised that the apparent ability of the Germans to retaliate within days of the D-Day Invasion with new, startling and very frightening weapons, did undermine Allied confidence and reduce some of the public euphoria about the Invasion itself.

1944 defence plan.

As a defence for London against the V1 (since there would/could be no defence against the V2), 376 heavy guns and 576 40mm guns were deployed in a belt from Maidstone to East Grinstead. Tunbridge Wells was situated broadly in the middle of this belt. Other defences included light anti-aircraft weapons on the South Coast and barrage balloons along the ridge of the North Downs.

The British Government had been aware of these new weapons for some time. As early as November 1939 a report by SIS had been submitted to the Air Ministry, that the Germans were developing secret aerial weapons and as a result, the RAF had been bombing test sites such as Peenemunde and launch sites under construction, since early 1943.

But this knowledge was highly secret and kept from the British public. It was not until 26th April 1944 that a notice was distributed to all police stations, and Royal Observer Corps and warden's posts in Southern England 'to prevent publication of any report which would indicate where missiles may (have) fall(en)' and such events were to be regarded as secret. In particular, there were to be no press reports.

The existence of these new weapons was eventually revealed (but in a somewhat uncertain manner) to the British public by a Ministry of Home Security (MOHS) Circular was issued to local authorities some ten days later on 6th May 1944, which stated:

> *'The enemy is known to be experimenting with pilotless aircraft and he may attempt to use this weapon against targets in the South of England from sites in Northern France'.*

Two days after the first V1 fell, Herbert Morrison, the Home Secretary, confirmed on 16th June 1944 that there was a new German 'Air Weapon'.

126

The first Flying Bomb or V1, to be reported in the Borough of Tunbridge Wells, was recorded on 26th June 1944, at 04.45 hours. It was shot down by Anti-Aircraft fire, and fell at Little Bayhall Farm, causing extensive damage to a farm house, farm buildings, and four cottages. There were no casualties.

In one school log book (St. Barnabas's), an entry records:

'A new device, a pilotless plane is being sent over by the enemy, this affected attendance of the children. Children take cover under desks'

Another school (Tunbridge Wells and Blackheath High School) reported that pupils taking public examinations had many trying experiences during June and July. Tunbridge Wells was directly under as many as 5 or 6 flight-paths of the V1s and V2s and it has been estimated that as many as 2000 flew over or near the Town.

For me, the V-weapons meant that the family moved back into the air-raid shelter in the garden every night, although my strongest memory for the period is being ill with whooping cough. We had no warning of V2s, but V1s could be heard some way off and one listened for the cut-out of its engine. If it happened above or beyond you, you were safe since (hopefully) it would take several miles to glide to its destination.

R.A.F. fighters were used to destroy the V1s. The pilots initially shot down the V1s in the conventional manner being able to match in a shallow dive, the 350 mph speed of the V1. But later they developed a technique of flying alongside a V1 and putting the fighter wing-tip under the wing of the V1 and flipping it over, causing the V1's gyroscope to be destabilized and for the V1 to crash far from its intended urban target.

Unfortunately, one V1 which was 'shot down' in this manner on Wednesday 5th July, crashed on a Canadian Army Camp situated on Crowborough Golf Course, which resulted in nine soldiers being killed and seventeen injured. They were members of the Lincoln and Welland Regiment, and today there is a simple memorial to them near the spot. Two roads in Crowborough also bear these names, and there is also a Garden of Remembrance in Church Road. Besides the tented army camp, many of the houses in the surrounding district had been requisitioned for use as army billets.

In all, 13 V1s fell around Tunbridge Wells, and many more in the surrounding areas of Kent and Sussex. The six that fell in the Borough caused 1,662 houses to be damaged to some degree; and by 23rd August 1944, it was reported that 21 houses had been severely damaged, 980 slightly, 565 with broken glass, and 85 which were still to be recorded; 135 were damaged by cannon shells and splinters from shells.

V1s were frequently destroyed in the skies over Tunbridge Wells. All these incidents had to be recorded by the Civil Defence Services, which added to their heavy work-load. Shrapnel from the AA and aircraft-cannon shells wounded 8 persons- 4 seriously - since many of the shells did not explode until they hit the ground. Some lodged in buildings, and these were subject to official reports with a detailed map reference, which involved the Police and the Control Centre, and their removal by Bomb Disposal Services.

Crashed V1 which didn't explode.

On 28th July, a V1 crashed near Powder Mill Lane, High Brooms and did not explode. It became the first complete V1 which could be examined by the military.

It should be recognised that when a house was damaged, even indirectly, virtually every-thing in it was unusable. In particular, all food was likely to be contaminated by flying glass and other debris, and this was where the WVS Mobile Canteens came into their own. In the Tunbridge Wells area especially, heavy calls were made on the WVS as a result of flying bomb attacks. Canteens also fed the Civil Defence rescue workers at the scene. Members of the WVS Housewives Section helped to clear up and put in order the houses damaged by bombs and blast. In many houses, it was not possible for the owners to return until repairs had been carried out; and many householders were injured, or traumatised by their experience. In those days, there were no counselling services, as there are today.

As a result of the V1/V2 threat, public shelters were opened again, having been closed earlier in the War because the threat of bombing had disappeared and because the shelters were being used by vagrants and as rubbish tips. Earlier, when the vagrant/rubbish problem was first identified, the Emergency Committee had decided that all public shelters should be kept locked, except during air-raids,(although this did raise the question as to how quickly they could be unlocked in the event of a raid) and had asked the Town Clerk to draw up rules and regulations for the use of shelters. At one point in the debate, it was reported to the Emergency Committee that the public shelter in Albion Road was being used for 'immoral' purposes.

Demand for Morrison Shelters increased and queues formed at the Borough Surveyor's Office, for the issue of shelters. Reserve stocks of these shelters had been moved to be near the London, Reading and Tunbridge Wells Regions in October 1943.

On 6th August 1944, George Gearing of Stanley Road, who was sitting in one of the thatched seats on the Common, died from injuries he received when a V1 exploded nearby.

With the attacks from the V-1, it was decided once again to evacuate children from Tunbridge Wells. In July, evacuation plans

The thatched seat on Tunbridge Wells Common where George Gearing died.

were discussed by Head Teachers of schools in the Borough, at a meeting in the Town Clerk's Office.A party of twelve children from the High School set off for the West Country and were received by the Coborn School in Taunton, who had previously been evacuated from Bow in London. Colfe's School went to Frome. Many children from other schools also set off for the West Country and South Wales. Before evacuation, the children had to be registered. They returned home in December, looking a picture of health.

It is somewhat ironic that the Government announced the end of official evacuation on 7th September 1944, the day before the first V-2 rocket fell on London, but even this new type of attack failed to halt the steady return of evacuees to the cities, which reached its peak during the autumn of 1944.

Losses of aircraft and pilots continued to be reported during 1944. Amongst them were many bombers returning damaged from bombing raids on Germany. Some of the crews were killed, others who were injured were treated at local hospitals, including those in Tunbridge Wells, but fortunately some escaped injury altogether. Luckily most of the planes crashed in open country, the wreckage of which was collected by the RAF 'Salvage Gang' of 49 Maintenance Unit.[111]

The summers of 1944 and 1945 were both very hot, with Tunbridge Wells recording one of the highest temperatures of 32C [90F] in both summers.

The King spoke to the nation on D-Day 6th June 1944:

'Once again what is demanded from us all is something more than courage, more than endurance: we need a revival of spirit, a new unconquerable resolve. After nearly five years of toil and suffering, we must renew that crusading impulse on which we entered the war and met its darkest hour'.

In August 1944, as a clear indication that the War was expected to end both shortly and successfully, there was a meeting outside Washington of the Allied Powers and it was agreed to set up an organization, later to be called the United Nations, which would supersede the defunct League of Nations.

Capt. Queripel

In September, Operation MARKET GARDEN took place, which was the largest airborne operation *of all time*. It involved 35,000 troops, 15,000 being landed by glider and 20,000 by parachute behind the enemy lines, in order to secure the bridge at Arnhem over the Rhine, which was a strategic necessity for the invasion of Germany. It was a gallant failure, dubbed subsequently as being 'a bridge too far'. The operation lead to the award of the Victoria Cross to a Tunbridge Wells man, Capt. Lionel Queripel of the 10th Battalion, Parachute Regiment and The Royal Sussex Regiment. He was killed at Arnhem on 19th September 1944, aged 24 and is buried at Oosterbeek Cemetery. He is commemorated in the Book of Remembrance in the Town Hall. The citation of his award was published in The London Gazette on 1st January 1945:

In Holland on September 19th 1944, Captain Queripel was acting as Company Commander. When advancing on Arnhem, heavy and continuous enemy fire caused his Company to split up on both sides of the road, and inflicted considerable losses.

---

[111] *'Bombers over Sussex' by Burgess and Saunders, pub 1995.*

Repeatedly crossing and re-crossing the road under sustained and accurate fire, Capt. Queripel not only immediately re-organized his force, but carried a wounded sergeant to the Regimental Aid Post, and was himself wounded in the face. Nevertheless he personally lead an attack on the strong point blocking their progress, and killed the occupants, thereby enabling the advance to continue.

Later Capt. Queripel found himself cut off with a small party. Although by then additionally wounded in both arms, he continued to inspire his men to resist until increasing enemy pressure forced him to order their withdrawal. He insisted on remaining behind to cover their retreat with pistol fire and hand grenades, and was not seen again. During nine hours of confused and bitter fighting, Capt. Queripel unceasingly displayed gallantry of the highest order. His courage, leadership and devotion to duty were magnificent and inspiring.

His parents, Leslie and Sybil Queripel, lived for many years at 52, Warwick Park. Although he had been killed in September, it appears that from the minutes of the Town Council of 7th February 1945, that he had not been officially reported dead, as the Council expressed their hope that his parents would soon receive official news of their son's death.

At the Meeting of the Tunbridge Wells Borough Council on 4th October 1944, it was reported that a letter had been sent by the Mayor to General Montgomery who had recently been promoted to Field Marshal, congratulating him on his appointment. The Mayor's letter was formal and appropriately succinct – some 27 words in total. The new Field Marshal's reply was equally formal and polite and even more succinct - and amounted to 15 words. In some ways it was surprising that they even received a reply, bearing in mind that Montgomery was in the middle of Operation MARKET GARDEN.

A meeting of members of the WVS from all over the South Eastern Region was held at the Assembly Hall in early November 1944. The Regional Commissioner, Lord Monsell, who could not attend the meeting in person, sent a message which included the following compliment:

'A fine, noble job of work of which you can ever be proud'

These words summed up the unselfish, unremitting and often heroic work of the WVS during the war years.

As the Allies advanced into Europe, news was coming through of local men, who had been prisoners of war, being released.[112]

Although the war was still being fought in Europe and the Far East, many local organizations which had been created for defence, were being 'stood down' i.e. disbanded, as there was no longer any fear or threat of invasion. Each organization held a 'Stand Down' Parade in the Town. The Home Guard stood down on 8th December 1944, followed by Civil Defence General Services on 2nd May 1945, Civil Defence (an event organised by the Borough Council) on 24th June and Tunbridge Wells Special Constables on 3rd October.

'Stand-Down' Parade for Home Guard and Civil Defence in Calverley Grounds.

Far from Tunbridge Wells, another local man Capt R.F. Jolly, a Skinners' Old Boy, was awarded the Military Cross for the part he played in Burma in the Battle of Kohima (April-June 1944). The 4th Battalion, Royal West Kent (RWK) was in this battle, the same battalion which had been involved near Dunkirk in 1940, and many of the men were from the local area.

The King in his Christmas Message in December 1944 said:

> *'We do not know what awaits us when we open the door of 1945. But if we look back to those earlier Christmas days of the war, we can surely say that the darkness daily grows less and less.'*

1945

1945 opened with increased optimism that the end of the war was in sight. However, the V1 and V2 attacks continued until March when the last V1 and V2 fell.

During March the Council received a letter from Lord Monsell announcing his resignation as Regional Commissioner and saying that he would be handing over to his Deputy, Mr. Arthur Bottomley.[113]

---

[112] *The Courier 4 May 1945 p 6 reported the names of British PoWs from Tunbridge Wells being released in the European theatre. An issue in September did the same for the Far Eastern PoWs.*
[113] *Council minutes Vol 420 p. 14.*

From 1st April, elementary (i.e. primary) schools which came under the Tunbridge Wells Education Authority were taken over by a new authority, the Kent County Council (KCC) Education Committee. The chairman of the Borough Education Committee, Alderman Saunders, reported to the Council's monthly meeting on the work which had been carried out by the Committee during the past 40 years. He said that the committee had ceased to function as an Authority for elementary education in the Borough on the 31st March 1945 and had been superseded by the KCC. He expressed his appreciation of the co-operation he had at all times received from Members of the Committee, the Officials, and Teachers of the Elementary Schools in the Borough.[114]

In March, there was a report in *The Courier* that Blackheath High School which had evacuated to Tunbridge Wells in 1939 would be returning to Blackheath in the Autumn. So in August 1945 the planned return of the High School to Blackheath started, with the school reopening on 20th. September in its premises in Wemyss Road, Blackheath, London, although only six months earlier the buildings had been damaged, when a V2 rocket which fell near by. I had been a pupil at the combined Blackheath High School/Tunbridge Wells High School for the past four years and so when it was announced that Blackheath was 'returning home', my parents decided that I should stay with Blackheath High School and so I became a boarder at Blackheath for the next four years.

The Allies continued to advance through France, Belgium and Holland and finally entered Germany in March. Two months later, following Hitler's suicide at the end of April, hostilities ceased as the German High Command in the West surrendered on Luneburg Heath to Field-Marshal Sir Bernard Montgomery.

It was announced in *The Courier*[115] that plans were been made for 20,000 Dutch children to be received in this country for a stay of five months. It was hoped that Tunbridge Wells would welcome sixty-five children and the Mayor asked for the names of families who would give free hospitality. A local Reception Committee was formed, with Mr S.H.W. Fowle as secretary, to oversee the arrangements, and on the 10th December 1945, 65 children arrived in the Town.[116] They were welcomed by the Mayor in the Council Chamber and later entertained to tea in the Assembly Hall lounge. It was estimated that each child would cost in the region of £8 for expenses relating to medical checks, entertainment and clothing, which would be paid by the Committee.

---

[114] *Council minutes Vol 420 p. 15.*
[115] *The Courier 20 April 1945 p 6.*
[116] *The Courier 14 Dec 1945 p 5.*

The Ministry of Home Security had fixed Wednesday 2nd May 1945 as the 'appointed day' for the commencement of the disbandment of Civil Defence Organisations.[117] Fireguard (i.e. firewatch) Orders had ceased from 30th April. In schools as early as February, workmen had been removing 'blast walls' and un-boarding classroom windows, and it was reported that the noise of the work had caused classes to be disrupted.[118]

Instructions were also received to put into action the Government plan for the return of evacuees to London.

VE DAY

As May started, everyone was waiting eagerly for news that the war in Europe was over. On the 7th May at 7pm, it was announced that Germany had surrendered and that the next day, the 8th, had been declared 'Victory in Europe' (VE) Day, with Sunday 13th *Victory Thanksgiving Day* .

The King addressed the War Cabinet and Chiefs of Staff on the 8th. May, VE Day:

> *'On a famous occasion five years ago - which to most of us seems like fifty - you told us that we would get nothing but blood, sweat, and tears. Looking back, I should say that is a fair estimate of what we did get'*

And to the Public in the evening at 9 pm, he said:

> *'So let us resolved to bring to the tasks which lie ahead the same high confidence in our mission. Much hard work awaits us, both in the restoration of our own country after the ravages of war and in helping to restore peace and sanity to a shattered world.'*

Churchill spoke to the Nation earlier in the day at 3pm:

> *'The lights went out and the bombs came down. But every man, woman and child in the country had no thought of quitting the struggle. London can take it. So we came back after long months from the jaws of death, out of the mouth of hell, while all the world wondered. When shall the reputation*

---

[117] *Council minutes 2 May 1945 p 18.*
[118] *St. Barnabas's School log book.*

and faith of this generation of English men and women fail? I say that in the long years to come not only will the people of this island, but of the world, wherever the bird of freedom chirps in human hearts, look back to what we've done and they will say 'do not despair, do not yield to violence and tyranny, march   straight forward and die if need be-unconquered'. Now we have emerged from one deadly struggle – a terrible foe has been cast on the ground and awaits our judgment and our mercy'.

The 9th and 10th May were also proclaimed to be Public Holidays and everybody celebrated with street parties, gatherings and parades.

Nursery Road, High Brooms – VE Day street party.

On 15th August, following the dropping of two atomic bombs on Hiroshima and Nagasaki in early August, Japan surrendered, although the formal surrender ceremony was not performed until 2nd September 1945 aboard the battleship USS Missouri in Tokyo Bay. Nonetheless, 15th August was declared to be Victory over Japan [VJ] Day and another two days were proclaimed to be Public Holidays.

VE Day celebrations in Calverley Grounds.

July 1945 was to see the resignation from the WVS of Miss Muriel Wells, with effect from 4th August, and it was announced that the WVS Centre in Tunbridge Wells would close from that date. The sale of 18 WVS motor vehicles raised £1,389 – an average of £77 each.

But while the Tunbridge Wells Centre might be closing down, it was certainly not the end of the WVS, which thrives to this day as the WRVS – the Women's Royal Voluntary Service.

Wounded servicemen were being treated at the Kent and Sussex Hospital and other local hospitals. Many, while recuperating, were seen in 'Hospital Blues' about the Town, including patients from the famous McIndoe Burns Unit at East Grinstead Hospital.

166 names of local men who had been killed during the War were to be added to the 776 already on the War Memorial from the First World War. In May 1948, a Service of Dedication was held at Holy Trinity Church, but it was not until June 1951 that Viscount De L'Isle and Dudley unveiled the additional names on the Memorial.

Dunorlan Park restored in 2005.

Dunorlan Park fountain.

On 5th June 1945, the Council completed the purchase for just under £43,000 of Dunorlan House and grounds, which had some 78 acres, including a six-acre lake, between Pembury Road and Halls Hole Road; and so laid the foundations for what is now one of its 'jewels', Dunorlan Park. Dunorlan House and grounds had been 'requisitioned' in 1941 and occupied, both sequentially and in parallel, by the Army, the National Fire Service (as its HQ), the War Damage Commission (as its HQ) and the Ministry of Works. The Council did not achieve full possession until 1957. The House itself was demolished in 1958 on the grounds that it was 'beyond restoration' due to a fire in April 1946, a view which would probably be disputed today. The Park was 'restored to its former glory' in 2005 at a cost of £2.9 million, most of which came from a Heritage Lottery Grant of £2.1 million.

GENERAL ELECTION JULY 1945

A General Election was held on 5th July 1945, the first since 1935, and a Labour Government was returned with a majority of 146, and Clement Attlee became Prime Minister. The result of the election came as a major shock to the Conservatives, given the heroic status of Winston Churchill as

John Bull passing the cricket ball to Attlee. Cartoon by Illingworth.

war leader, but it reflected the voters' belief that the Labour Party were better able to rebuild the country following the war, than the Conservatives. (It should be remembered that the British Government from 1931-1945 had been a National i.e. a 'coalition' Government, with the Cabinet drawn from all three parties, although the Conservatives had dominated it. So there had been no *single* party as such, in control of the British Government for 14 years.)

Clement Attlee.

137

But Tunbridge Wells [or more precisely the Tonbridge constituency, of which Tunbridge Wells was then part] remained staunchly Conservative, and Lt. Commander Gerald Williams RNVR was returned as the local M.P.[119]

 On 6th June 1945, the Council formally thanked the Mayor, Alderman Charles Westbrook O.B.E. J.P. for his achievements as Mayor from 1938 to 1945. He had first been elected to the Council in 1910, and became an Alderman in 1921. He was elected Mayor for first time in 1925 and subsequently in 1926, and was awarded the OBE in 1936. He was made a Freeman of the Borough in January 1938, and elected for his third term as Mayor in November 1938. Because of the War, he continued as Mayor for another six terms, establishing a record for the office, which can never be bettered. He was further honoured in November 1950 by the Council when Miss Muriel Wells, the Mayor, declared with only the slightest exaggeration that during the War Years, 'he was to this Town what Churchill was to this Nation – a tower of strength and an inspiration.' He retired from the Council in 1952, after 42 years of service, and died in June 1958.[120]

Two others were honoured by the Council in 1945. John Whitehead, who had been Town Clerk of the Borough of Tunbridge Wells since July 1925 and Sub-Controller of the ARP during the war years, together with Councillor Robert H. Burslem, JP, were made Honorary Freemen of the Borough of Tunbridge Wells at a special meeting of the Council at the Assembly Hall in October 1945.

In November 1945, the first Borough Elections since 1938 took place. The Mayor, Alderman Charles Westbrook O.B.E. J.P., understandably did not seek re-election.

On 9th November, Alderman T. C. Allen succeeded Westbrook as Mayor.[121] It was also at this meeting that the Council made the following Proclamation:

> *"The Council desires to express its deep gratitude and thanks to the men and women who served or are serving in HM Forces... and also in the Civil Defence Services"*

---

[119] *He would remain MP for Tonbridge until 7th May 1956, when he retired from Parliament by taking the Stewardship of the Chiltern Hundreds, on the grounds of ill-health. He died, 33 years later, in 1989 at the age of 85.*
[120] *The Courier 3rd November 195 p 5; and obituary The Courier 27th. June 1958.*
[121] *Council Minutes 6 June 1945.*

So the war years ended, but it was not the end of shortages and rationing for the people of Tunbridge Wells. In fact in many ways, it became much worse, although at least the bombing and the killing had stopped.

The whole country faced another ten years of real economic austerity, although on a decreasing scale, and it was to be 1954 before Tunbridge Wells could enjoy a completely ration-free life.

Unofficially, the Nevill Golf Club had heard, that the War Office was considering incorporating the 7 holes which had been requisitioned by them in 1942, into a permanent Army range. The Club had applied for de-requisitioning of the land.[122] While there is no official report of the outcome, it is clear that since the Club now operates an 18-hole course, that they were successful in their application. The only relic of the War is that on the 8th hole, traces of a gun emplacement can still be seen to this day.

Canadian Troops

The first Canadian troops had arrived in Britain in December 1939, and many were to be stationed to the south of Tunbridge Wells, mainly in Sussex, from 1940.

The presence of so many Canadian troops in the Tunbridge Wells area for up to five years, obviously had an impact in a number of ways.

Many settled in the area after the war, choosing not to return to Canada.[123] Others (it is said 40,000) chose to marry local girls and take them back to Canada.

In 1945, the 'Canadian War Brides' of Tunbridge Wells, 84 in number, had their own club which had been set up by the Canadian Army, while they were awaiting passage to Canada to join their husbands.

Later in 1947, a letter to the Courier[124] from a Canadian ex-serviceman complained that the parents of army wives were trying to persuade their daughters to return to England and this was leading to broken homes in Canada.

---

[122] *The Courier 27 July 1945 p 5.*
[123] *'The Maple Leaf Army in Britain' by P. Longstaff-Tyrrell Published 2002.*
[124] *The Courier, 18 July 1947 p 3.*

Rehabilitation

The rehabilitation of returning ex-Servicemen and women to civilian life was a new and important issue. In July, a Ministry of Labour Resettlement Advice Bureau was opened at 24, Grosvenor Road and in the first six months dealt with 3,000 inquiries from ex-servicemen and women.[125]

Additionally, a 'Welcome Home Fund' had been proposed and in October, the Mayor asked for donations and hoped there would be a formal opening ceremony early in the New Year.

Housing

With many servicemen returning home, no new houses having been built and many houses destroyed, there was an acute shortage of housing in Tunbridge Wells.

This caused some local people to try and solve the problem for themselves. A group of so-called Vigilantes, who seemed to be based in Brighton under the leadership of a 'Guv'nor' called Mr. Cowley, installed L/Cpl Simpkins RASC, his wife and two children in an empty house at 315 Upper Grosvenor Road over a weekend in July.[126]

At a Council meeting, it was agreed that another 100 houses should be built[127] and it was estimated that the cost of preparing the site would amount to £23,858. Under new laws, local authorities had been given powers to requisition empty houses in their area, and the Housing Committee was seeking information on fifty such properties in the Borough.

The Tunbridge Wells Food Control Committee, was formed to provide representation of all those involved in the food chain – local government, local traders and consumers. They were appointed each January from 1946 to 1951.[128]

1945 saw awards announced for the many achievements of local men and women. Among these was the Legion of Merit awarded to Major Harry King of the Royal Artillery, son of Lt. Col. H. King of Frant Road, by the White House.[129] The citation was one of the last to be signed by

[125] *The Courier 11 Jan 1946 p 5.*
[126] *The Courier 27 July1945 p 6 (picture p 3); 3 August 1945 p 2.*
[127] *The Courier 27 July 1945 p 5 for Council Report.*
[128] *General Purposes Committee minutes 5 December 1945.*
[129] *The Courier 24 August 1945 p 6.*

the President, Franklin D. Roosevelt, before his death. It was given for 'exceptionally meritorious conduct from 1942 to 1944 as the AA Liaison Officer, 2nd Bombardment Division'. Another award of the Croix de Guerre was to Sergeant Neville Carey, who was parachuted into enemy-occupied France in August 1944. (Other awards to Tunbridge Wells men will be found in Appendix 2)

THE CIVIC ASSOCIATION PROPOSALS
The Civic Association [the forerunner of *The Royal Tunbridge Wells Civic Society*] had been invited by the Town Council in November 1943 to prepare proposals for the post-war development of the Town.

Their proposals were discussed internally within the Association during 1943 and 1944 and published in 1945 in a report of some 80 pages, which was edited by Helen Spalding. Sketches and plans for many major projects were put forward, including the rebuilding and refurbishment of the Pantiles; a repertory theatre; a Winter Garden; development of the High Street; and plans for housing, traffic, schools, playing fields, sport facilities, and car parks were also covered in the report.

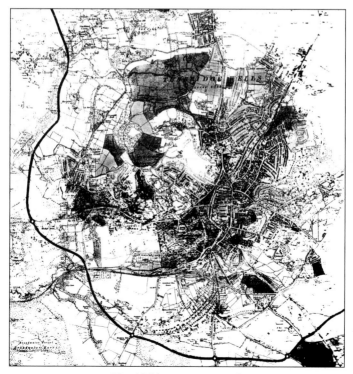

The A26 by-pass proposal.

141

Plans for housing included a somewhat extreme proposal for the demolition and rebuilding of the whole of the St. Peter's area, possibly influenced by the fact that that area had suffered more bombs than most and might therefore be more suitable for redevelopment. The flow of traffic was discussed and it was suggested that many major roads in the Town should be widened, particularly in the shopping areas, and a by-pass of the Town to the South West, should also be built to relieve the A26, which was considered to be overcrowded even in 1942/43. A municipal airport was also considered, possibly at Penshurst, with helicopters being the visionary choice of aircraft.[130]

Even then, the Civic Association was not happy with the Cinema site at the top of Mount Pleasant, although when it had been opened in 1934, the Mayor Councillor E. B. Weeks described it as the most luxurious in Kent.[131]

Although many of the proposals make sense even today (although some do not!), none of them have yet seen the light of day, probably because they were 'buried' in the turmoil of post-War Britain and were not economically or financially feasible in the stringent circumstances of Austerity Britain.

THE TUNBRIDGE WELLS BURIAL BOARD

Another Council sub-committee which had been actively engaged in making many decisions connected with the war, was the Burial Board.[132] They were responsible for the burial of military, civilian and enemy personnel who had been killed in the area. Not only did they receive directives from the Ministry of Health, but also from the Imperial War Graves Commission (later to be renamed the Commonwealth War Grave Commission).

The work of their Emergency Mortuary Service was not confined to the local area. In a letter received from the Senior Regional Officer of the Ministry of Health in September 1943, the Superintendent and his staff were thanked for their valuable help given to an unnamed 'Sussex Town', following an air raid in July 1943.

The Borough Cemetery did not escape the attention of the Luftwaffe. In

---

[130] *In 1935, there had been a landing strip at Penshurst and a RAF bomber had had to make a forced landing there with a wing on fire [The Courier 26 July 1935 p15].*
[131] *The Courier 7 December 1934.*
[132] *Burial Board Minutes (Tunbridge Wells archives).*

September 1940, the eastern wall was damaged 'by enemy action' and later other buildings were damaged.

The unfilled/undedicated land in the Cemetery grounds was also put to good use, with the growing of potatoes and tomatoes, which were then sold. It was reported by the Board that for the years 1942-43-44 a profit of £305-13-1d (approximately £9,000 at 2009 values) had been made on these sales.

As early as February 1939, the old Mortuary at the Borough Cemetery had been converted into an ARP shelter. The Mortuary and Chapel crypt at Woodbury Park Cemetery were also used as an ARP Post and listening post.[133] In 1987 after the 'Big Storm', a vault was 'revealed' in the Woodbury Park crypt, which was found to contain guns and Mills bombs, dating from the Second World War, and these had to be removed by the Police and Army bomb disposal experts.

After the War, in 1946, it was proposed by the War Graves Commission that the work of erecting permanent headstones would begin and a letter from them to the Burial Board requesting permission to start work was received. In a meeting held on 11th April 1946, the Council approved the request.

In the King's Christmas Message for 1945, he said:

> 'For six years past I have spoken at Christmas to an Empire at war. During all those years of sorrow and danger, of weariness and strife, you and I have been upheld by a vision of a world at peace.'

---

[133] *Woodbury Park Cemetery Newsletter 2008.*

The Cost of Civil Defence to Tunbridge Wells

The threat of war, and war itself, created significant additional costs for individuals, families, businesses, organisations, and government, both central and local. Much of this additional cost is impossible to calculate and not all of it was monetary.

Individuals and families could count the cost of additional Blackout material or a Morrison or Anderson shelter; but not the cost of delays, or being on ARP duty three nights a week.

While much cannot be counted, we are able to count the cost – the direct cost – of ARP/Civil Defence in Tunbridge Wells because it was recorded in the Borough Accounts and in the Rates which the householder paid; and as a percentage, it is remarkably modest at about 5%.

KCC had decided before the War that the cost of ARP and Civil Defence Services would be borne by the District, and not the County, and so Tunbridge Wells had to bear the cost, less the Central Government Grant. The Emergency Committee reported to the Council each year the amount actually paid and these were:

Year	Council ARP/CD Expend.	Gov't Grant	Net Council Expenditure	Additional ARP/CD Poundage	Total Rate Poundage
1938-9	£694	–	£694	$^1\!/_2$d	10s4d
1939-40	£38,127	£31,898	£6,229	6d	10s10d
1940-1	£28,308	£16,725	£7,534	6d	10s10d
1941-2	£70,402	£58,281	£12,121	5d	11s3d
1942-3	*	*	*	*	10s10d
1943-4	£68,043	£60,695	£7,348	4d	11s5d
1944-5	£51,874	£43,999	£7,875	4d	11s5d
1945-6	£13,300	*	*	*	13s6d

* Despite extensive research, no precise data has been found.

It is worth noting that the War does not seem to have caused a significant rise in the Rates – an increase from 10s 4d to 11s 5d is only roughly 10% over 7 years – and the big increase (of over 15% in just one year) to 13s 6d in the first post-war year was attributed to KCC, who increased their levy by £47,125 to £305,370.

To put the above figures in 2009 perspective in terms of value, they should be multiplied by 38 for 1939 values and 30 for 1945 values. So total annual expenditure by the RTWBC on ARP and Civil Defence at 2009 values would have been approximately £1,450,000 in 1939, £2,135,000 in 1942 and £1,550,000.

1944–45 CHRONOLOGY

1944   Jan 1   Soviet troops advance into Poland.
           Jan 22   Allies land at Anzio in Italy.
           Jan 27   Leningrad relieved after almost 900-day siege.
           Mar-Jul   Japanese Army decisively defeated at Imphal/
                       Kohima in India.
           June 5   Allies enter Rome.
           June 6   D-Day landings in Normandy.
           June 13   First V-1 lands on London.
           June   Battle of Philippine Sea – Japanese Aircraft
                       Carriers annihilated.
           Aug 25   Liberation of Paris.
           Sept 8   First V-2 rocket lands on London.
           Sept 17-25 Operation Market Garden – battle of Arnhem.
           Oct 25   Battle of Leyte Gulf – heavy Japanese losses.
           Dec 16   Battle of the Bulge in the Ardennes starts.

1945   Jan 1-17   German forces withdraw from the Ardennes.
           Feb 4   Yalta Conference – Roosevelt, Churchill, Stalin.
           Feb 11-13   Dresden destroyed by mass bombing.
           Mar 27-28   Last V-1 and V-2 land on London.
           Mar 30   Soviet troops capture Danzig.
           Apr 12   Death of US President Franklin D. Roosevelt;
                       succeeded by Harry S. Truman.
           Apr 18   German forces in Ruhr surrender.
           Apr 25   San Francisco Conference agrees to set up United
                       Nations to succeed League of Nations.
           Apr 28   Mussolini and mistress captured and both
                       hanged by Italian Partisans.
           Apr 30   Hitler commits suicide in Berlin.
           May 2   German troops in Italy surrender.
           May 2   Fall of Berlin.
           May 7   Unconditional surrender of all German forces.
           May 8   VE (Victory in Europe) Day.
           July 5   UK General Election-Labour Government
                       returned.
           Aug 6&9   Atomic bombs dropped on Hiroshima & Nagasaki.
           Aug 14   Unconditional surrender by Japan.
           Aug 15   VJ (Victory over Japan) Day in Britain.
           Aug 15   Nationalisation of coal mines announced.
           Aug 21   President Truman suspends Lend-Lease
                       programme to UK.
           Oct 4-Nov 5 Dock strike in UK.
           Dec 27   International Monetary Fund and World Bank
                       established.

1946-53 CHRONOLOGY

1945–48		Jewish terrorism in Palestine.
1946	Mar 5	Churchill delivers 'Iron Curtain' speech in Fulton, Missouri.
	Mar 21	Plans for National Health Service unveiled.
	May 30	Bread rationing introduced.
	Nov 12	Nationalisation of all transport (rail, ports, canals, long-distance road transport) announced.
1946-54		First Indo-China War.
1947 June 5-**1948** Mar 31		Marshall Aid Plan established.
	Aug 15	India partitioned; India and Pakistan independent states.
	Oct 21	Nationalisation of gas industry announced.
	Nov 8	Potato rationing introduced.
1948-1960		Malayan Emergency.
1948	Jan 1	Railways and Transport nationalised.
	Jan 30	Gandhi assassinated in Delhi.
	Apr 1	Electricity Industry nationalised.
	May	Establishment of State of Israel; first Arab-Israeli War.
	Jun 21	'Empire Windrush' arrives with first Jamaican immigrants.
Jun 26-**1949** May 12		Berlin Airlift.
	Jul 5	National Health Service inaugurated.
	Jul 29-Aug 14	XIVth Olympic Games held in London.
1949	Mar15	Clothes rationing ends.
	April 4	North Atlantic Treaty Organisation (NATO) inaugurated.
	May 1	Gas industry nationalised.
	August	USSR tests its first Atomic Bomb.
	Sept 18	Devaluation of £ – falls from $4.03 to $2.80 to £.
	Oct 1	Formal inauguration of People's Republic of China.
1950	Feb 23	General Election: Labour returned with majority of 5
1950 June 25-**1953** July 27		Korean War.
1951	Feb 15	Iron & Steel industry nationalised.
	May 3	Festival of Britain opens on London's South Bank
	Oct 25	General Election: Conservatives win with majority of 17.
	Oct 26	Churchill becomes Prime Minister again.
1952	Feb 6	Death of King George VI; Accession of Queen Elizabeth II.
	Feb 21	Wartime Identity Cards abolished.
	June 16	European Coal & Steel Community (forerunner of EU) set up.
	July 23	Military coup in Egypt by Col. Nasser overthrows King Farouk.
	August	Start of Mau-Mau activity in Kenya.
	Oct 3	First British Atomic Bomb tested.
	Nov 5	General Eisenhower elected President of the USA.
1953	March 5	Death of Joseph Stalin, who was succeeded by Malenkov, and then very quickly by Bulganin and Krushchev.
	May 29	Mount Everest conquered by Hillary and Tensing.
	June 6	Coronation of Queen Elizabeth II.
	June 17	Uprising in East Germany.
	July 27	End of Korean War.
	Aug 12	USSR tests an H-Bomb.
	Nov 5	Announcement that all rationing to end in 1954.

PART 2 TUNBRIDGE WELLS IN THE YEARS OF AUSTERITY

CHAPTER 8

POST-WAR AUSTERITY 1945 -1949

Post-War Tunbridge Wells was dominated by a number of issues – the Nationalisation of its Gas, Electricity and the Health Services; the rationing of Goods and Services, but particularly food; the provision of Housing, which included the issue of 'Squatting'; Education and the need for new and upgraded Schools; the Weather which was abnormally severe; and the presence of a large number of Prisoners-of War in the area. All of these caused concern, if not problems.

NATIONALISATION

The Labour Party entered government with the firm determination to implement what was a key policy for them – the nationalisation of key industries into public ownership. During the six years of the Labour Government [1945-1951] many key industries, such as Gas, Electricity, Iron & Steel, Railways and Coal-mining, were nationalised; and services such as doctors and hospitals were coordinated and concentrated into a National Health Service.

Tunbridge Wells Electricity Generating Station.

This had a considerable impact on Tunbridge Wells and its Borough Council, which as a very enterprising, forward-looking and self-sufficient Town since its creation less than 60 years before, had actually set up the utility companies which supplied gas and electricity to the Town; and had initiated three hospitals – the Kent and Sussex, Homeopathic and Pembury Hospitals – which up till now had been privately run with funds raised by the Town's inhabitants.

Tunbridge Wells Gas Generating Plant.

The Lighting Committee of the Borough Council was very concerned about the Electricity Bill which was introduced by the Labour Government to nationalise electricity supplies. The local electricity company had been set

147

up in 1895 and was owned by the Council, who had over time made a capital investment of £956,220 in the company. It was proposed that in taking over the electricity company, the Government would pay only £29,958 in compensation, which the Council understandably thought very unfair.

Similar circumstances also applied to the Gas Works. Again the Council was worried about the low compensation that would be paid by the Government. Gas was nationalized by the Gas Act of 1948 but no record can be found of how much compensation was actually received by the Borough Council.

When in 1948 the Kent and Sussex Hospital, the Homoeopathic Hospital in Church Road, and Pembury Hospital became part of the National Health Service, much dismay was shown by the local population.[134] The accounts[135] for the Hospital showed that the cash balance was £10,000 *[£295,000 at 2009 values]* with investments amounting to £52,000 *(£1,535,000)*, and the building and equipment being valued at over half a million pounds *(£14,750,000)*. Again no record can be found of how much compensation was paid.

Peanut Club Badge.

A particular cause of public dissatisfaction over the Hospital was that the inhabitants of Tunbridge Wells, as well as many outsiders, had contributed substantially during the previous 20 years, through organizations such as the Pea-Nut Club, to fund-raising for the building of the Kent & Sussex Hospital, which had opened in 1934 as a 'state-of-the-art' hospital and there was a strong feeling of 'we wuz robbed' about its nationalisation.[136]

Additionally, the Kent and Sussex Hospital was reported to be in financial difficulties owing to an understandable drop in donations, with expenses possibly reaching £90,000.[137] To offset this, the Kent and

---

[134] *The Courier 30 April 1948 p 4*

[135] *The Courier 18 June 1948 p 7*

[136] *A significant contributor to the Hospital funding was the Pea-Nut Club, which was the biggest and most successful money-raising scheme for the Hospital. The Club was started in the early 1930s by accident, and almost as a joke, by The Courier and the Club was run by 'Aunt Agatha'. Membership cost 1/- and there were 31,000 members in 1937, including the Archbishop of Canterbury, Shirley Temple and the entire crew of a British warship. In 1938, nearly 43,000 people .attended a four-day funfair organised by the Club which raised nearly £10,000 (equivalent in 2009 to about £390,000)*

[137] *The Courier 10 May 1946*

Sussex Hospital had sold in October 1947 some of it assets and three wards had had to be closed because of the lack of nurses.[138]

RATIONING

In 1946, food rationing which had been in force since January 1940 became more stringent than ever. Bread, which had never been rationed during the war, was rationed for the first time in July 1946. As an exclusively post-war phenomenon, bread rationing was seen by many to be the result of Government 'incompetence', rather than economic necessity. Nonetheless, the public accepted it as part of the 'fair-shares-for-all' concept, which was seen as the basic justification of the need for rationing in wartime Britain. Much to the disquiet of bakers and housewives, bread was to remain rationed for the next two years.

A thinner John Bull reflects the impact of rationing. Cartoon by Illingworth.

Potato rationing was also introduced in 1947 – an almost unbelievable course of action for an essentially home-grown crop. There was even a suggestion that other greengrocery would be rationed. The Ministry of Food continued to give guidance through its food preparation advertisements – one of which famously had the headline: *'Five ways on how to use stale bread'.*

Coal/coke rationing which had been introduced in July 1941 and they were to remain in restricted supply until 1958 – the last products to be returned to 'free supply'. The importance of coal/coke to an average British household during World War II (and before) cannot be underestimated – it was then the primary source of both heating and cooking. Few households had central heating of any sort and coal fires/coke stoves were the principal source of heat and hot water. While gas and electricity were developing as heating/cooking fuels in terms of the number of households using them, coal/coke was still the primary fuel.

---

[138] *The Courier 3 Oct 1947 p 4*

The Divisional Food Office was in Bishops Down, with Mr Vidal and Mr Barrett as the Divisional Food Officers. The Regional Food Office was at Mount Ephraim House with Major General Dalison CB OBE as Regional Food Officer.

In May 1946 the office was visited by Dr. Edith Summerskill, M.P. the Under-Secretary at the Ministry of Food. The Ministry was responsible for buying food imports in bulk and distributing supplies through the local food offices. They also issued Ration Books annually.

But there were signs that rationing was beginning to ease up and supplies were going back to normal, although the picture was very uneven.

The Emmanuel Canteen run by the Emmanuel Church *(demolished in 1974)* on Mount Ephraim closed at the end of January 1946 after six years of service to the Forces, and it was estimated that between 600,000 and 700,000 men had been served during that time. The canteen was one of many in the Town.

The two British Restaurants in Calverley Grounds and Grosvenor Recreation Grounds had served about 3,000 meals a week (an average of just over 2,000 in Calverley and just under 1,000 in Grosvenor) since being established in late 1942. They were transferred to the KCC Education Committee at the beginning of April. Later in the month, the Grosvenor Recreation Ground restaurant became a school canteen, with 50 children from St. Barnabas' School attending.[139]

Shipments of oranges, lemons and bananas arrived in December 1945, the first since 1940. For many younger children, this was the first time that they had seen or tasted the fruit.

Early in 1946, buffet cars were re-instated on the trains to Hastings for the first time since 1941.

Some unusual but unrationed items also went on the market in 1947 – horse meat, whale meat and tinned 'snoek', which was described as a species of South African pike or perch. The Ministry of Food had bought 3,850 tons of 'snoek', but the great British public decided that, regardless of the shortages, it was not for them and left it on the shelves. It was said that the solution found for this problem was to re-label the tins, calling it 'Rock Salmon' with a flash saying 'Guaranteed _not_ to go pink in the tin'.

---

[139] *St. Barnabas' School Log Book p 309*

HOUSING

During the whole period, there was a severe housing shortage in the Town (and indeed in the whole country), caused by bomb damage and no new houses being built during the War, and compounded by population growth and shifts in the distribution of population. This was to remain a major problem for many years to come. Before the War, the Council had built 493 Council houses. Post-War, up to 1953, they were to build a further 313 houses, 237 flats, and 100 'pre-fabs' (prefabricated bungalows) – a total of 650 – and they also provided accommodation for a further 153 families in (what were presumably short-term) requisitioned houses – so they were providing accommodation for a total of 803 tenants.[140] In total up to 1953, the Council undertook the construction of 888 dwellings on four Council estates. There were therefore a further 238 'units' under construction, but not completed in 1953, making a total of 888 constructed. But, regrettably, the demand was much greater than this.

Housing Register
The Housing Register, recorded in the Health and Housing Committee's Minutes, lists the number of housing applicants at given dates, although not all categories are minuted on all dates:

At:	Couples with children	Couples without children	Elderly	Total
1 Jan 1943	148			
1 Jan 1944	204			
1 Jan 1945	285			
1 Jan 1946	847			
April 1946				950
Dec 1946				1,165
19 Nov 1947	1,039	323	50	1,412
19 Jan 1948				1,444
17 Jan 1949				1,576
17 Jun 1949	929	402	61	1,392
16 Jan 1950		284		1,462

Clearly, there was a massive increase in the number of applicants on the Register immediately after the end of the War, with which no building

---

[140] *Carole Tyrell: article in Civic Society Newsletter, Summer & Autumn 2001*

programme could cope. It was obviously an enormous surprise to Tunbridge Wells Council, and no doubt to many other Councils as well.

The Council used it powers to requisition many empty houses in the Town, and a hundred or more houses, flats and cottages were acquired. They included St. Mark's Army Camp near St. Mark's Church in Broadwater Down which consisted of 20 Nissen[141] huts with basic sanitation. These were used to house seventy five families over the next seven years. They were gradually re-housed in Council houses in other parts of the Town.[142] [143]

Hawkenbury Close

The Health and Housing Committee[144] had acquired ground between Napier Road and The Convalescent Home in Hawkenbury for 'temporary

housing.' i.e. for what would become known colloquially as 'pre-fabs' – a single-storey prefabricated house. German PoWs did much of the work preparing the site. Named Hawkenbury Close, the first 'prefabs' arrived at the end of January 1946 and in March the first tenants moved in.[145] It was to be 1979 before these were demolished and a new estate built on the site.[146]

A pre-fab estate.

Powder Mill Lane

Tenders were accepted in February 1946[147] for 114 new houses in Powder Mill Lane, and in August 1946, the builders were ready to start.

---

[141] *Nissen huts, which were semi-circular in profile and made of overlapping corrugated iron, had been developed by Colonel Nissen of the Canadian Army during the First World War and were the standard barrack-room hut in the Second World War.*
[142] *See article by Kathleen Strange: Bygone Kent vol. 7 no 4 1986*
[143] *Council minutes 16 Feb 1945*
[144] *Council minutes 16 Feb 1945*
[145] *The Courier 25 Jan 1946 and article in 'Bygone Kent' vol 15, p 137 – 139 by Kathleen Strange.*
[146] *Oral history: Jack Luxford*
[147] *The Courier, 8 February 1946 p.6*

Building work on the Council's estate in Powder Mill Lane was delayed by the bad weather of early 1947, and it was reported that the estate would not be finished until 1948. In May 1947, the estate was inspected by Sir William Douglas, Permanent Secretary of the Ministry of Health.[148]

During the summer of 1947, the first tenants moved into the new houses on the council estate in Powder Mill Lane. The names of the roads reflected the war years – Cunningham, and Montgomery and Tedder, three wartime leaders of the Navy, the Army and the RAF. After there had been a rent strike in October by tenants who thought that the rents were too high, the Council agreed to reconsider them, but the Council eventually refused to alter them.

The Powder Mill Lane Estate was nearing completion in October 1948 and it was declared that another 50 acres of land in the Borough were required for more houses.

Ramslye Estate
In February 1946 the Council approved a plan for 380 houses on the Ramslye Farm Estate off the Eridge Road, with a school, community centre, public house and at least 8 shops and a post office.[149] In July 1946 the Marquis of Abergavenny in a letter to the Council, objected to the Council's Compulsory Purchase Order for approximately 60 acres of land forming part of the Ramslye Farm; he stated that it was good farming land, which was needed for food production in a time when there were severe food shortages. A further 50 houses at Ramslye were approved in May 1947. In 1949, the first tenants moved into the new houses on the Ramslye Estate.

Sherwood estate.

Sherwood Estate
In 1949, a new Council Estate of 394 houses was proposed at the junction of Sandhurst and Pembury Roads, which later became known as the Sherwood Estate. In June 1949, the land had been valued at

---

[148] *The Courier 2 June1947 p 5*
[149] *The Courier 7 Feb 1947 p 5*

£6,285, (approximately £190,000 at 2009 values, but worth considerably more today because of the inflation of land values) and the Housing Committee agreed to issue a Compulsory Purchase Order for it. On earlier council estates, local building firms had tendered for the work, but as only two contractors had tendered on this new project, consent was obtained from the Ministry of Housing and Local Government to use direct labour.[150] November saw the plans approved for 60 single-bed , 272 two-bed and 68 three-bed dwellings and work started. By October 1952, the first tenants moved in, and the keys were handed over by Alderman F. S. Harries.[151]

It is worth recording the proposed weekly rents and rates for the Sherwood Estate in 1952:[152]

Type	Rent	Rates	Total	2009 Equiv.
3-bed house	£1-10s-01d	11s-7d	£2- 1s-8d	£45.43
2-bed house	£1- 5s-10d	10s-9d	£1-16s-7d	£39.97
1-bed flat	£0- 15s-08d	7s-6d	£1-3s-2d	£25.33

❖❖❖❖❖

Contracted construction continued on the Ramslye Estate, which had been delayed earlier in the year because of the shortage of building materials.

Throughout the building of the many new houses in the Borough, damage including graffiti and theft of builder's materials, was caused by children. It was said that this was through lack of parental discipline and control. Damage and theft to the buildings on the Manor Road site in Southborough was also caused by youths, amounting to over £500.

One Southborough Councillor had been reported as saying: *'They should be up-ended and soundly smacked'.*[153] This was in the days before the one-sided and currently-prevalent concept of 'political correctness' (individual rights put before individual and collective responsibilities) had been developed.

---

[150] *Bygone Kent Vol.17 1996 and Civic Society Newsletter Summer and Autumn 2001*
[151] *Courier 7 Oct 1952; Civic Society Newsletter, Summer and Autumn 2001*
[152] *Carole Tyrell: article in Civic Society Newsletter, Summer & Autumn 2001*
[153] *The Courier 12 Dec 1947 p 4 ;30 Sept 1949 p 4*

At Somerhill, 30 of the PoW buildings were converted to form 60 bungalows and there were requests that there should be a church as well.

Kent & Sussex Housing Association

There was one short-lived attempt to solve the housing problem from the 'private' sector. In January 1947, a Mr William Finnigan proposed a Kent and Sussex Housing Association. He said at a meeting that 800 people were required to join.[154] In February, the Association was incorporated with a nominal capital of £5,000 and the directors were William Finnigan, Frederick Rowlands, and Tom Higgins. But by July, the Association was causing the Borough Council concern. By December 1949, the scheme had run in to difficulties with large debts and was declared bankrupt.[155]

Squatters

'Squatters' had been a housing problem since the end of the War. 'Squatters' are homeless people who take the law into their own hands and occupy empty buildings generally by breaking in, to provide accommodation for themselves and their families. Post-War, there were a large number of homeless – mostly homeless through no fault of their own – and there was much sympathy for them. English Law somewhat quirkily provides them with protection under certain conditions, so Squatters' Rights can and do exist to this very day.

Homeless families had moved into the Great Bounds Army Camp in Southborough.[156] In January 1947 the Regional Office of the Ministry of Health, decided that the occupiers of the huts who were paying rent, should also be charged with the cost of electricity, and the supply cut off to those who refused to pay.[157] Later in May 1947, the Southborough Urban District Council criticised the repair bill specification for weatherproofing the huts at Great Bounds.[158] The squatters' camp at Great Bounds was demolished in September 1950.[159]

There were more 'Squatters' in the Agricultural Show Ground at Eridge Road.[160] A family had occupied a hut since November 1947. The huts

[154] *The Courier 24 Jan 1947 p 5*
[155] *The Courier 16 Dec 1949 p 3 and Council minutes.*
[156] *Amongst the army units stationed at the camp during the war had been the Scottish Horse and Royal Artillery. See picture The Courier 30 May 1947*
[157] *The Courier 3 Jan 1947 p 6*
[158] *The Courier, 30 May 1947, p 4*
[159] *The Courier 8 Sept 1950 p 5*
[160] *Council Minute 27 July 1948*

which were permanent structures had been used during the pre-war Agricultural Shows to house the show animals. The Borough Council had received a letter from the Housing Officer of the Ministry of Health asking the Council to rehouse the occupants, or control the hut on the Ministry's behalf, until such time that the family could be rehoused. The Show did not return to its traditional ground until 1951.

EDUCATION

Along with the housing shortage, there was a lack of school places in the Town. Many local schools, some of which had been built in the 19th century, were in need of replacement, or at least refurbishment. Historically, a large number of these schools were Church Schools.

In a lecture given in June 1947 by Mr W. Moore, West Kent Divisional Education Officer, at Culverden House, the Adult Education Centre, a large audience heard his outline of the plan for the future for local schools[161] in the area.

It was suggested that Huntley's in Culverden Down, the former home of Sir John Blunt, which previously had been a secretarial college and during the war a military hospital, had been bought by KCC. (This was later denied by Sir John Blunt.) In January 1948, there were further discussions with the Church on a £12,000 venture for a school at Huntleys.[162] After three years of delays, the future of Huntley's was still not decided in June 1950.[163]

But in October 1950 it was reported that the plan would go forward with an appeal for £10,000.[164] In 1952, Mr James Nicholson took over as Headmaster when King Charles, Royal Victoria, and St James Schools were amalgamated, but it was not until 1956 that the new School moved to its new site.

Infant and primary schools were also needed on the new housing estates of Banner Farm, Ramslye, Powder Mill Lane, and Sherwood. Amongst other schools to be built or opened during the post war period was Bennett Memorial School. Ridgeway School, Southborough was built in 1955. The West Kent Technical High School for Boys in St John's Road was built in 1956 and Sandown Court School opened in 1960, replacing a number of smaller schools.

---

[161] *The Courier 6 June 1947 p 5 and 27 June1947 p 5.*
[162] *The Courier 23 Jan 1948 p 5*
[163] *The Courier 16 June 1950 p 5*
[164] *The Courier 6 Oct 1950 p 5*

During 1946-8, many problems were hitting schools in the area. The long hard winters disrupted time tables, with teachers unable to get into schools as the roads were impassable; and much absenteeism and illness was reported amongst both the children and staff, and there was the continuing universal paper shortage.

During the latter part of 1947, concern was shown over an outbreak of Infantile Paralysis, more familiarly known as 'polio', in the Town. Five cases were confirmed, with the deaths of Mrs Grace Price, a school teacher, and Mr R.H. Leaney. The Medical Officer of Health stated that there was no cause for alarm.[165] In 1949, 14 new cases of 'polio' were reported in South West Kent, but fortunately none were in the Tunbridge Wells area. The outbreaks caused many restrictions to be imposed, especially at swimming baths.

❖❖❖❖❖

THE WEATHER

The winter of 1945/46 was very hard and in January 1946, there was recorded -9°C (16°F) of frost in the Town. Heavy demand resulted in electricity cuts; and caused disruption in local schools, and to transport and food deliveries in general.

A bleak realistic view of 1947, Cartoon by Illingworth.

The New Year of 1947 introduced another hard winter, known popularly as the 'Shinwell Winter' [after Emmanuel Shinwell MP, the Minister of Fuel and Power, who masterminded the nationalisation of the coal industry).

In retrospect, it was very unfortunate that nationalization, coupled with coal rationing which would remain in force until 1958, should have been introduced on 1st January 1947, days before the start of the coldest winter for fifty years. Snow fell and was to remain on the ground for 6-8 weeks. On the night of 23rd February, the temperature recorded in Tunbridge Wells was -19° C [2° F]. The countryside was 'locked in an icy

---

[165] *The Courier 14 Nov 1947 p 5*

grip' with heavy snowfalls and many schools were closed. The bad weather understandably caused much absenteeism amongst both teachers and pupils.

A major problem was water pipes freezing. St. Barnabas's School[166] reported that all the lavatories and pipes were frozen, and when a sudden thaw happened, the pipes burst, flooding the cloakrooms. There were major gas and electricity cuts everyday, and prison was threatened for anyone found wasting electricity. It was recommended that everyone should only have one bath a week to save fuel and ease electricity consumption. Older people remember having to walk from the Town to the local coal companies which had depots at the High Brooms sidings, to collect their coal supply in old prams or hand carts.[167]

After the long hard winter of 1946-47, it was estimated that the cost to the Council for clearing the snow had amounted to nearly £10,000 [£300,000 at 2009 values]. It was not until the middle of March that the temperature rose, but with higher temperatures, came gales and heavy rain and flooding. Many crops had been ruined after six weeks of snow, and vegetables became scarce. Later there was to be a long hot dry summer, which in its own way caused different problems.

Double Summer Time, which had first been introduced as a safety measure during the War to extend the daylight hours of a normal summer day, was reintroduced in March 1947.

For the first time in many years, the winter of 1947-1948 was comparatively mild. The Spring was very dry, and by early June, the Council was appealing to people to save water, once again. But only two weeks later, there was a severe storm in the area with many houses being struck by lighting and there was flooding in the lower parts of the town. Reports of this appeared, somewhat paradoxically, juxtaposed to the 'save water' advertisements in *The Courier*. In August 1948, there was a heat-wave followed again by heavy rain, and later in the month, a 70 mile-an-hour gale struck the South East. To finish the year, December saw the worst fog, (or 'pea-souper' as they were then called), for 40 years.

In 1949, the weather again played an important part in the Town's year. Rainfall since 1939 had been below average every year except 1948, and there was a shortage of water throughout Kent, the worst for 20 years. Local residents were asked to save water and announcements were made on how this could be achieved, including advice on the depth of

---

[166] *St. Barnabas' School logbook*
[167] *Oral history: Pamela Taylor (née Bates)*

water in baths, although how this could be checked within the bounds of decorum was anybody's guess.

But by September 1949 there were severe storms once again and many traders' premises in the Town were flooded.

PRISONERS-OF-WAR (PoWs)

Somerhill PoW camp.

The prisoner-of-war camp at Somerhill, near Tonbridge [known as Working Camp 40], was capable of holding 1,500 prisoners. Many German prisoners of war were still being held there as late as 1948. (The Italian PoWs were repatriated much earlier than the Germans, because they had become Allies in the last months of the War and because Italy had not suffered the same degree of urban destruction as Germany.)

Because of the labour shortage, many German PoWs were put to work on farms, building sites, and roads; and all were paid a modest remuneration for their work. As an illustration, some 15 were used on the Eridge Road development [Ramslye Estate], but were withdrawn in March 1948. Some were also employed on the Powder Mill Road estate. When the camp was finally empty, the huts were used for temporary housing.

February 1948 saw 'Squatters' invading Somerhill. The Commanding Officer (CO) of the Camp was Colonel Ord, who had been appointed at the end of the War. He had joined the Army in 1916 and was a regular soldier with 33 years' service. He was a popular CO amongst the many prisoners. The huts were still occupied by the PoWs and for a short time the 'Squatters' were locked behind the barbed wire fencing intended for the PoWs. After five hours, Colonel Ord was able to persuade the 'Squatters' to 'surrender',[168] their 'invasion' having been watched, probably somewhat incredulously, by many of the PoWs. In April 1948, it was decided that the Camp could not be released for housing.[169] But later in February 1949, permission was given for some 30 huts in the camp to be used as temporary housing, and by November 1949 the huts had been converted which impressed Councillors when they inspected the camp.[170]

---

[168] *The Courier 13 Feb 1948 p3 and Frank Chapman Nostalgia Column, 2 March 2001*
[169] *Tonbridge Free Press and The Courier 4 April 1948 p 4*
[170] *The Courier 18 Nov 1948 p 4 and picture*

In all, some 24,000 PoWs (4.3% of all PoWs in the UK) chose not to go home, mainly because they had or were going to marry English girls.

After the War, German PoW's started to play a part in the Town's life. In April 1947 they had sung at the Salvation Citadel in Varney Street (now under the Royal Victoria Place) and in October a Church service had been held in German and English in a local Tonbridge church.[171] Many were still working on housing sites, roads and farms. There was public concern about this, but the public was assured by the authorities that the prisoners were always 'under control'.

In September 1947, a woman was gaoled, the Police describing her as 'a perfect nuisance to the PoWs at their camp at Somerhill'.[172]

In October 1950, the future of Mabledon Park was under discussion. In 1941, its owner, John Francis Deacon [of Deacon's Bank], had died and in his will, bequeathed the house to be used as a rest home for clergy,

laymen and laywomen. However because of wartime constraints, it had been requisitioned and used during the war as both a 'battle school' and a prisoner-of-war camp (numbered No. 629, so it was a much later foundation than the nearby Somerhill which was numbered No.40). In the post-war years, it was used as a hospital and rehabilitation centre for displaced persons and Polish ex-servicemen.[173]

Mabledon Park.

---

[171] *The Courier 24 Oct 1948 p 4*
[172] *The Courier 26 Sept 1947*
[173] *2WW File, Tunbridge Wells Reference Library*

1945

The Tunbridge Wells War Comfort Association closed. *The Tunbridge Wells Advertiser* reported[174] that during the war years, it had provided many thousands of cigarettes and parcels, to servicemen and women. It was finally wound up in February 1946 with the final funds amounting to £58 – 15 – 7d [about £1,750 at 2009 values) which was divided between the Soldiers, Sailors, and Air Force Association (SSAFA) and the Soldiers, Sailors and Airmen Help Society (SSA).

In June, the Council launched a Welcome Home Fund to provide for returning servicemen. As in the previous years, many special weeks were held. It was announced that National Savings in Tunbridge Wells had reached the £10 million mark, [£200 million at today's values] and a new target for National Savings was set amounting to £700,000 in the coming twelve months [equivalent to £14 million today].

Councillor McNab was awarded the MBE for his work in the National Savings Movement in the New Year Honours List of 1946. He had been the Chairman of the Local War Savings Movement, of which the Mayor, Alderman Westbrook had been President.

A Road Safety Week was planned with events being held each day. There had been a Road Safety Conference held at Maidstone in April which was attended by the Mayor, Cllr. T. C. Allen, and Chief Inspector Sly. Anxiety was growing about safety on the roads and the police started visiting schools giving talks, demonstrations and showing films on road safety to pupils. The talks were to continue in the coming years.[175]

In September, a Safety First Tour of Tunbridge Wells was made. The conclusion was that pedestrians were the worst offenders, with the elderly and women being the worst.[176]

---

[174] *The Tunbridge Wells Advertiser 2 Feb 1945*
[175] *St. Barnabas's School log book*
[176] *The Courier 27 Sept 1946 p 5*

1946

Mr. Aneurin Bevan, the Health Minister, attended a conference on Housing early in February 1946, held at the Assembly Hall.[177]

The Chamber of Trade appealed for unity in post-war planning and called for a Civic Week to be held.

In March, the Council had acquired the Freehold of 'the 12 acres or thereabouts' of the Nevill Ground from the 'struggling' Tunbridge Wells Cricket, Football and Athletics Club Ltd. for a consideration of £2,850 [about £85,000, or £7,000 an acre, at 2009 values].

Also in March 1946, a RAF Mosquito fighter-bomber crashed in Rusthall near to two schools. It is thought that the pilot did not bale out because, as a local man, he knew about the schools and made sure that he did not hit them. Fortunately none of the children were hurt, although the pilot, Squadron Ldr. Kenneth Dart, DFC, was killed.[178] He had been awarded the DFC in October 1941 when at the age of 20 years, he had carried out a reconnaissance mission in a Sunderland flying boat, in which his aircraft was damaged and three of the crew wounded.[179] There is now a memorial garden in his honour at the school.[180] In August 1941, he had married Meryl Maldwyn Jones, the 'Charter Queen' of the 1939 Jubilee celebrations and daughter of Rev. I. Maldwyn Jones, Minister of the Mount Pleasant Congregational Church *(later to be Habitat and now Cotswold)*.

But amid all the uncertainties, there were some bright spots. On 8th June 1946, the Victory Day anniversary celebrations were held with a three-day holiday being declared over the Whitsun Weekend[181]; a V-Day Pageant was held in London; and in Tunbridge Wells, a Fireworks display took place in the Calverley Grounds in the evening, at which many old people of the Town were entertained by the Mayor.

Cricket Week was also held in June. The Open Tennis Tournament was revived and held in July for the first time for many years; the Tunbridge Wells Bowls Tournament was restored after a lapse during the war years, and local football was once again in the news. November saw Bonfire Night celebrated. And a Festival of Remembrance was held in the

---

[177] *The Courier 8 February 1946, p. 6*
[178] *The Courier 22 March 1946*
[179] *Citation : London Gazette 31 Oct 1941*
[180] *Kent Messenger Extra and Courier 14 Nov 2008*
[181] *The Courier 14 June 1946 page 3*

Assembly Hall.[182] All these were events which had not been held during the War years.

The Soroptimists

Revival was also to be seen in new organizations being formed. In June 1946, a group of Tunbridge Wells' most influential and formidable women signed a petition to form a Soroptimist Club in the Town. A Charter Dinner was held on the 26th October at the Royal Mount Ephraim Hotel *(now The Royal Wells)* and Sir Robert Gower, former Mayor and MP and the principal guest, said at the dinner:

> *'The establishment of a Soroptimist Club in Tunbridge Wells will no doubt benefit the whole population. I hope it will go from strength to strength.'*

The Soroptimists continue to be very active to this day in Tunbridge Wells.

At the other end of the spectrum of female involvement, recruiting advertisements for the Women's Land Army appeared in April 1946, asking for women between the ages of 17 – 40 years to volunteer.[183] They were required to enlist for 2 years service, the rate of pay being 50/- [£2-50p, or £74 at 2009 values] for a 48 hour week, plus overtime.

At the beginning of October, Alderman E.B. Weekes, who had been Mayor from 1934-1936 and was the owner of Weekes, the Tunbridge Wells department store, announced his retirement from the Council at the age of 80 after over 20 years' service. James A. Sargeant was elected Alderman in his place.

An exhibition of industrial design entitled 'Britain Can Make It' was held at the Victoria and Albert Museum in London in 1946; surprising, given that so many restrictions were still in place, it attracted over one and a half million visitors.

In November 1946, plans were published by the Civic Association for a new War Memorial and Garden of Remembrance, designed by Mr H. A. Humphrey, the Chairman of the Association. The scheme would include

---

[182] *The Courier 22 Nov 1946, p. 4*
[183] *The Courier 17 April 1946, p. 6*

a spacious assembly hall, a theatre, playing fields, a sports pavilion and committee rooms for ex-service organisations. The Centre was to be built at Dunorlan. The plans were approved by the British Legion in March 1947 at an estimated cost of £70,000 [£2,065,000 at 2009 values) and later approved by the Council, but by April because of the lack of public interest or more probably, lack of funds, the scheme was dropped.

Two other schemes proposed at the time were for a new ex-servicemen's club, and a plan by Cecil Burns, a leading architect of the Town, for the improvement of the existing war memorial, but neither were implemented.

Away from the Town, the Conservators of Ashdown Forest asked the Borough Council for their support in preventing the military authorities from taking over part of the Forest as a permanent training area. Much of the Forest had been used during the War for army exercises[184] and the Army sought to perpetuate this. Although the outcome of this was not reported, it would seem that the Army were not successful in their application.

At Christmas, 1946, the King' in his Christmas message said:

'Better days lie ahead. We must not concentrate too much on the difficulties of the present – they will pass. Let us rather think of the possibilities that the future may hold for us.'

1947

The ambition of the Tunbridge Wells Chamber of Trade was to make the Borough a 'Front Line Town' with a first class shopping centre, and in the Autumn it was chosen by the National Chambers of Trade for their annual conference.

There were reporting and newsprint restrictions throughout the period and *The Courier* consisted of just 8 broadsheet pages. Ironically, it had been increased from 8 to 10 pages the previous year. Schools were also hit by the paper shortage, and it was not until 1953 that all restrictions on paper use and consumption were removed.

---

[184] *The Courier 20 Sept 1946 p 6*

Now Rayon Parachutes for the HOME !

Ideal for makln. lr.to CURTAINS, BEDSPREADS, CUSHION COVERS and other items for the home. Suitable for LININGS, etc. Available In attractive colours — Gold, Green/Blue, and Red.

PRICE — Complete with 24 panels, each 2ft. 6ins. wide at base and appp·x. 11ft. long . . . . **£6 12s. 0d.**
Each separate panel (6 panels will make a Bedspread) **5s. 9d.**

R. W. WEEKES Ltd.

Opp. Central Station   TUNBRIDGE WELLS   Phone 2727

Other uses found for redundent materials.

The first WVS 'Meals on Wheels'
in Tunbridge Wells, 1947

Other shortages included cloth- ing. Weekes, Tunbridge Wells's department store, advertised in March 1947 rayon parachutes for sale at £6 – 12 – 0d each [*£6.60 p, or about £180 at 2009 values*] and the women of Tunbridge Wells set to work with a will, to make new underwear from it.

During the winter months, members of the WVS in Tunbridge Wells started 'Meals on Wheels', the first service of its kind not only in Kent but in the whole country, providing two meals a week at a cost of 1/- [5p, or £1.50 at 2009 values] This was subsequently to become a country-wide service and continues to be an estab- lished part of Social Services for the elderly and bed-ridden to this day.

The public were asked to make other economies and savings, among which was a nationwide call for recycling empty jam jars.[185]

The Council thanked the Trans- port and Food Service workers for their untiring efforts during the severe weather.[186]

The Assembly Hall had been opened for two hours every morning and afternoon by the Red Cross for light refreshments for the old folk of the Town.

On 2nd March 1947, the death of Mrs Fahie was announced. She was Pauline Gower, the younger daughter of Sir Robert Gower, KCVO, Mayor of Royal Tunbridge Wells from 1917-1919 and MP for the Gillingham

---

[185] *The Courier 11 April 1947 p 5*
[186] *RTWBC Council minute 5 March 1947*

Pauline Gower.

Division of Rochester from 1929-1945. She was one of Britain's most famous pioneer women pilots. Before the War, she had been a partner in the first women's air taxi service across the Wash to Skegness and by 1938 had flown some 10,000 miles. A distinguished career followed during the war when she organised and became the Commander of the Women's section of the Air Transport Auxiliary (ATA). She was awarded the MBE for this in 1942. She subsequently became a Director of BOAC and was the author of numerous publications including 'Women with Wings' in 1938.[187]

Many major conferences were held in Tunbridge Wells at this time. This may have been due to Tunbridge Wells's position as a Regional Centre of Government, or to its pleasant ambience and location for such events. But it is a practice which has now declined almost completely and this is to be regretted, since to be a Conference Town was of both economic and reputational (image) value. One major conference in this period was the South Eastern Regional Conference for Fuel and Power, which was held in October 1947, and was attended by Hugh Gaitskell, MP, then Fuel Minister, and later the Leader of the Labour Party. At this conference, calls were made, not surprisingly, for domestic and industrial fuel economies.

Hugh Gaitskell.

August 1947 saw the Chancellor of the Exchequer, Sir Stafford Cripps, announcing an Austerity Plan which involved higher taxation; the banning of travel abroad and the use of cars for pleasure; the reduction of imports and the increase of exports, with the motto 'Export or Die'. The cuts in imports caused reductions in the meat and butter rations. A local butcher, John Spicer of 61 St. John's Road, who was

Sir Stafford Cripps.

---

[187] *The Courier 8 June 1945 p 6; also 'Spitfire Women' by Giles Whittell, Harper Press, 2007; and the Dictionary of National Biography.*

also Chairman of the Tunbridge Wells Butchers' Buying Committee, was fined £120 on 8 summonses (£3,500 at 2009 values) in January 1947 for contravening a Ministry of Food Order under the Defence (General Regulations) Act of 1939. His defence was 'It was a mistake.' Later in the year another trader was fined £350 [approximately £10,000 at 2009 values] in connection with the sale of oatmeal, over supplying and not keeping proper records.

On a somewhat lighter note, a visit to Kent was made by the Mayors of Dunkirk, Calais, Boulogne and Arras in early June and Tunbridge Wells was included in their itinerary, but the purpose of their visit was never declared.

June also saw a cull of grey squirrels which were sold for human consumption. It was said that they tasted like rabbit when cooked.

At Christmas, Tunbridge Wells (along with many other towns) received food parcels from Wellington, New Zealand, and Tasmania, including 50 cases of jam and tinned fruit; and 7 cwts of rolled oats.

Power cuts lasting 3 hours in the morning and 2 hours in the afternoon were a regular occurrence.

The petrol allowance for private cars which had been 270 miles per

Princess Elizabeth and the Duke of Edinburgh.

month in 1946, was withdrawn totally in August 1947. In December,[188] it was reported that 12,000 had applied at the Regional Petroleum Office in Tunbridge Wells for petrol coupons since September, and that the staff had been overwhelmed. The allowance, but for only 90 miles a month, was restored in August 1948 and petrol rationing was only finally ended in the Spring of 1950.

Royal Wedding
A major event which helped relieve some of the gloom of Austerity was a Royal Wedding. On 20th November 1947 at Westminster Abbey, Princess Elizabeth (later to be Queen Elizabeth II) married Lt. Philip Mountbatten RN,

[188] *The Courier 12 December 1947 p.5*

who was her Third Cousin, and who was made Prince Philip, Duke of Edinburgh, just before the wedding. It was reported in *The Courier* that some of the orchids used in her bouquet were grown at a Jarvis Brook Nursery, and Wallace Nurseries of Bayham Road were to give tulip bulbs as a wedding present.[189]

ENTERTAINMENT

Before the Second World War, most people found and made their own entertainments in the home, or locally. Quite a large number had a piano, even more by 1939 had a radio; and events such as the Agricultural Show, the Flower Show, Cricket Week, Tennis Week, and Bowls Week thrived on what was a largely-local and relatively captive audience. Most hoped to take an annual holiday, but certainly not all did. That holiday for nearly everybody was in Britain, not abroad, and for most it was a week, not a fortnight, and particularly at the seaside. For many, it was only a relatively local 'day out' or a series of 'days out', since the cost of overnight B&B accommodation, although relatively inexpensive, was something many could not afford.

The Opera House.

The Ritz.

When the War came, many of these 'local' pleasures were curtailed –travel was severely restricted, 'holidays' became almost impossible for nearly everyone and major local events were cancelled. As a family, we had our last holiday in the summer of 1939 at Camber Sands. It was not until the late 1940's that I went on another 'away-from-Tunbridge-Wells' holiday, this time with school friends, and it was not until 1962 that I went abroad for the first time. My experience of this is fairly typical.

Cinema had become the mass entertainment of the British Public during the 1930's and became even more so during the War, when most people went at least once a week. Average weekly cinema admissions throughout the War were over 30 million.[190]

---

[189] *The Courier 21 & 28 November 1947, p 3*
[190] *Admissions were to decline to 26 million in 1951, 8 million in 1961 and 3 million in 1971, almost entirely due to the growth of TV ownership.*

During the War, Tunbridge Wells had four cinemas, all of them with a single screen (since multi-screen was a development of the 1970s) – the Ritz (opposite the Town Hall); the Opera House (which showed films for 9-10 months of the year); the Kosmos in Calverley Road (which closed in March 1960); and the Great Hall in Mount Pleasant (which closed in 1958). There had also been two other cinemas, in Camden Road, which closed before the War.

They had a total seating capacity of about 5,000 (the Ritz and the Opera House alone had about 3,500) and frequently played to full houses. There were generally 2-3 entrance prices, ranging from 1/6d (7$\frac{1}{2}$p, equivalent to about £2.25 in 2009) to 2/9d (13$\frac{3}{4}$p, or £4.17 at 2009 values) for the best seats.

They generally played what was called a 'double bill' – in other words, two feature films (the 'A' main film of about 85-105 minutes, the 'B' supporting film of about 60-85 minutes), plus a newsreel (10 minutes) and often a 'short' of about 5-15 minutes, which was usually a cartoon, short comedy or informational/documentary film, and there were also the trailers for next week's programme (5-10 minutes). So the whole programme, which was continuous *with no interval*, lasted 3-3$\frac{3}{4}$ hours – which was very good value-for-money.

Because it was continuous, the start–time (apart from the day's start-time) was not advertised as it is today (because today all performances are quite separate); and so many customers would see the programme round somewhat more than once, particularly if they had enjoyed it, or had arrived in the middle of one of the films.

Programmes were changed at least once a week and in many cinemas twice a week, so if one wanted to see a specific film, rather than 'have a night out at the flicks' (as they were colloquially known for their originally 'flickering' and silent images), it was wise to see it as quickly as you could.

The other major local attractions in Tunbridge Wells were a series of traditional events which had run for years, but which had been disrupted by the War and were slowly being revived. These included Cricket Week, the Open Tennis Tournament, and the Bowls Tournament; and in 1947 the Town's Music Festival was revived in May after nine years and the Agricultural Show was restored to Down Farm, St John's Road, and attracted large crowds.[191]

---

[191] *The Courier,27 June 1947, p.5*

The King in his Christmas Message in 1947 said:

> 'Here, at home, the greatness of our contribution
> to victory is the measure our present difficulties'

The cost of fighting the war had been huge, and it was said that it had cost Britain a quarter of the country's economy as a result.

1948

So another Year started, but there was to be little or no improvement in living conditions.

The prospects for 1948,
Illingworth Cartoon.

Internationally, there was a great deal of tension, called 'The Cold War' by the media, between the Western Allies and the USSR, and the 'Berlin Air Lift' was started on June 27, 1948 to cope with one of the Russians' ploys. Another area of tension was Palestine, still a British Mandate which had been set up after the First World War. A guerrilla war by Jewish Liberationists against the British had started in 1946 (it was possibly the first of many such wars which would occur in the second half of the 20th Century) and would not end until the independent state of Israel was set up in 1948.

Many local men were involved in both the Berlin Airlift and the Palestine conflict and reported their experiences to *The Courier*.[192] In April it was reported that Mildred Marston, formerly of Upper Grosvenor Road, had been killed by an Arab sniper in Jerusalem.

As a result of these tensions and conflict, Britain re-introduced conscription for 18 year-olds under the name of National Service, initially for 12 months, then extended it to 18 months and finally to 2 years. National Service was not to be ended until 1963. There was a TA recruiting drive in the Town as fears of another war increased. The Government introduced a new Civil Defence Act in 1948, but it was not until May 1950 that the Council formed a new Civil Defence Committee with Councillor Glanfield as Chairman.[193]

Murder

Away from the international news, the Town was gripped by the news of the murder of Mrs Phyllis Gorringe on New Year's Eve/New Year's Day.[194] She was a young woman from High Brooms whose body was

---

[192] *The Courier, 9 July 1948*
[193] *Committee minute book 10 April 1951 – 16 Nov 1962*
[194] *The Courier 2 Jan 1948*

Phyllis Gorringe.

found in a yard off Crescent Road, close to the Assembly Hall, by a lorry driver. Phyllis Gorringe had spent the previous evening, New Year's Eve, dancing at the Assembly Hall. Her husband, Bob, who was an employee of the Gas Company, had reported her missing.

The following week, Gorringe was charged with his wife's murder at the Tunbridge Wells Magistrates' Court before Sir Robert Gower and Mr Hobbs and remanded in custody. An inquest was held at the Kent and Sussex Hospital, where a post-mortem was also held which was attended by Keith Simpson, the Home office pathologist. Chief of Kent CID, Supt. F. Smead from Maidstone was called to give evidence.[195] Gorringe was again remanded in custody, and a queue of 100 people waited outside the Court.[196] In the first week of February,[197] he was before the bench again when he reserved his defence and was sent for trial at Kent Assizes. At the trial later in the month, he was found guilty and sentenced to death.[198] The execution was set for Wednesday 24th. March.

On 12th March, *The Courier* reported that 11,000 had signed a petition for clemency for Gorringe and the petition had been sent to the Home Secretary. A week later, the King granted a reprieve and his parents were allowed monthly visits to Wandsworth Prison.

Five months after being reprieved, it was reported that Gorringe was still full of hope 'that everything will come right in the end'. He had been moved from Wandsworth Prison to Wakefield and was being instructed in engineering, and received a copy of *The Courier* every week. His parents were able to visit him on a number of occasions, and were saving to launch another appeal. They continued to believe that he was innocent.

In a letter to The Courier, Gorringe wrote ' I wish to thank you all for your kindness and for your help to my Mother and Father. I cannot find words enough to thank you, but one day in the future I hope I will be able to thank you in person.'[199] Since then, he appears, as they say, to have disappeared quite understandably 'off the radar'.

---

[195] *The Courier 9 Jan 1948 p 3*
[196] *The Courier 16 Jan 1948*
[197] *The Courier 6 Feb 1948 p 3*
[198] *The Courier 27 Feb 1948 p 3*
[199] *The Courier 30 July 1948 p 3*

Olympic Games

Wembley Stadium 1948.

A major event in Britain in 1948 was the XIVth Olympic Games which were held in London from 29th July-14th August 1948, and were opened at Wembley Stadium by King George VI, before 85,000 spectators. The Games were shown on television, but it was a television service very different from today. It was in black and white, had a screen definition of only 405 lines and had only one channel, what is now BBC1. TV ownership was very low, with less than 1 million sets in the UK. My parents did not then own a TV, but I can remember watching

Olympic games poster.

some of the Games on a cousin's set. With such low TV coverage, it was not surprising that the Games, which were also much smaller in terms of both the number of events and the number of countries participating, than they are today, seemed to have had relatively little effect on the everyday life of the Town, or the Country as a whole, coinciding as they did with the August Bank Holiday, which was the major and traditional holiday period, when many took their holidays or at least, day trips to the coast.

King George VI opens the games.

There were food shortages particularly of tinned food stuffs and traders said that there were too many points chasing too few goods and bakers warned of a bread shortage in the Autumn owing to the bad weather. In June, a state of emergency had been declared because of a countrywide dock strike.

The international situation was very tense throughout 1948, with the developing Communist guerilla emergency in Malaya, and the continuing fear about the risk of atomic warfare.

Toward the end of the war, The Ministry of Works, South East Region, had opened the Civil Service Regional HQ at Hawkenbury, the building of which had begun in 1941. Later the offices of the Ministry of Pensions were in the same building.

During the early part of the war it had been used as a Hospital for Italian PoWs and the huts were converted into government buildings.[200] Another building on the site, which was known locally as 'The Bunker' or 'The Kremlin', was built in 1951 as a War Room. This was intended to be a Regional Centre of UK Government in case of war.[201] It was joined in 1963 by an eight-storey office building, Curtis House, which was to dominate the Tunbridge Wells skyline for the next 34 years. Beneath the Bunker were *reputedly* eight floors of offices and accommodation. Fortunately, the Tunbridge Wells War Room ceased to be used for its original purpose in 1956/7, when it became the home for the first ever National Police Computer, and later a document store, before being demolished in 1997.

Its demolition in the Autumn which was supposed to take only 2-3 weeks, actually took about 12 weeks of pneumatic drilling and minor explosions. It is thought that many of the underground rooms at the lowest level remain intact. The site is now occupied by the Land Registry Office, and some of the site was sold for private housing.

As the winter approached it was again feared that there would fuel, electricity and other shortages. There was also an increase of TB in the Town.

The King in his Christmas message referred mainly to his personal and family life, rather than world events.

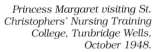

Princess Margaret visiting St. Christophers' Nursing Training College, Tunbridge Wells, October 1948.

---

[200] *The Courier 1 Oct 1948*
[201] *See Subterranea Britannica web site for details*

1949

1949 started with the Council seeking to expand the Borough boundaries to include Southborough, Bidborough, Speldhurst, and Pembury under the Local Government Commission Act of 1945. In retrospect, this was a very sensible proposal and it would have increased the population (by42%) from 38,080 to 54,064. But the plan was strongly opposed by all the Parishes involved. Later in the year, the Boundary Commission was suddenly wound up, and the plan was dropped. This was a great pity, since the solution which was eventually devised in the Local Government re-organisation of 1974, created the current Borough of Tunbridge Wells which has all the Parishes which opposed it in 1949; has a population of over 100,000; and stretches across more than 20 miles to Cranbrook, which is an awkward and unmanageable shape to administer. It also takes no account of the fact that most movement for Tunbridge Wells is North-South, rather than East-West.

In February, The High Brooms Brick Works accepted a Government order for three million hand-made facing bricks for the new power station to be built at Southwick, near Brighton.

Traders in the Town were hoping for a better year with fewer controls and the easing of difficulties in the coming months.

It is surprising (astonishing?) that when there was no fear of enemy attack, it took four years for the wartime restrictions on street lighting to be lifted, which eventually happened in April 1949. Obviously, there must have been other considerations.

The rationing of clothing which had been introduced in 1941 ended in November 1949. The number of coupons initially allowed per person had been 60 points a year, and as an example, a lady's winter coat required 15 points. But the total number of points had been reduced from 60 in 1941 to 35 in 1945.

On 'demob', servicemen were fitted out free and given a further 223 points 'for additional clothing'. Servicewomen were given no free clothing but 146 points, probably because the vagaries of female clothing were too abstruse to monitor or control, together with an unspecified money grant, and a further 219 coupons. The rationale for the difference between the terminal 223 points and free clothing for men and the terminal 365 points but no free clothing for women, is now 'lost in the sands of time' and does it matter? In either case, these points should be compared with the much-lower civilian allowance which started at 60 points in 1941 and ended up at 35 points in 1945. The Chamber of Trade was alarmed at the growth of 'no waiting' restrictions in the Town and the traffic problem in the main shopping streets.

The 'Berlin Air Lift' finished on 12th May, 1949 after 11 months in which the Allies called the Russian bluff. Although the Russians climbed down and allowed unrestricted access of goods to Berlin, this did not remove the fear of an atomic war. In July, there were plans for bringing Civil Defence up-to-date with an Atomic Warfare Syllabus being discussed. It was proposed that a new recruiting drive for Civil Defence should be started in the Autumn. The previous autumn had seen a recruiting drive for the Territorial Army (TA). April had also seen the creation of the North Atlantic Treaty Organisation (NATO) as a defence against the Russians.

In May 1949, the first woman Mayor of Tunbridge Wells, Miss Muriel Wells, was elected. She was nominated by Alderman Westbrook and served as Mayor for two terms until 1951, when she was elected an Alderman. During the war she had been district head of the WVS. She died in July 1953.[202]

Miss Muriel Wells.

Tunbridge Wells was again proving a popular place for conferences. Those held included the SE Division of the Local Education Authorities Association, addressed by the Minister of Education, Mr. George Tomlinson. 2000 members of the British Legion attended the County Rally and Parade. It was decided that The County's Building Week Exhibition would also be held in the Town during the Autumn.

The Medical Officer's report for 1949 stated that the death rate in Tunbridge Wells was higher than average, with 350 females and 235 males dying, possibly reflecting the somewhat older age of the population and an imbalance in the ratio between men and women living in the Town. Pembury Hospital was reported to be uneconomical, and it was also reported that local hospitals required 386 more nurses.

Throughout the Autumn, unemployment in Tunbridge Wells had been gradually increasing, with 144 men and 73 women registered as unemployed in November 1949,[203] but there were 120 vacancies mainly in building and domestic service.

---

202 *The Courier 10 July 1949 p 4*
203 *The Courier, 2 December,1949, p 4*

In the late post-War 1940s, two things happened which at least made the lives of British women somewhat easier and less stressful.

Drawing seams.

The first *British-made*, American-style, nylon stockings went on sale, although the quantities available were initially very limited.

Nylon was a new synthetic fibre patented by Dupont in the USA and shown for the first time at the World Trade Fair in New York in 1939. The NY from New York, provided the first two letters of the name nylon, which Dupont deliberately did not register, as they wished it to become the generic term for all artificial fibres. In this, they succeeded. The first nylon stockings appeared in New York stores in 1940 and were an instant success.

However once the USA entered World War II, nearly all production of nylon went into the war effort for products such as parachutes and glider tow-ropes; and nylon stockings became very hard to obtain, even in the USA – during this time, women were known to draw/paint 'seams' on the back of their legs instead, so it appeared as if they were wearing nylon stockings (which in those days, had seams).

Some nylon stockings did reach Britain via the American armed forces, who used them to seduce as many English girls as they could. Nylon stockings were very, very desirable and there was a 'black market' in them. So when after the War, ICI which held the English rights for nylon from Dupont, started production, suddenly British women could buy British-made nylon stockings. But they were expensive and nowhere near as good quality as today, so if you 'laddered' your nylon stockings, you could either buy a nylon stocking repair kit, or get them repaired (both are an unthinkable idea today), and I remember that many dress shops in the Town provided this service.

Nylon stocking repair kit.

The second post-War development which improved women's lives was the introduction of a new product – a *detergent* washing powder, which was demonstrably better than the soap, soap flakes or soap powder used up until then in washing dirty clothes, insofar as it cleaned better in hard water and did not leave any scum.

TIDE was the brand name of the first heavy-duty synthetic detergent, which was introduced in the USA by Procter and Gamble in 1946 and to Britain by its subsidiary, Thomas Hedley & Co. of Newcastle-upon-Tyne, in 1948 and it caused quite a sensation. It would be followed by its other detergent brands – Ariel, Bold and Fairy – and competitors and their detergent brands – Unilever with Omo, Rinso and Surf (Unilever's existing Persil and Lux brands successfully remained soap powders); and Colgate Palmolive with Fab and Ajax. The highly-competitive nature of the washing powder market has ensured its dominant presence in the British advertising scene. This could be seen even in Tunbridge Wells – since even *The Courier* carried detergent advertising in the 1950's.

❖❖❖❖❖

As Christmas approached, 1,000 young fir trees, the property of the Marquess of Abergavenny, were stolen from Broadwater Forest. Retribution was swift. In January 1950, the thieves were tried and sent to prison.[204]

During 1949 the King had been seriously ill and in his Christmas message, he said:

> *'Difficult days bring to my peoples the opportunity of showing the great qualities of human nature – courage, perseverance, endurance, unselfishness, and public spirit. These are the qualities by which in our long history, the sons and daughters of our race have met and overcome many crises.'*

---

[204] *The Courier 13 Jan 1950 p6*

CHAPTER 9

TUNBRIDGE WELLS: THE PROMISE OF A BETTER FUTURE
1950–1953

1950

As the decade of the 40s ended and the 1950s began, many things started to return to somewhere near normal.

In January, the biggest-ever dog show was held at the Assembly Hall.

The weather was also in the news in April when there were heavy snowfalls in the area. These caused the Station clock to stop, and it was not restarted until September.

The Ministry of Health reported to the Council that the Town's water was unsatisfactory 'owing to its iron content and its aggressive nature' (a surprising statement, since they should have known that Tunbridge Wells's origin and existence depended on its chalybeate springs) and throughout May, this report continued apparently to cause considerable concern. Other topics discussed during the year included the establishment of a new school at Huntley's, the future of which was still uncertain.

The Pump Room.

Petrol was derationed in June 1950 and the ensuing increase in traffic was said to be causing problems in many streets. The Regional Petroleum Office in the Pump Room was closed in July, and the fate of the building was unknown. It was suggested that the Pantiles Association might acquire the building. The Pump Room was eventually to be demolished in 1964 and Union Square built on the site.

June saw a crowd of 10,000 attend a fete in Dunorlan Park. In July, the 75th S.E. Counties Agricultural Show[205] again attracted large crowds at Down Farm. The Tennis Tournament in August[206] was described as the

---

[205] *The Courier 21 July 1950 p.5*
[206] *The Courier 4 August 1950 p.5*

best ever, although during the tournament, there was a lightning strike near some of the spectators, who had a lucky escape.

Unemployment in Tunbridge Wells[207] was said to be 247 in October,[208] with a shortage of workers in the building trades again being reported.

Ministry officials again visited the Town during 1950, since many regional offices were still in Tunbridge Wells.

Amongst them was Mr F. T. Willey from the Ministry of Food who visited the Regional Food Office.[209] He was met by the Regional Food Officer, Major General J. B. Dalison CB OBE.[210] His visit included the inspection of Romany's Biscuit factory in Eridge Road.

One personality who brought a little light relief to Tunbridge Wells from 1940 was an Irish doctor, Dr. Eric St. John Lyburn. He was evacuated from Hastings, and set up a clinic in Ferndale, and later in Broadwater Down. He was in and out of the news for many years, particularly regarding his relationship with the NHS and the General Medical Council. He died in 1977.[211]

The Assembly Hall continued to be the venue for conferences, including the National Conference of the Council for the Preservation of Rural England (CPRE).

The Korean War
On 25th June 1950, the Korean War started when North Korean troops invaded South Korea. The USA and Britain immediately came to the aid

The 'Bunker'.

of South Korea and a number of local men were to be involved: and, as a result, the length of National Service was increased from 18 months to two years.

Other areas of conflict were Malaya (now Malaysia)[212] and Kenya. Because of the threat of nuclear war, 'The Bunker' at Hawkenbury was constructed.

---

[207] The Courier 27 October 1950 p.5
[208] The Courier, 27 October 1950 p 5
[209] The Courier 19 May 1950 p 3
[210] Dalison had had a distinguished career in India before 1947.
[211] Tales of Old Tunbridge Wells, by F. Chapman p 113; and various Courier references
[212] The Courier 2 Nov 1951 p5

This was intended to be a Regional Centre of Government in the event of a war, but with the advance of nuclear technology, it was never used for this purpose and it became redundant. Later it was used as a police communications centre, the home of the first National Police Computer, and a document store. It was finally demolished, with some difficulty, in 1998.

Civil Defence

The fear of Atomic Warfare had superceded the fear of Invasion which had dominated nearly everybody's thinking during the first three years of the Second World War. I have to say that I was never afraid during the Second World War, probably because I was well-protected by my parents, but I was really afraid when the consequences and likelihood of Atomic Warfare became so apparent while I was a teenager.

A new Civil Defence Committee was formed in May 1950. At its first meeting the Mayor, Miss Muriel Wells, was in the Chair, and Councillor Glanfield was appointed Chairman of the Committee. In the following year, eleven meetings were held.

The Committee was responsible for training of staff, emergency feeding and recruitment and dismissal of staff and all functions under the Civil Defence Acts 1937 to 1948, not covered by the functions of other committees.

The Civil Defence HQ was behind the Great Hall and it was decided that a portrait of H.M. Queen should be placed in the HQ.

Lt Cmdr G. W. Morgan MBE RN [Rtr] was appointed as the new Civil Defence Officer in June 1951, but he resigned within two years – in June 1953.[213]

Another appointment made was that of Col C.W. Tandy-Green, GC, as District Chief Warden, on 15 May 1951.[214] In April 1952, he also tendered his letter of resignation to the Committee.

His successor was Mr K.G. Robertson of 35 Birling Road, who was a member of the Civil Defence Corps and who 'stayed the course' and was awarded the MBE in 1962. By September recruits were wanted, with further advertisements appearing in December. On 2nd October 1952

---

[213] *Civil Defence Committee minutes and The Courier 15 June 1951 p 4 and 6 July p 5*
[214] *The Times 9 May 1934 p 14; obit. 29 September 1978, p 18; London Gazette 19 June 1934. He had been awarded the Empire Gallantry Medal, later to become the George Cross, in May 1934 when he foiled an assassination attempt on the Governor of Bengal.*

the Home Secretary had broadcast an appeal for recruits in connection with the Autumn/Winter Civil Defence recruiting campaign. By 1952, the establishment of the Borough Civil Defence Corps was 371 persons.

During the year, plans for a school on the site of Huntley House had been in the news. Finally in December it was agreed that the future of a School on the site was assured, but the Town would have to raise £8,900.

Though the international situation was tense, with the threat of a nuclear war, the population of Tunbridge Wells seemed to be more concerned with the continuing shortages.

In November 1950, there had been electricity cuts about which the Town's traders expressed concern. Early December saw the first big freeze of the winter causing traffic chaos in the Town; and bus services were suspended because of the icy roads.

The electricity generating plant which had been owned by the Council was finally nationalised and the Council received a cheque from the Government for £11,067, which many considered a profit of £874,000 for the State on the book-value of the investment.[215]

The King in his Christmas message of 1950 said:-

> 'Since I spoke to you last Christmas, storms have begun to cloud the horizon in spite of all our hopes and endeavours. It is hard to feel the happiness and merriment which naturally belong to Christmas when the grim shadow of war hangs over the world'

He also referred to 'The Pilgrims Progress'.

At the end of 1950, there were still shortages, reference was made to the meat ration being reduced, and fuel was in short supply.

---

[215] *The Courier 1 Dec 1950 p 5*

1951

The 'Festival of Britain', which was planned to be a morale-boosting post-War celebration, mirroring the achievements of the Great Exhibition of 1851, opened in May 1951 on London's South Bank. Like the Great Exhibition, it introduced new ideas and designs in Architecture, Industry, Science and the Arts.

Skylon and Dome of Discovery on the South Bank.

Festival logo.

Tunbridge Wells celebrated the event, with illuminations which were switched on at 9pm on Thursday 3rd May, and on the following Sunday, a United Service was held in Calverley Grounds. The Borough Entertainments Department arranged a full programme of events including a Band Season on the Pantiles. (See opposite page.) There were a series of stage shows at the Assembly Hall, the main one being Harold Fielding's *'Music for the Millions'* with many famous stars of Stage, Screen and Radio appearing, including Anne Ziegler and Webster Booth, Max Wall, Charlie Chester, Richard Murdoch, Rob Wilton, The Western Brothers, Jack Train, Anona Winn, Winifred Atwell, The Beverley Sisters, Rawicz and Landauer, Semprini, and Ted, Barbara and *Julie* Andrews. The Festival Diary also listed many events taking place in the surrounding area.

June 1951 saw the unveiling of the 1939-1945 additions to the War Memorial by Viscount De L'Isle and Dudley, VC, KG. Other events held in June were the first carnival for 14 years, a music festival and a shopping week. The Agricultural Show returned to its permanent show site in Eridge Road [now the Showfields Housing Estate] and the Mayor attended a special service for the Show at Holy Trinity on the 22nd July.[216] Other events which took place during the summer were the

---

[216] *The Showground had been requisitioned during the war for military purposes and in November 1951, six years after the end of the War, an anti-tank ammunition dump was found there.*

ROYAL TUNBRIDGE WELLS ENTERTAINMENTS DEPARTMENT

FESTIVAL ★ YEAR
★ ATTRACTIONS ★

— WILL INCLUDE —

ASSEMBLY HALL —

April 30th—May 4th   BALLET EROS
May 18th   FESTIVAL BALL 8 p.m. to 2 a.m.
June 18th—23rd   'STARLIGHT RENDEZVOUS" (prior to their Season at Bexhill)

June 25th—30th   The Tunbridge Wells Amateur Operatic and Dramatic Society presents " MERRIE ENGLAND "

October 8th—13th   THE YOUNG VIC COMPANY

FOR A SEASON—Tunbridge Wells Corporation present HAROLD FIELDING'S

"MUSIC FOR THE MILLIONS"

each Thursday, Friday and Saturday commencing Thursday, July 12th, ending Saturday, Sept. 22nd, excluding August 30th, 31st and Sept. 1st.
Among the stars of radio and stage who will appear are

Anne Ziegler & Webster Booth ; Peter Cavanagh ; Jack Train ; Anona Winn ; Robert Moreton ; Julie Andrews ; Ted & Barbara Andrews ; Winifred Atwell ; The Western Brothers ; Elsie & Doris Waters ; Richard Murdoch ; Bob & Alf Pearson ; Ronald Chesney ; Semprini ; Clifford Stanton ; The Kordites ; Rawicz & Landauer ; Suzette Tarri ; Alfred Swain ; Carroll Gibbons ; Rene Strange ; Robb Wilton ; Harry Hemsley ; Marion Sanders ; The Beverley Sisters, etc.

Other events arranged include a presentation by the Tunbridge Wells Drama Club of "THE MERRY WIVES OF WINDSOR " on The Pantiles, 28th May—2nd June, and the TUNBRIDGE WELLS DRAMA FESTIVAL OF ONE-ACT PLAYS, October 15th—20th, at the Assembly Hall.

BAND SEASON —

May 13th and 14th   THE ROYAL TUNBRIDGE WELLS HOME GUARD BAND

July 1st—7th   CENTRAL BAND OF THE ROYAL AIR FORCE

July 8th—14th   BAND OF H.M. ROYAL HORSE GUARDS (" THE BLUES ")

July 15th—21st   BAND OF THE ROYAL SCOTS (ROYAL REGIMENT) WITH PIPER AND HIGHLAND DANCERS

July 22nd—28th   THE FAIREY AVIATION WORKS BAND

July 29th—August 4th   BAND OF THE IRISH GUARDS

August 5th—11th   THE STAFF BAND, ROYAL ELECTRICAL AND MECHANICAL ENGINEERS

August 12th—18th   FODENS MOTOR WORKS BAND

August 19th—25th   THE BAND OF THE ROYAL REGIMENT OF ARTILLERY

Advertisement in The Courier showing Festival Year attractions in Tunbridge Wells.

traditional Cricket Week and a Festival Rally celebrating 50 Years of Motoring, which was organised by the Tunbridge Wells Motor Club.

In September, a South Eastern Regional Civil Defence Conference was held at the Town Hall and the Council sent a representative.

The return of the Pilot – a famous cartoon comparison with one of Bismarck in the late 19th century. Cartoon by Illingworth.

Gerald Williams was again returned as the Member of Parliament for the Tonbridge Constituency in the General Election held in October 1951, when the Conservatives were returned with Churchill becoming Prime Minister once again. He had been the Member of Parliament for the Tonbridge Parliamentary Constituency (of which Tunbridge Wells was then, but is no longer part) since the General Election of July 1945 but was to resign from Parliament by taking the Stewardship of the Chiltern Hundreds in 1956 on the grounds of ill-health.

The first Population Census for twenty years was taken in April, the last having been taken in 1931. The population of Tunbridge Wells was recorded as 38,397, compared with 35,367 in 1931 – a net and modest increase of 3,030 people, or an average of just over 150 per year.

During 1951 and 1952, there had been two serious accidents in the Town. At the Gas Works, there was a collapse of bricks which caused two workmen to be killed and three injured.[217] At North Farm Sewage Works, one man was killed.

In schools the common illnesses of children continued to cause much absenteeism. Early in 1951, there was an outbreak of Scarlet Fever, at St. Barnabas' Infant School. Because of this, the Medical Officer of Health, Dr. Crowley, visited the School daily to inspect the children.

The King's 1951 Christmas message, which was to be his last, included these words:-

> *'Though we live in hard and critical times,*
> *Christmas is and always will be, a time*
> *when we can count our blessings'*

---

[217] *The Courier 17 Aug 1951 p 3*

1952

The year started with a major international drama for Tunbridge Wells.

'The Flying Enterprise'

The sinking 'Flying Enterprise' with the tug 'Turmoil'.

The end of December 1951 and the beginning of January 1952 saw one of the worst storms to hit the Atlantic in many years, and the arrival of a new Tunbridge Wells hero, 27 year-old Ken Dancy of Hook Green. He became a household name internationally, watched by the world's media, as he tried together with Captain Carlsen to save the American freighter 'Flying Enterprise' from sinking. He was an old boy of Skinner's School[218] and at the time he was First Mate of the salvage tug 'Turmoil' which had gone to the aid of the 'Flying Enterprise' which was listing badly. On returning home, he was given a Civic Reception after being driven around the Town in an open-top car accompanied by police outriders.[219] The guests at the Reception included two Admirals, Sir Percy Noble-Henley and Sir Cecil Harcourt, and Gerald Williams, the MP for the constituency. In his speech at the Reception, the Mayor, Alderman F. S. Harries, said:

> *'All of us followed with intense interest the wonderful struggle of Captain Carlsen, yourself and Captain Parker, to save the Flying Enterprise. That your efforts were not successful takes no whit away from the grand qualities you and they displayed in the perilous task'.*

---

[218] *The Courier 11 Jan 1952 p 5*
[219] *The Courier 18 January 1952 p 5*

The Mayor toasts Ken Dancy.

Dancy in a short speech replied :

'I was only doing my job for which I am paid.... I think if any one of you had seen Captain Carlsen alone in that ship, you would have had a great urge to join him. I saw the opportunity and took it'.[220]

Even six years after the war had ended, there was talk of a reduction in the meat ration. Early in 1952 there was also an outbreak of foot and mouth disease, which caused further concern about the supply of meat and there was still a fuel shortage.

With the continuing critical international situation, recruitment of men aged between 18-65 years for the Home Guard was started once again, but there was a slow response at the start and by the end of February, only 1,100 had enrolled in the whole of Kent.[221]

The Council announced that there had been good progress in the provision of housing in the Borough during the past two to three years. Up to the middle of December 1951, a total of 502 housing units – 100 prefabs, 250 houses, and 152 flats – had been provided, and 167 families had been moved into requisitioned premises. So 679 families had been accommodated, but 1,250 applicants still remained on the Housing Register. In August 1952[222] the Council considered the building of a further 500 new houses on the Sherwood site near Pembury Road.

---

[220] *Civic Society Newsletter – Winter 2006 – p 6, for a detailed article.*
[221] *The Courier 25 Jan 1952 p5*
[222] *The Courier 1 August 1953 p 5*

It was reported that in the South East Region, 30,444 people had been rehoused since the end of the War.

The death of King George VI on 6th February 1952, and the accession of Queen Elizabeth II and her Coronation the following year on 2nd June 1953, served as a psychological break in public attitude to the Second World War, the Years of Austerity and to Britain's future prospects. The long dark years of war and the post-war years of austerity seemed to be over at last, even though the international situation remained uncertain. People started to talk of a 'New Elizabethan Age' and there arose a feeling of optimism and expectation about the future, which invigorated the nation and would lead in due course to the 'you've never had it so good' euphoria of the late 1950s and early 1960s.

Three local links with the past were in the news in 1952-3 and endorsed this change of mood:

- May saw Alderman Westbrook retire from the Borough Council[223] after 42 years' service.

- In November, W. C. Cripps died at the age of 97 years. Born in 1855, he had been in 1889 the first Town Clerk of the Borough of Tunbridge Wells.[224] In February 1948, he retired from being a KCC Councillor at the age of 93.[225]

- The following March, Sir Robert Gower died at the age of 72. Born in 1881, he was first elected to the Council in 1909. He was Mayor of the Town three times and also a Member of Parliament for 15 years (but not for Tunbridge Wells). He was Chairman of the RSPCA and received many honours for his public service. He was also the father of Pauline Gower, the pioneer woman aviator.[226]

The Queen in her first Christmas message in December 1952 said:

> *'Many grave problems and difficulties confront us all, but with a new faith in the old and splendid beliefs given to us all by our forefathers, and the strength to venture beyond the safeties of the past, I know we shall be worthy of our duty'.*

---

[223] *The Courier 2 May 1952 p 5*
[224] *The Courier 21 November 1952 p 3*
[225] *The Courier 20 February 1948 p 3*
[226] *The Courier 13 Mar 1953 p 5*

1953

Queen Elizabeth II and the Duke of Edinburgh.

In line with the rest of the country, Tunbridge Wells and the surrounding villages mounted an enormous number of events to celebrate the Coronation. *The Courier* of 29th May 1953[227] records 66 towns, villages and hamlets within a 20-mile radius, organising no less than 332 events, mainly on Tuesday 2nd June, but also during Coronation Week (Sunday 31st May – Saturday 6th June). These events ranged from Dances and Balls; to Parades and Processions, (both Fancy Dress and conventional); Tableaux; Fancy Dress Competitions; Sports (both Children and Adult); Cricket matches (and even a football match [in June!]); planting of commemorative trees; old-time, country and modern dancing; and Bonfires and Fireworks.

But for nearly everybody, the highlight was actually watching the Coronation *live* from Westminster Abbey on television, which was in those days in black-and-white. Television was still a novelty for most people and the opportunity to see the Coronation for the first time live,

Coronation decorations in Calverley Street.

---

[227] *The Courier 29 May 1953 p 5*

was to prove a tremendous fillip to television sales and ownership. Those who did not have a TV, which was still the majority, were invited by family, friends and neighbours to view the broadcast, which was about six hours from the Queen setting off from Buckingham Palace to her returning there; and so an audience for the Coronation of 15-30 people per set was not unusual. In the case of my own family, we already had a TV and so my mother's father, sister and husband came to us for the day. My mother had prepared a lunch which we could eat while watching the Ceremony, but it was not Coronation Chicken, which was then an unknown recipe!

Coronation decorations in the High Street.

After the end of the transmission, my father and I went out to look around the Town which was deserted, probably because everybody was recovering from watching the Coronation, although many events had been organised for the evening. The weather which was gloomy – wet and cold – could not dampen our high spirits.

In the context of post-war anxieties, it should also be recorded that on Coronation Sunday 31st May 1953, 53 Civil Defence members in uniform took part in the parade held in the Calverley Grounds.

The international situation was to continue to cause concern but that is an unchanging scenario in almost any decade or century. What is more important is that from an internal perspective, Britain's economy continued its steady recovery from the ravages of the Second World War and it was possible only six years later, for Harold Macmillan, the Prime Minister, to declare:

'You've never had it so good.'

And that was largely true for Tunbridge Wells,
as well as for everybody else.

POSTSCRIPT

No sooner had World War II ended, than the political situation throughout the world set fresh challenges for the defence of Britain. While austerity was to be the prevailing consideration in Britain until the mid-1950s, it was matched by similar inhibiting international constraints – the tension and potential conflict with the Communist world, and particularly the USSR, which led to the development of the 'Iron Curtain', 'the Cold War', the Berlin Airlift and the Korean War, all of which kept Britain in a state of anxiety which would last, to a greater or a lesser extent, until 1989 and the fall of the Berlin Wall and the subsequent collapse of Communism. Particularly during the Cuban Missile Crisis of 1962, an atomic attack by the Soviet Union was a very real threat.

The nature and speed-of-delivery of atomic warfare meant that the invasion of Britain from the sea was extremely unlikely and so Kent and Sussex, with Tunbridge Wells at its centre, were not in the same strategic position as they had been in 1940. The Civil Defence organization had been revived in 1950 and put on alert once more, but Tunbridge Wells was not, quite understandably, to be the Regional Centre of Government, which was somewhat inexplicably established in the tunnels and caves at Dover. It was later to be transferred to Crowborough in 1984, which also seems equally inexplicable.

However as a reflection of the continuing prevalence of WWII strategic thinking, Tunbridge Wells was still initially thought of as a Regional Centre of Government. A bunkered HQ had been built at Hawkenbury in Tunbridge Wells in 1951, with a County Control Centre at Springfield, Maidstone and a network of local control centres, as each essential service had its own control room. The Royal Observer Corps had also been given a new role of monitoring the pattern of nuclear bursts and radiation fallout.

So while outwardly life in Britain seemed increasingly good, there were still continual and continuing challenges being made to the safety of Western Europe. But the realities of modern warfare are such that the old structures and methods no longer have the same relevance and eventually Civil Defence in 1968 and the Royal Observer Corps in 1991 were disbanded. Today we have different systems and methods to face a different set of dangers.

APPENDIX 1

PROPERTIES REQUISITIONED IN TUNBRIDGE WELLS DURING WORLD WAR II AND THE POST WAR YEARS

This list is as comprehensive as records allow:

ARMY

Ashurst Place, Langton Green	RASC
Boyne Park	Military Billet
Broadwater Down	No.2 Army 'O' Traffic Control Centre, 12 Corps Postal Unit
6,8, 10	Army H. Q. XII Corps
16,21	Army Signallers Centre
22	Used by KCC during war as an emergency maternity home
35a	12 Corps Signals
30	
38	
44 [Broadwater Court]	MTC 12 Corps
Calverley Park No.23	USA and Canadian Troops prior to D-Day
Camden Park, No.4	HQ RE
Court Road	Military Billet
Earls Road	Military Billet
Frant Road No.49	HQ RA
Great Bounds Southborough	Army Camp
Grove Hill Rd, [Mountfield]	Army Billet, Tunnel Corps
Huntley's, Culverden Down	'O' Sp CMP [TC]
Knocklofty	Army Billet
Madeira Park No.58	Army Billet
Manor Grange House Hurstwood Lane	Army Billet
Molyneux Park Road No.19	HQ for RE Tunnel Corps
Mount Edgecombe	172 Tunnelling Co RE
Nevill Gate, Chimneys	Army Billet
St. John's Rd. Drill Hall	265 Field Park Co.
The Pantiles No. 44	RE Bomb disposal
The Pantiles (No. unknown)	Officer's Club
Upper Cumberland Walk, Brook Cottage	Army Billet
Warwick Park No.8	41 FS Section
10	Army Billet
18 Oak Cottage	Army Billet
53	108 PRO Coy.
69	Army Billet
86	Army Billet
88	RAMC
Warwick Park [No. unknown]	HQ ATS
Public Swimming Baths	Facilities required for Military Authorities

For security reasons, the occupants of the billets were not stated, but it is now known, for example, that 69 Warwick Park was occupied by the GOC, Brook Cottage by the CRA (Commander, Royal Artillery), Knocklofty by his G2 RA, Oak Cottage by the i/c PRO, Chimneys by the Assistant Commander Signals, 10 Warwick Park by i/c DADOS Corps Tps; and 88 Warwick Park by the Chief Medical Officer.

CIVIL DEFENCE

Council Minute re Requisitioning of premises – An Instruction from Government, stating that the power should only be used where premises were essential for the efficient working of the Civil Defence. As circumstances proved, the needs of Civil Defence could be defined fairly widely.

The Beacon Hostel	Spanish and Jewish refugees [not actually requisitioned]
Bishop's Down Grange	used by Council – idea dropped [Sir Hildred Carlisle]
5 and 8 Bishop's Down	Ministry Food Offices
3 Boyne Park	Tunbridge Wells Food Office
15 Boyne Park	Evacuation Hostel Health and Housing Committee
17 Boyne Park	
Bredbury, 12 Mt.Ephraim	HQ Civil Defence SE Region no 12
Broomhill Bank	Nurses Home, also to be used by casualties from Rusthall
24 Calverley Park	Blackheath and Tunbridge Wells High School
49 Calverley Road	Requisition re Defence regulation 1939
3 Carlton Road	use unknown
22 Church Road	Evacuation, central enquiry office for evacuees Billeting office – W V S clothing store
49 Claremont Road	Warden's Post
Culverden House,	
Culverden Park Rd School	Greenwich Blue Coat School – owned by Skinner's School
Danemore Park, Speldhurst	Thought to be a training centre for Civil Defence
Drill Hall, Albion Road	ARP Depot
Ferndale Point	Hostel for difficult boys
31 Ferndale	Hostel for evacuees, requisitioned 25 Oct 1939
Fonthill, The Common	Council Decontamination centre. Also laundry.
Woodlands	Decontamination of clothing [Gas]
25 Frant Road	Hospital for evacuees [In 1948 used as Petroleum Office annex]
15/17 Grange Rd, Rusthall	Rusthall ARP depot personnel, canteen and rest room
Hamsell Manor, Eridge	Evacuee Hostel
Hawkenbury Centre	SE Regional Pensions HQ – Ministry of Pensions 1943 (also Italian PoW's)

Holly Bank, Crescent Road	London NFS billet
17 Lansdowne Road	War time nursery, Ministry of Health, closed 1950
1 Langton Road	Warden's Post
21 London Road	Public shelter, requisitioned 3 Oct 1939
St. Helena 'Cave' under London Road	Public shelter
81 London Road	ARP HQ Office; WVS Civil Defence centre Miss M. B. Wells organizer
Flat 6a Lower Green Road	Fire Brigade use
Mabledon	Polish patients/PoW/battle site and rehabilitation centre
Manor Grange House, Hurstwood Lane	Auxiliary Hospital for treatment of minor infectious ailments
Meadow Road	Baltic Saw Mills yard – Fire Brigade vehicles
22 Molyneux Park Road	Hostel for 'difficult' Mothers and children
30 Molyneux Park Road	Folkestone Gas and Coke Co. (why?)
Mount Ephraim House	Regional Food Office, de-requisitioned 1951.
5 Nevill Park	Ministry of Health, Government evacuation scheme
10 Nevill Street	Council used as storage of furniture from bombed-out premises
16 Pantiles	WVS clothing store moved from 22 Church Road
46a Pantiles	Auxiliary Fire Station, requisitioned under Reg. 51 of Defence Regulations 1939
Pantiles Information Bureau [No. unknown]	Used as clearing house for evacuees
Pump Room Pantiles	Evacuation reception centre and subsequently Regional Petroleum Office
St. Barnabas Parish Hall [basement]	ARP
Blackhurst, Pembury Road	Nurses training school
St Christopher's Pembury Rd	Reception Centre for babies and children from London
Pembury Grange	First KCC Old Peoples' Home opened 1937
The Wilderness [Stables] Pembury Road	Contaminated foodstuffs
Rustwick, Rusthall	Empty house requisitioned by Emergency Committee May 1944
28/30 St. John's Road	ARP Depot [access via Culverden Square]
David Salomon's House	Used for wounded servicemen. Given by Sir Davis Salomon to KCC in 1936 and opened as convalescent home for Kent people in 1937. County emergency store for supplies e.g. medical and household during WW II
Somerhill	PoW Camp
8 Upper Grosvenor Road	Depot
225 Upper Grosvenor Road	Government evacuation scheme
39 Woodbury Park Road	Rescue School

APPENDIX 2

AWARDS AND HONOURS

With reference to men and women from Tunbridge Wells.

This list does not claim to be comprehensive.

MILITARY

Name	Award and Date	Reference
W/O Albert E. Brown RAF	Belgian Croix de Guerre & Palme 1947 MID for service in Palestine	Courier 30.07.1948
Sergt. Neville Carey	French Croix de Guerre MID in Burma	Courier 27.08.1946
F/O C. F. Guest	DFM [when Sergt] May 1942	Courier 25.08.1944
F/O K. Dart [later S/Ldr]	DFC	London Gazette 31.10.1941 issue 35334 p6367/8
CPO Arthur Holme	George Medal	London Gazette 04.07.1941 issue 35212 p3915 Courier 4/18.07.1941
Capt R. F. Jolley	Military Cross	Courier 04.08.1944
Lt F. J. King	DSC [mine sweeping in Channel]	Courier 29.06.1945
Major Harry King	Legion of Merit USA	Courier 24.08.1945
Lt Eric B. Marland RNVR	DSC 1940 and Bar 1943	London Gazette 09.04.1943 issue 35978 p1699
Capt Lionel Queripel	VC	London Gazette 01.01.1945 Courier 09.02.1945
F/O 'Pat' Smyth [later Wing/Cdr]	DFC	Courier 10.05.1940
S/Ldr Eric H. Thomas	DFC	Courier 1941
Henry Wenham	Military Medal MID	19.07.1944 Courier 23.01.1948

DFC	– Distinguished Flying Cross	CPO	– Chief Petty Officer
DFM	– Distinguished Flying Medal	F/O	– Flying Officer
DSC	– Distinguished Service Cross	S/Ldr	– Squadron Leader
MID	– Mentioned in Dispatches	W/O	– Warrant Officer
VC	– Victoria Cross		

CIVILIAN

Mrs K. M. Stewart Anderson	MBE Jan 1946	Courier 06.01.1946
Arthur S. Charlton	OBE 1943 – CBE 1952	Courier 06.06.1952
Veronica M. M. Cox	MBE – OBE Jan 1946	Courier 06.01.1946
Cllr. J.A. McNab	MBE Jan1946	Courier 6 Jan 1946
Pauline Gower [Mrs Cusack Fahie]	OBE Jan 1942	Courier 02.01.1942 Courier 07.03.1947 'obit'
Miss M. A. Payne	OBE Jan 1946	Courier 06.01.1946
Walter Hyland	MBE Jan 1946	Courier 06.01.1946
Platoon Sgt D. O. Scrace HG	BEM	Courier 21.01.1944

BEM – British Empire Medal
CBE – Commander of the Order of the British Empire
MBE – Member of the Order of the British Empire
OBE – Officer of the Order of the British Empire

APPENDIX 3

SOURCES

1. PRIMARY SOURCES

D. A. Barmby	Typescript – Memories [Tunbridge Wells Reference Library]
Evacuee Diary – 17 Boyne Park	G. Copus [photocopy, Tunbridge Wells Reference Library]
St Barnabas School Log Books 1939-1972	G.Copus Collection
Tunbridge BC Archives	Council Minutes 1930 – 1954
	Emergency Committee Minutes 1939 – 1945
	Other Council Committees, passim
Tunbridge Wells Borough Cemetery	Burial Grants and Committee Minutes 1939-1945
War Memorial research file	Tunbridge Wells Reference Library : Richard Gosling

Papers and Photographs in private collections

2. ARCHIVES

Centre for Kentish Studies, Maidstone	www.kentarchives.gov.uk
East Sussex Record Office Lewes	www.eastsussex.gov.uk
Tunbridge Wells Museum and Art Gallery	photographic collections
Tunbridge Wells Reference Library	document collections and cutting files

3. BIBLIOGAPHY OF SELECTED BOOKS

Author	Title	Publisher	Year
Colin Alexander	Ironside's Line	Historic Military Press	1999
R. Arnold	A very Quiet War		1962
Jane Bakowski	Calm Amidst the Waves	Gresham Books	2004
H. S. Banner	Kentish Fire	Hurst & Blackett	1944
H. P. Pratt Boorman	Kent Unconquered	Kent Messenger	1951
Edward B. S. Clarke	From Kent to Kohima	Gale & Polden	1951
The Courier	Civil Defence 1939-1945	A Supplement	
K.R.Gulvin	Kent Home Guard. A History	North Kent Books	1980
Peter Howlett	Fighting with Figures – A Statistical Digest of the Second World War	HMSO	1995
S. Hylton	From Rationing to Rock		1998
S. Hylton	Kent and Sussex 1940	Pen and Sword	2004
Roy Ingleton	Gentlemen at War – Policing in Britain 1939 – 1945	Cranbourne	

Author	Title	Publisher	Year
Roy Ingleton	Policing in Kent 1800 – 2000	Phillimore	2002
KAHRS*	Buzz Bomb Diary		
KAHRS	Aircraft Casualties in Kent Part 1 1939-1940**	Meresborough Books	1990
KAHRS	Wings Over Kent	Meresborough Books	1983
KCC Civil Defence Dpt.	Enemy Action in Kent		
King George VI	Speeches to His Peoples	John Murray	1952
David Kynaston	Austerity Britain 1945 – 1951	Bloomsbury Publishing	2007
D. Lampe	Last Ditch	Cassell	1968
J. D. Lewis	WVS in Kent 1939-1945	Kent Messenger	1947
Norman Longmate	How we lived then	Hutchinson	1971
P. Longstaff-Tyrrell	The Maple Leaf Army in Britain	Gote House Pubs.	2002
S.P.Mackenzie	The Home Guard	OUP	1995
Ted Marchant	One Cog – History of St. Augustine's Church		1995
E. Melling	History of the KCC 1889-1974	KCC	1975
T. H. O'Brian	Civil Defence	HMSO	1955
Bob Ogley	Doodlebugs and Rockets	Froglets Publications	1992
Bob Ogley	Kent at War	Kent Messenger Group	1994
Bob Ogley	The Kent Weather Book	Froglets Publications	1991
W. L. Platts	Kent: the County Administration in WWII	KCC	1946
Erica Prean	Beacon Hostel: A History	published privately	200?
Victor Smith	Front Line Kent	KCC	2001
Saunders and Smith	West Kent Defence Heritage Gazetteer		2001
Editor: H. Spalding	Tunbridge Wells – A Report	TW Civic Assoc.	1945
F. C. Squirrel	Civil Defence in Tunbridge Wells		
C. E. Washbrook	Civil Defence in Tunbridge Wells	Courier Group	1945
Giles Whittell	Spitfire Women of WW II	Harper Press	2007
Henry Wills	Pill Boxes	Leo Cooper/Secker Warburg	1985
	Who Was Who	A & C Black passim	

Kent Aviation Historical Research Society
*** Compiled by G.G. Baxter, K. A. Owen, and P. Baldock*
Also many others that have brief references to Tunbridge Wells and the local area.

4. NEWSPAPERS AND JOURNALS

Bygone Kent: passim [Tunbridge Wells Reference Library]
Frank Chapman: Warwick Column [The Courier]: passim
Hastings and St Leonard's Observer [on film Hastings Reference Library and WWII cuttings)
Kent and Sussex Courier 1930 – 1953 [on film Tunbridge Wells Reference Library]
The Kent Messenger: passim
Oxford Dictionary of National Biography [New Edition 2004] online
Sussex Express and County Herald : passim
The Times 'Obituaries' online
Tonbridge Free Press: passim: Tonbridge Reference Library
Tunbridge Wells Advertiser
'Who was Who': names associated with Tunbridge Wells in the years 1930 – 1953

Various Journals, including the RTW Civic Society Newsletter: passim

5. WEB SITES

BBC History, life in Britain in WWII	www.bbc.co.uk/
Centre for Kentish Studies	www.kentarchives.gov.uk
Commonwealth War Graves Commission	www.cwgc.org includes Civilian war deaths]
East Sussex Record Office Lewes	www.eastsussex.gov.uk
Imperial War Museum [photographic collection]	www.iwm.org.uk
Kent Police Museum	www.kent-police-museum.co.uk
London Gazette	www.gazettes-online [award citations]
The National Archives Kew	www.nationalarchives.gov.uk/a2a
Subterranea Britannica	www.subbrit.org.uk/sb-/sites/t/tunbridge-wells
Tunbridge Wells Borough Cemetery	www.deceasedonline.com

APPENDIX 4

ACRONYMS AND ABBREVIATIONS

ADC	Aide-de-Camp
AFS	Auxiliary Fire Service
ARP	Air Raid Precautions
ATS	Auxiliary Territorial Service
ATA	Air Transport Auxiliary
BEF	British Expeditionary Force
C-in-C	Commander-in-Chief
CD	Civil Defence
CKS	Centre for Kentish Studies
D-DAY	6 June 1944
EHS	Emergency Hospital Scheme
EMS	Emergency Medical Services
ESRO	East Sussex Record Office
GHQ	General Headquarters
GOC	General Officer Commanding
HE	High Explosive Bombs
HG	Home Guard
HQ	Headquarters
KCC	Kent County Council
LCC	London County Council
LDV	Local Defence Volunteers
LHG	Local History Group of RTWCS
NFS	National Fire Service
OC[ROC]	Observer Corps [later Royal)
PoW's	Prisoners of War
RA	Royal Artillery
RTWCS	Royal Tunbridge Wells Civic Society
RADAR	Radio Detection and Ranging
TA	Territorial Army
TNA	The National Archives (Kew)
TW	Tunbridge Wells
TWBC	Tunbridge Wells Borough Council
TWODS	TW Operatic and Dramatic Society
V1&V2s	Flying Bombs
VAD	Voluntary Aid Detachments
VE Day	Victory in Europe Day
VJ Day	Victory over Japan Day
WAAF	Women's Auxiliary Air Force
WLA	Women's Land Army
WRNS	Women's Royal Naval Service
WVS	Women's Voluntary Service [later Royal)

APPENDIX 5

CONVERSION OF EARLIER £ STERLING VALUES INTO 2009 VALUES

The Tunbridge Wells Reference Library holds a detailed, authoritative, but unattributed, conversion table of the value of the £ (Pound Sterling) from 1270 to 1996 and this has been used in this study, to convert 1938 costs/prices/ expenditure into 2009 values, which are not *necessarily equivalent.*

To bring it up-to-date from 1996 to 2009, an increment of 42% has been added to the 1996 figures, which reflects the 42% increase in the UK Retail Price Index (RPI) over this period, and hence a further devaluation in the value of the 1938 Pound Sterling.

So:

£1 in						
1938	=	£27.46	@ September 1996	=	£38.99 in 2009
1939	=	£26.98		=	£38.27
1940	=	£23.30		=	£33.09
1941	=	£21.36		=	£30.33
1942	=	£21.36		=	£30.33
1943	=	£21.36		=	£30.33
1944	=	£21.36		=	£30.33
1945	=	£21.07		=	£29.92
1946	=	£20.78		=	£29.51
1947	=	£20.78		=	£29.51
1948	=	£19.47		=	£27.65
1949	=	£18.99		=	£26.97
1950	=	£18.31		=	£26.00
1951	=	£16.90		=	£24.00
1952	=	£15.38		=	£21.84
1953	=	£14.93		=	£21.20
1954	=	£14.65		=	£20.80

It should be recognised that while the table above is a mathematic conversion of values, real values for individual products/services may vary considerably over the period. For example, land values over the past 60 years have increased out of proportion to any technical conversion of values. The reader is advised that as a broad rule-of-thumb, they should multiply any 1938-1953 values quoted, by a factor of 20-25, to establish 2009 comparative values/cost.

ACKNOWLEDGMENTS

The publishers have sought to establish the copyright holders of all illustrations in this book. If they have failed unwittingly, they offer their apologies and will rectify their mistake in any reprinting.

Many old prints, photographs, maps and postcards are generally by their age 'out-of-copyright'; and since each can be found in a number of public and private collections, it is not realistic to attribute any one collection as a source or copyright holder.

But we would like to acknowledge the following as the sources of many of the illustrations reproduced in this book:

> The Tunbridge Wells Museum and Art Gallery
> The Tunbridge Wells Reference Library
> The Tunbridge Wells Courier
> The Kent Messenger

as well as private collections which have been made available to us, we would like to thank them all for permission to reproduce from the copies they own.

We would also like to thank the staff of:

Tunbridge Wells Library
Tunbridge Wells Borough Cemetery
Many other Libraries and Archives, including:

> Sevenoaks
> Tonbridge
> Hastings
> Crowborough

and:

Dr. Ian Beavis of the Tunbridge Wells Museum and Art Gallery;
Members of the RTW Civic Society Local History Group Committee, and particularly John Cunningham, one of the founders and the Chairman of the RTWCS Local History Group, who has been the Editor of this monograph.

INDEX

A

Abergavenny Estate   177
Agricultural Show
(Ground)   62,63,169,178,182
Air Raid Precautions (ARP)
   Exercises   79
   Posts   75,80
   Shelters   34,75,81,99
   Warning Sirens   34
Albrighton Hall   74
Allen, Alderman T. C.   138,161
Anderson, Sir John   33,87
Anderson Shelters   33,64
Anschluss, Die   3,6
Arlington House   59
Army Camps   121
Arnold, Capt. Ralph   91,93
Ashdown Forest   121,164
Assembly Hall   68,76,163,164,179
Associations
   Merchant Navy Ship
   Adoption Society   119
   POW Depot   83
   TW Knitting Society   83
   TW War Comforts Association
      82,161
   TW War Savings Association   83
   TW Waste Paper Recovery
   Association   83
Atom Bomb   135
Attlee, Clement, MP, Deputy
   Prime Minister   88,137
Aultmore, Kingswood Road   66
Auxiliary Fire Service AFS –
   see Voluntary Services
Auxiliary Territorial Service (ATS) 23
'Auxiliary/Observation
   Units'   47,100-101

B

Baillie, Sir A. MP   58,114
Baltic Saw Mills   57
Basinghall Street   97
Basque Children   57
Battle of the Atlantic   11
Battle of Britain   44-46,54,86,93-98
BBC   21,90
Beacon Hostel [Hotel]   57
Beaverbrook, Lord   112

Beech Street   99
Bell ringing ban   95,98
Berlin Air Lift   170,175
Bevan, Aneurin,MP   162
Bevin, Ernest,MP   24
Billeting   72,121
Black Broadcasting   90
Blackford, Bob   103
Blackheath High
   School for Girls   72,119,128,133
Black Markets   12
Blackout   18-20
Black Shirts   56
Blakeway, Henry   101
Blitz, The   86,98-99
Blitzkrieg   10
Blunt Sir John   156
Bolt M. H.   107
Bomb damage   54
Bombs dropped on TW   54,104
Book Drive   116,118
Boorman, Bernard. J.   108-9
Borough Surveyor's Office   74-75,
     81,130
Bottomley, Arthur   114,132
Bowls   63,82,162,169
Boyne Park, No.5   99
Bredbury   54,65
British Expeditionary
   Force (BEF)   47,82,89
British Restaurants   17,114,150
British Ship Adoption Society   119
British Union of Fascists   56
Broadhead, Lt. J.   101
Brooke, Gen. Sir Alan   48,66,93
Bunker, The   173,179
Burial Board   97
Burns, Cecil   164
Burslem, Cllr.   67,138
Burslem, Mrs.   72
Bus services   74,112

C

Caley [Mary] Recreation Ground
   61,81
Calverley Grounds   61,75,95,162
Camden, Lord   68,98
Camden, Marchioness   68
Camden Road   99
Canadian Army   52-53,92,127,139

Canadian War Brides 139
Canterbury, Archbishop of 64
Carey, Sgt, Neville 141,194
Carlsen Capt. 185
Carlton Guy 87,118
Cemetery Borough 142-3
          Woodbury Park 143
Chamberlain, Neville 6-7
Christmas Day 1,7
Chronology (Time
     Lines) 3,86,117,121,145,146
Churchill, Randolph 114
Churchill, Winston 1,6,115,117,
          131,137,145
Churn, Wally 101
Cinemas in Tunbridge Wells 168-169
Civic Association 141-2,163-4
Civil Defence
     (CD) 119,123,146,180-181,184
Civil Defence Regions 12,22,64,67
Civilian Protection and Safety 32-35
Collins, Carteret 106-107
Commonwealth War Graves
     Commission [CWGC] 142
Conscription, men and women 23-25,
          67,110
Cost of Civil Defence 144
Courier, The Kent and Sussex –
     passim
Crescent Road, 'Holly Bank' 57
Cricket Week 63,82,162,168,184
Cripps, Sir Stafford,MP 165
Cripps, W. C. 186
Crossfield, Miss Fanny 99
Crowley, Dr. 183
Culverden House 73
Curfews 20,48,98
Curtis House 172

D

Dalison, Maj. Gen. J. B. 149,178
Dancy, Ken 184-185
Dart, Sq. Ldr. K. RAF 162,195
David Salomon's House 78,193
Dawnay, Maj. Christopher (Kit) 105
D-Day 53,54,123
De La Warr, Earl 100
De L'Isle and Dudley, Viscount
     136,182
'Demob' 25
Dennis, Miss Dorothy 99
Detergents 175-176

Doodlebugs, see V1s/V2s
Dornden – US Army 123
Double Summer Time 157
Dowding, Air Chief Marshal
     Sir Hugh 93
Dragon's Teeth 75,88,94
Duke of Windsor 65 (footnote)
Dunkirk 54,89-90,93
Dunorlan (House,
     Park) 106-7,137,164,178
Duprez, June 68

E

Eating Out 17
Eden Sir Anthony 88
Education 72-74,155-6
Education Committee 59,73,133
El Alamein 110,117
Elementary Schools 73,133
Elim Cottages 99
Emergency Committee 67,87,94,
          112,113,116,119,128
Emmanuel Canteen 149
Entertainment 167-8
Evacuees 54,71-74

F

Fascists 56
Festival of Britain 182-184
Fire prevention orders 134
Fire watchers 103-5
First Aid Posts 76,80
First World War – passim
Fifth Column 91
Five Ways 96
Flying Bombs – see V1/V2
Flying Enterprise 185-6
Fonthill 76
Food Rationing 13-4,78,87
'Four Feathers,The' 68
|Fowle, S.H.W. 133

G

Gammell Maj. Gen J. A. H. 106
Gas attacks 32,58-9,103
Gas masks 32,60,77,84
Geddes, Sir Auckland 65,69,75,
          84,107,109
Gearing George 129
General Election 1945 137-8
               1951 184

German Navy 11,38
German-Soviet Pact 46
GHQ – Line 65,66
Goodwin, John 110
Gorringe, Mrs Phyllis 170-171
Gower, Pauline 30,165-6
Gower, Sir Robert,MP 30,72,162, 165,171,186
Great Hall 169
Grosvenor Recreation Ground 114-115
Grosvenor Road 96
Guernica 7,10
Guy's Hospital 74,77,84

H

Halifax, Lord 64,70
Hall's Bookshop 93
Handley, Tommy (ITMA) 99
Hardinge, Lord 69
Haskins, Miss M. L. 84
Hawkenbury 108,117,172
Hayward Mr. 103
Heritage Lottery Grant 137
Hilbert Recreation Ground 61,81
Hillman, Cllr. 67
Hindenburg 5
Hiroshima 135
Hitler, Adolf 5,7,133
HMS Brilliant 37,112,118
Hoare, Sir Samuel 60
Hobart, Maj. Gen. Percy (Hobo) 106 (footnote)
Hobart, R.T., JP 106
Holme CPO Arthur – RN 109
Homeopathic Hospital – see Hospital
Home Guard (HG) 29-30,88,100, 101,119,186
Hope-Paley, Miss E. 59
Hospital
    Homeopathic 76,79,99
    Kent and Sussex 96,136
    Pembury 78
Housing 140,150-156,186
Housing Estates
    Hawkenbury Close 151
    Powder Mill Lane 151
    Ramslye 152
    Sherwood 152-153
Housing Register 150-151
Huntley House 156,178,181

I

Identity Cards 21-22
Infantile Paralysis (Polio) 157
Inflation 17
Ironside, Gen. Sir Edmund 47-48, 65,91,93,94
'Ironside Line' 88

J

Japan 109,135
Jewish Children 57
Jolly Capt. R. F. 132
Johnson, Amy 30
Jones Miss Meryl M. 68,162
Jubilee Celebrations 1939 68-69

K

Kempster & Sons 109
Kent & Sussex Hospital – see Hospital
Kent County Council (KCC) 71,78,144
Kent Education Committee 133
Kent
    Duke of 107,114
    Duchess of 107,114
Kent and Sussex Housing Association 155
Kenya 178
Kindertransport 57
King Charles the Martyr 113
King George V 7,8
King George VI 8,63,70,71,84,100, 104,110,116,120,130,132,134, 143,164,168,170,172,173,181, 184,187
King, Major Harry 141,195
Kings Standing 90
Kingswood Road 66
Kirkdale Road 99
Knollys Lord 65,87
Knox Brig. H. O. 88
Kohima 132
Korean War 178

L

Labour Exchange 105
Land Army (WLA) – see Voluntary Services
LDV – see Home Guard

Lend Lease 35,52
Lincoln and Welland Regiment 127
Lines of Defence/Nodal Points 49,65
Linton Dr. F. C. 60
Little Bayhall Farm 127
London Road, No.81 66
Lyburn Dr. E. St J. 179

M

Mabledon 39,159
Macmillan, Harold 188
Maidstone and District
  Bus Services 62
Malaya 172,179
Maldwyn-Jones, Meryl 68,162
Maldwyn-Jones, Rev. I 162
Marriott, Sir John 57
McIndoe Burns Unit 136
Mechanised Transport
  Corps [MTC] 104
Messerschmidt 36,95,97
McNab, Cllr 112,161,195
Montgomery, Lt. Gen
  Sir Bernard 49,50,51-52,93,
    101,104-105,131,133
Montgomery, Betty [née Hobart] 106
Monsell, Lord 65. 109,131,132
Moon, Herbert 96
Morgan Lt. Cmdr. G. W. 180
Morrison, Herbert, MP,
  Home Secretary 33,107,126
Morrison shelters 33,129
Mosley, Sir Oswald 56
Munich agreement 63
  Crisis 6,59,60,72

N

Nagasaki 135
National Archives (TNA) 43
National Fire Service (NFS)
  107,111,122
National Fuel Campaign 112
National Identity Cards 21-22,78
National Registration Act 1939 21,73
National Savings 35-37,160
National Savings Weeks 35-37
  Salute the Soldier Week 1944
    37,123
  The Spitfire Fund, 1939 36,98
  Warship Week, 1942 37,112
  War Weapons Week, 1940 36,98

Wings for Victory Week, 1943
    37,118
  Thanksgiving Week, 1945 37
National Service Act (No.2) 1941
    24,82,124
Nationalisation 146-149,156,181
Nevill Golf Club 139
Newhaven-Hoo Peninsular Line
    65,66
Nodal points 49,65
Norman Road 99
North Atlantic Treaty Organisation
  (NATO) 174
Nursery Road, High Brooms 135
Nylon 175

O

'Observation/Auxiliary Units'
  47,100-101
Observer Corps, Royal 27
Olympic Games 1948 172
Oosterbeek War Cemetery 130
Opera House 75
Operation
  Barbarossa 46
  Dynamo 89
  Eagle 44
  'Market Garden' 130-131
  Overlord(D-Day) 53
  Sea Lion 43-44,46,93
Ord, Colonel 159

P

Pantiles 57,81
Paget Lt. Gen. Sir Bernard 48,50
Parker, Major G. L. 60
Pattenden,Charles 96
Paying for the War 35-37
Pea Nut Club 68
Peace of Versailles,1919 4
Pearl Harbour 52,110
Peck, Kenneth 97
Pembury Hospital – see Hospital
Perrins, Capt. Alan 93
Petrol rationing 16,112,122,167,178
Phoney War, The 85,86
Pill Boxes 94
Population 9
Postlethwaite, J. R. P. 66,100
Post Office 74
Powdermill Lane – see Housing
  Estates

POW's   38-39,159-160
   British   38
   German   38-39,159-160
   Italian   38-39,117
Pratley, Harry   93
Princess Margaret   173
Princess Mary, Princess
   Royal   114
Pump Room   72,178

Q

Queen Elizabeth II   187-8
Queen's Own Royal West
   Kent Regiment   89,132
Queriple, Capt Lionel.
   VC   130-131,195
Queues at Bus Stops   111

R

Radar   34
RAF   44-46,54,69,127
RAF 'Salvage Gang'   130
Ration Books   14,119,125,149
Rationing   12-16,149
   Clothing   15-16,173
   Food   12,13
   Petrol   16
Rawson's Garage   111
Read, A. B. H.   60,66,114
Reading, Lady   28
Redman, Lincoln   97
Regional Government,
   Centre of   54
Regulation and Control   21-22
Removal of Signs
   Order 1940   94
Resettlement Bureau   140
Restrictions   18-21
Rhodes-Moorhouse, Fl.Lt.,
   DFC, RAF   97-98
Ritz Cinema   167
Road accidents   75
Robertson, K. G.   180
Romany Biscuits   179
Romer Lt. Gen. Sir Cecil   88
Rommel, Gen. Erhardt   52,106
Roosevelt   141,145
Royal Tunbridge Wells
   Civic Society   141
Royal Wedding   166-167

Rusthall
   ARP   79
   Beacon   57
   Common   99
   Lodge   119-120
   Lower Green Road   57

S

St Augustine's Catholic Church
                                    91,96
St Christopher's Nursery College,
   Pembury Road   57,108,118
St. John's Recreation
   Ground   61
St Mark's Primary School   77
Salute the Soldier Week
   – see National Savings Weeks
Salvage   112-114
Schools
   Blackheath High School
   for Girls/TW High School
   for Girls   72,119,133
   Blue Coat School for Girls   73
   Clyde Street   73
   Coborn   129
   Colfe's   73,129
   Deptford RC Boys' School   73
   Down Lane Infants   73
   Invicta   73
   Lee, South East London   73
   LCC Invicta   73
   Notting Hill London   73
   Randell Place Greenwich   73
   Rusthall Infants and
   Girls' School   73
   St. Barnabas   73,77,114,127,
                              149,157,183
   St. James Senior   73
   St Stephens   73
   Sacred Heart [Beechwood]   74
   Skinners' School   60,67,73,74,
                                 132,184
Shawcross, Sir Hartley   65,108
Shelters
   Anderson   33
   Morrison   33-34
   Private   81
   Public   81
Sherwood Park   77
Shinwell, Emmanuel, MP   156
Shortages   12-18

Simpkins, L/Cpl RASC 140
Sly, Sergeant/Inspector 87,161
Smyth P/O / W.Cdr. J. P. S.,
  RAF 89,115
'Snoek' 149
Soady J. H. 110
Somerhill, Tonbridge 39,159-160
Soroptimists, The 163
South-Eastern Command 50,52,92
Soviet-German Friendship
  Pact 46
Spalding, Helen 141
Spanish Civil War 7,57
Spitfire Fund
  – see National Saving Weeks
Springfield Gardens 99
Squatters 154-5,158-9
Squirrell, Sergeant F. C. 114
S.S.A.F.A. and S.S.A 161
'Stand-down' (disbandment) 132,134
Static Water Tanks 118
Strange, Mr 57
Subterranea Britanica
  Society 103
Summerskill Dr E. MP 150

T

Tandy-Green, Col C. W., GC 179
Taylor, H. T. 60
Television 20-21
Tennis Week/Tournament
  63,82,161,177,187-188
Territorial Army Units 61-62
Thorne, Lt. Gen. A. F. A. N.
  41,47,50,92,93,104
Tide 175-6
Toop the Butchers 98
Travel 20,121
Trench Scheme 77
Tunbridge Wells passim
  Burial Board 97,142-3
  Opera & Dramatic Society
  (TWODS) 69
Tutty's Farm 107

U

United Nations 130
'U' Boats 11
Upper Grosvenor Road 90

V

VE Day 134-136
VJ Day 135
Vidal, Mr. 150
Vigilantes 140
V-1's and V-2's 54,99,124-129,
  132,133
Voluntary Services and Local
  Defence 26-31
  AFS Auxiliary Fire Service
  26,29,31,57,107,110
  ARP Air Raid Precautions
  26,27-28,31,55,58,
  66,69,70,77,79,106,145
  ATA Air Transport Auxiliary
  26,30,31,166
  ROC Royal Observer Corps
  26,27,31,34,77,126
  VAD Voluntary Aid
  Detachments 59
  WLA Women's Land Army
  26,28,31,132
  WVS Women's Voluntary Service
  26,28,31,62-63,67,77,107,
  128,131,136,165

W

Wakefield Prison 171
Walker, L/Cpl J., ATS 106
Wallis, Hollier and Lee 97
Wandsworth Prison 171
War Budget 71
War Comforts Association 161
War Damage Commission 107
War Memorial 55,136,182
Warship Week
  – see National Savings Weeks
War Weapons Week
  – see National Savings Weeks
Warwick Park 105
Waste Paper 112-113
Weather, The 82,87,130,156-8
Weekes, Alderman E.B.
  113,162,163
Welcome Home Fund 140,161
Wells,Miss Muriel 62,136,175,180
Westbrook, Alderman
  Charles, J. P. 67,82,100,109,115,
  138,161,187
Whitehead, John, Town
  Clerk 138

Wilderness, The   101,103
Williams, Gerald MP   138,184,185
Windmill Street, No.21   96
Wings for Victory
   – see National Savings Weeks
Women's Auxiliary Air Force
   (WAAF)   23,71
Women's Land Army (WLA)
   – see Voluntary Services
Women's Royal Naval Service
   (WRNS)   23
Woodruff, Eric   103

Woolton, Lord   118
World War I passim
World War II passim
Worsley, Lady   67
WVS – see Voluntary Services

XYZ

XII Corps HQ   40-42,43,47,50,
    51,52,54,64,92,93,100,101
   Divisions   41-42
Zeppelin   10

LOCAL HISTORY GROUP PUBLICATIONS

The Local History Group of the Royal Tunbridge Wells Civic Society was founded in 2002 and since then has published some ten Local History Monographs, as follows:

'Decimus Burton, Esquire: Architect and Gentleman'
– by Dr. Philip Whitbourn. Our first Monograph and a best-seller, first published in 2003. The life of Decimus Burton and his work in Tunbridge Wells and elsewhere. A5 format, perfect-bound, laminated cover. 88 pages, 90 illustrations. Now in its second edition (2006). ISBN 0-9545343-6-0 Price £5.95.

'Researching Royal Tunbridge Wells'
– by Susan Brown, the Tunbridge Wells Reference Librarian. A bibliography of historical sources, which is an absolutely invaluable reference work for any one researching local or family history. A5 format, laminated cover. 64 pages, 30 illustrations. Published in 2003. ISBN 0-9545343-1-X Price £4.95.

'The Skinners' School. Its controversial origin and its landmark buildings'
– by Cecil Beeby and Philip Whitbourn. A fascinating insight into a Victorian 'storm in a teacup' which lasted 17 years and had Tonbridge and Tunbridge Wells at each others' throats, together with a history and assessment of its landmark buildings. A5 format, perfect-bound, laminated cover. 96pp, 48 illustrations. Published October 2004. ISBN 0-9545343-2-8 Price £4.95.

'The Residential Parks of Tunbridge Wells'
– by six LHG members – Ann Bates, Sue Brown, Geoffrey and Brenda Copus, John Cunningham and Dr. Philip Whitbourn. A history of the development of the Park concept which came through Decimus Burton and John Ward from Regent's Park to Tunbridge Wells, and which led to Calverley, Nevill and Hungershall, Camden, Bishop's Down, Woodbury, Grosvenor, Boyne, Molyneux, Ferndale, Sherwood, Sandown, Sandhurst and Liptraps Parks; and to Warwick, Madeira, Linden and Culverden Parks. It is the first comprehensive history of the property development which has created so much of the style and character of the Tunbridge Wells. A5 format, perfect-bound, laminated cover. 100pp, 60 illustrations and maps. Published December 2004. ISBN 0-9545343-3-6 Price £5.95.

Souvenir Calendar for the Fourth Centenary in 2006
– featuring in full colour some 13 old paintings and prints of Tunbridge Wells, with a backboard containing notes on each of the illustrations. Approx. 12" x 11", with a separate page for each month, wirebound, with hanger. Published July 2005. ISBN 0-9545343-4-4 Price £4.95.

'400 Years of the Wells'
published to mark the Fourth Centenary of the Discovery of the Wells in 1606, is a History of our Town from inception to the present day. It has been written by a number of members of the Local History Group – Lionel Anderson, John Arkell, Ann Bates, Ian Beavis, Geoffrey Copus, John Cunningham, Chris Jones and Philip Whitbourn. A5 format, perfect-bound, laminated cover. 200 pp, 146 illustrations. Published November 2005. ISBN 0-9545343-5-2 Price £7.95.

'The Origins of Warwick Park and the Nevill Ground'
by John Cunningham. The story of how and why the Home Farm Estate of the
Marquess of Abergavenny became in the 1890's the Warwick Park Estate and the
Nevill Cricket Ground, as researched in the Archives of both the Marquess and
the Tunbridge Wells Borough Council. A5 format, perfect-bound, laminated
cover. 183 pp, 80 illustrations and maps. Published July 2007. ISBN 978-0-
9545343-7-0 Price £7.95.

'An Historical Atlas of Tunbridge Wells'
– edited by John Cunningham. An Atlas of some 79 maps of Tunbridge Wells and
its immediate area, from 16th. to 20th. centuries. A3 format. Perfect-bound.
Laminated colour cover. 136 pp, 116 Plates (28 of them in colour). Published
December 2007. ISBN 978-0-9545343-8-7 Price: £16.95.

**'Tunbridge Wells in Literature An Anthology of a spa town in literature
from 17th to 20th Century'**
– compiled by Susan Brown. A5 format. Perfect-bound, laminated cover. 116
pages. 51 illustrations. Published May 2008. ISBN 978-0-9545343-9-4 Price
£6.95

'Tunbridge Wells in 1909: The Year we became Royal' – by Chris Jones, A5
Format. Perfect Bound, laminated cover. 214 pages, 148 illustrations.
Published November 2008. ISBN 978-0-9560944-0-7. Price £8.95

'By Royal Appointment' or 'Why Do They Call It Royal Tunbridge Wells' –
by Chris Jones, A4 Format. Perfect bound, laminated cover. 40 pages, 64
illustrations. Published February 2009. ISBN 978-0-9560944-1-4. Price £5.95

*All titles can be obtained at all good bookshops, or from the Royal Tunbridge
Wells Civic Society, whose address can be found on its website –
www.thecivicsociety.org*